REMINISCENCES THE STORY OF AN EMIGRANT • MATTSON, HANS

Publisher's Note

Purchase of this book entitles you to a free trial membership in the publisher's book club at www.rarebooksclub.com. (Time limited offer.) Simply enter the barcode number from the back cover onto the membership form on our home page. The book club entitles you to select from millions of books at no additional charge. You can also download a digital copy of this and related books to read on the go. Simply enter the title or subject onto the search form to find them.

Note: This is an historic book. Pages numbers, where present in the text, refer to the first edition of the book and may also be in indexes.

If you have any questions, could you please be so kind as to consult our Frequently Asked Questions page at www.rarebooksclub.com/faqs.cfm? You are also welcome to contact us there. Publisher: General Books LLC™, Memphis, TN, USA, 2012. ISBN: 9781153650564.

Proofreading: pgdp.net

✦ ✦ ✦ ✦ ✦ ✦ ✦ ✦

CONTENTS

CHAPTER I. 3
Ancestry and country home in Sweden—Home influences—My first school years—Christmas—Military life—Departure for America.

CHAPTER II. 7
Arrival at Boston—Adventures between Boston and New York—Buffalo—An Asylum—Return to New York—A Voyage—On the Farm in New Hampshire.

CHAPTER III. 11
The Arrival of my Father and Brother—Journey to Illinois—Work on a Railroad—The Ague—Doctor Ober—Religious Impressions—The Arrival of my Mother, Sister and her Husband—A Burning Railroad Train—We go to Minnesota—Our Experience as Wood Choppers and Pioneers.

CHAPTER IV. 16
Future Hopes—Farm Life—Norwegian Pioneers—The Condition of the Immigrant at the Beginning of the Fifties—Religious Meetings—The Growth of the Settlement—Vasa Township Organized—A Lutheran Church Established—My Wedding—Speculation—The Crisis of 1857—Study of Law in Red Wing—I am admitted to the Bar and elected County Auditor—Politics in 1860—War is Imminent.

CHAPTER V. 20
The Beginning of the Civil War—The Scandinavians taking part in it—Appeal in *Hemlandet* to the Scandinavians of Minnesota—Company D. Organized—The Expressions of the Press—The Departure—The March over the Cumberland Mountains—The Fate of the Third Regiment.

CHAPTER VI. 22
Events of 1863—The Siege of Vicksburg—Anecdotes about Gens. Logan, Stevenson and Grant—Little Rock Captured—Recruiting at Fort Snelling—The engagement at Fitzhugh's Woods—Pine Bluff—Winter Quarters at Duvall's Bluff—Death of Lincoln—Close of the War—The Third Regiment Disbanded.

CHAPTER VII. 26
Reconstruction in the South—Third Regiment Mustered Out—The Farewell Order—Sacrifices and Costs of the War.

CHAPTER VIII. 30
My Reason for Taking Part in the Civil War—The Dignity of Labor—The Firm Mattson & Webster—*Svenska Amerikanaren*, its Program and Reception—The State Emigration Bureau of Minnesota—Its Aim, Plan and Work.

CHAPTER IX. 33
Visit to Sweden in 1868-1869—The Object of my Journey—Experiences and Observations During the Same—Difference Between American and Swedish Customs—My Birth-place—Arrival and Visit There—Visit to Christianstad—Visit to Stockholm—The Swedish Parliament—My Return to America—Reflections on and Impressions of the Condition of the Bureaucracy of Sweden.

CHAPTER X. 36
The Importance of the Scandinavian Element—A Swede Elected Secretary of State in Minnesota—False Rumors of Indian Depredations—The Northern Pacific Railroad is Built—Trip to Philadelphia—The National Convention at Indianapolis—Delegation to Washington—A Swedish Colony in Mississippi Moved to Minnesota—The Second Voyage to Europe.

CHAPTER XI. 39
In Sweden Again—Reception at My Old Home—Visit to Northern Sweden—Field Maneuvers in Sweden—The Opening of Parliament—In Norway—Visit in Stockholm—Royal Palaces—The Göta Canal—A Trip to Finland and Russia—King Oscar II.—A Trip to Dalarne in the Winter.

CHAPTER XII. 41
Visit in Minnesota and Philadelphia—Conversation with Jay Cooke—The Crisis of 1873—Negotiations in Hol-

land—Draining of a Lake in Skåne—Icelandic Colony in Manitoba—Return to America.

CHAPTER XIII. 43
Grasshopper Ravages in Minnesota—The Presidential Election—Chosen Presidential Elector—Minnesota *Stats Tidning*—*Svenska Tribunen* in Chicago—Farm in Northwestern Minnesota—Journalistic Work.

CHAPTER XIV. 44
I am Appointed Consul-General to India—Assassination of Garfield—Departure for India—My Stay in Chicago and Washington—Paris and Versailles—Rome—Naples—Pompeii—From Naples to Alexandria—Interesting Acquaintances on the Voyage—The First Impressions in Egypt.

CHAPTER XV. 47
Alexandria and its Monuments—The Egyptian "Fellahs"—The Mohammedans and Their Religion—The Voyage Through the Suez Canal—The Red Sea—The Indian Ocean—The Arrival at Calcutta.

CHAPTER XVI. 49
India—Its People, Religion, Etc.—The Fertility of the Country—The Climate—The Dwellings—Punkah—Costumes—Calcutta—Dalhousie Square—Life in the Streets.

CHAPTER XVII. 52
The Promenades of the Fashionable World—Maidan—The Viceroy—British Dominions in India.

CHAPTER XVIII. 54
An Indian Fête—The Prince of Burdwan—Indian Luxury—The Riches and Romantic Life of an Indian Prince—Poverty and Riches.

CHAPTER XIX. 56
Allahabad—Sacred Places—Kumbh Mela—Pilgrimages—Bathing in the Ganges—Fakirs and Penitents—Sacred Rites—Superstitions.

CHAPTER XX. 58
Benares, the Holy City of the Hindoos—Its Temples and Worshipers—The Sacred Monkeys.

CHAPTER XXI. 61
Nimtoolaghat—Cremation in India—Parsee Funeral Rites.

CHAPTER XXII. 62
Heathenism and Christianity—The Religion of the Hindoos—Caste—The Brahmins—Their Tyranny—Superstition—The Influence of Christianity—Keshub-Chunder-Sen, the Indian Reformer—His faith and Influence.

CHAPTER XXIII. 65
Steamboating On the Ganges—Life on the River—The Greatest Business Firm in the World—Sceneries—Temples—Serampoor—Boat Races—An Excursion to the Himalayas—Darjieling and Himalaya Railroad—Tea Plantations—Darjieling—Llamas—View from the Mountains.

CHAPTER XXIV. 68
Cholera and other Diseases—The Causes of Cholera—How the Soldiers are Protected Against it—Sudden Deaths—Fevers—The Teraj—Contempt for Death—The Cholera Hospital—The Sisters of Mercy—The Princes Tagore—Hindoo Family Customs—Hindoo Gallantry—A Hindoo Fête.

CHAPTER XXV. 70
Agriculture, Manufacture and Architecture—Wheat Growing—The Farm Laborer—His Condition, Implements, etc. The Taj-Mahal—Jugglers—Snake Charmers—From My Journal.

CHAPTER XXVI. 75
The Women of India—The Widows—The American Zenana—Prizes Awarded in a Girl's School—Annandabai Joshee—Her Visit to America—Reports to the Government—Departure from India—Burmah—Ceylon—Arabia—Cairo.

CHAPTER XXVII. 79
Cairo—Cheop's Pyramid—Venice—The St. Gotthard Tunnel—On the Rhine—Visit in Holland and England—Father Nugent—Arrival at New York.

CHAPTER XXVIII. 81
Home from India—A Friendly Reception—Journey to New Mexico—The Maxwell Land Grant Company—Renewed Visits to England and Holland—Re-elected Secretary of State—Visit of the Swedish Officers in Minneapolis and St. Paul—Two Hundred and Fiftieth Anniversary of the Landing of the First Swedes in Delaware.

CHAPTER XXIX. 84
The Causes of Immigration—American Influence on Europe, and Especially on Sweden—The Condition of the Swedes in America—American Characteristics—Antipathy against Foreigners—The Swedish Press on America—American Heiresses.

CHAPTER XXX. 86
REVIEW.
NOTE.
These *reminiscences* were written from memory in such leisure moments as the author could spare from a busy life, and published in the Swedish language nearly a year ago. They were intended solely for Swedish readers in the mother country and America, but since their publication in that language it has been urged by many that they ought to be made accessible to English readers also. And this, principally, in order that the children of the old Swedish emigrants, who are more familiar with the English than the Swedish language, may have an opportunity to learn something of the early struggles of their fathers in this

country.

At the same time it was thought that the American reader in general might take pleasure in following the fortunes of one of the many emigrants who owes whatever he has accomplished in life to the opportunities offered by the free institutions of this country, and that it would especially interest him to read the account of oriental life, religion and characteristics as seen by the author during his residence in the wonderful land of the Hindoos.

As to literary finish no claim is made. In a few instances of a descriptive nature recourse has been had to the accounts of other observers. In all other respects the story is a plain recital of the personal experiences of the author, told without pretensions, as an humble contribution by an emigrant to the history of the emigrants, and of the settlement of the Great West.

THE AUTHOR.

Minneapolis, Minn., October, 1891.

CHAPTER I. 1
Ancestry and country home in Sweden—Home influences—My first school years—Christmas—Military life—Departure for America.

My childhood passed so quietly and smoothly that it would be superfluous to mention it at all, except for the fact that such omission would leave a gap in these reminiscences. For this reason, and, also, in order that the American reader may get some idea of a good country home in Sweden, I shall relate very briefly some incidents from that time.

My parents belonged to one of those old families of proprietary farmers, whose spirit of independence and never failing love of liberty, have, from time immemorial, placed Sweden, as a land of constitutional liberty, in the front rank among all the countries of the Old World.

Like the descendants of the old Scotch clans the ancestors of my father were noted for certain physical and mental qualities, which made them prominent among the inhabitants of the district of Villand, Skåne, where most of them had their home. They were independent freeholders and were generally reckoned among the leading men of their district. They were large and strong with broad shoulders, high and broad foreheads and other family characteristics. The christian names of the male members were generally Bonde, Trued, Lars, Matts, and Hans, and the family can be traced back in the parish records for more than two hundred years.

My mother was born on the island of Ifö, my father's family also came from that island and were the owners of the estate described by Du Chaillu in his "Land of the Midnight Sun" with the remarkable crypt built by Bishop Andreas Suneson [1] .... 0 and the estate still belongs to a second cousin of mine. My father inherited a small sum of money for which, at the time of his marriage, he bought a land in the parish of Önnestad near the city of Kristianstad. On this property he built a small house, barn, etc., and on the south side of the former a small flower garden was laid out at either end of which my father planted a spruce tree, one of which grew up into a fine, big tree, the only one of its kind in the whole neighborhood, and to which I shall refer farther on. In this unpretending little cabin I was born Dec. 23d, 1832, and under its lowly but peaceful roof I spent the first years of my childhood, together with an elder sister and a younger brother.

I can yet distinctly remember many incidents from my childhood as far back as my third and fourth year; all these memories are dear and exceedingly pleasant to me. There was no discord, no cause for sorrow and tears in my home during the time of my childhood. Everything bore the stamp of peace and calm, emanating from that spirit of genuine old Swedish honesty and sincere piety, which animated my parents. One of my very first recollections is of my father reading aloud the beautiful hymn: "The morning light shall wake me To the strains of sacred song," etc.

At the age of six my schooling commenced under the guidance of an itinerant schoolmaster by name of Bergdahl, who taught small children at their homes, stopping one day for each child at every house and keeping on in that way the whole term which lasted from three to four months. Old Bergdahl was a good and sensible man, far superior to the average men of his class. He seldom punished his pupils except by appealing to their better nature, and still maintained the best discipline that I have ever seen in any school of even greater pretensions.

My parents were doing well on their little farm, which they sold about this time, buying a larger one on the Önnestad Hills. Here they erected larger and more commodious buildings.

OUR HOME.

Near the house was a park, a creek, and some large rocks, all of which afforded welcome play-ground, and soon made this place dearer to me than the old home. We were followed by the schoolmaster who also settled down in our neighborhood. I continued reading another year under his guidance, after which I attended a private school, and at the age of eight was sent to the village school that was superintended by a lady teacher, a normal school graduate, who was considered one of the best teachers in that part of the country. My parents, desiring a more extensive field for their activity, also rented a large farm, called Kallsagard, near the village church, and we now moved into a still larger and better house. Meanwhile I continued my attendance at the village school until I had learned all that was taught there. During the vacations I worked on my father's farm at such light work as was suited to my age and strength. I had a decided fancy for horses, of which my father raised a large number, and was always happy for a chance to ride or drive in company with the hired men, and after my twelfth year I used to break the young colts to the saddle. At the same time I had a great taste for reading and never intended to remain long on the farm, but was always meditating on getting a higher education, which would prepare me for a larger field of action than a country farm could offer. At the age of fourteen I was sent to another school, located about three miles from my home. Here I was instructed in the common branches, and in a short time passed through the whole course of studies. I also received instruction from Rev. T. N. Hasselquist, who has played such a prominent part in the Swedish Lutheran Church of America, and took private lessons in arithmetic and writing of Mr. S. J. Willard, a bright young teacher, who afterwards married my only sister, and finally became my companion during our pioneer life in Minnesota.

Our last home offered many conveniences; the house was well furnished, and so large that the second story could be rented most of the time, and it was occupied alternately by a clergyman with his family, and a captain of the army. These people, and our numerous city friends, exerted a refining and elevating influence on the farm surroundings, and our home was widely noted for its hospitality. My father was a kind-hearted, noble-minded man, and was liked by all who knew him. My mother was a woman of strong character, and wielded a great influence over her surroundings. She managed a household of forty to fifty persons, and on Sundays there was always an extra table set for friends and visitors. Her good-will, however, extended not only to our - 5 - pleasant associates, but also to the poor, the suffering and the unfortunate. I cannot recall any period of my childhood when we did not harbor some poor, forsaken pauper, waif, orphan or cripple in my father's house.

Christmas has always been, and is yet, the greatest of all festivities or holidays among all the Scandinavian peoples. It is not merely a holiday like it is among Americans, but a festival lasting for many days. While the people in the different localities of the Scandinavian countries, at the time of my childhood, differed in many customs, they were all alike in making this season one of joyous hospitality, blended with religious worship. I shall endeavor to describe Christmas as celebrated in my home in Southern Sweden 50 years ago, and I venture to say that while matters of detail might differ in different parts of the country, the descriptions as a whole will apply to them all. The preparations for Christmas commenced in the beginning of December by butchering, brewing and baking, so as to lay in large stores of the essential elements for enjoyment and hospitality. The fattened animals were slaughtered, the tallow made into candles, the meat salted, smoked, and otherwise prepared for a whole year. The rich brown Yule-ale was made in large quantities, and poured in kegs and barrels. Bread of many varieties was baked for days and days, and stored away in proper places, a large share of it being intended for the poor, who began their rounds of calls a week before Christmas, receiving presents of brown and white loaves, large cuts of meats and cheese, rolls of sausage, etc. The school-master, the parish mid-wife, the village night watchman, and other semi-public characters of small degree were carefully remembered at this time. The village tailor with his journeymen and apprentices appeared a few weeks before Christmas and made the wearing apparel for the family and servants out of home-spun fabrics for the whole year. The village shoemaker - 6 - with his crowd of workmen followed close upon the former, and made up the boots and shoes out of leather which had been prepared to order, finishing up by repairing the stable harnesses, sometimes making new ones. It was a busy season; the house-wife was kept astir early and late to give directions, and superintending all these things.

Finally the day of Christmas Eve came, on which everything must be in readiness, pans and kettles be scoured, floors scrubbed and strewn with white sand and fresh juniper twigs, even the stables for the cattle receiving an extra scrubbing. The yard was swept and every nook and corner of the premises put in holiday attire, and last of all, the hired men and girls were expected to retire to their respective quarters for a similar cleaning, and make their appearance about five o'clock in the afternoon in clean linen and new clothes, ready for the great event, as for a marriage feast. In the mean time pots and kettles were boiling on the hearth in the great kitchen, baskets were being filled and sent off to the poor who were too feeble to call for their gifts; the family and servants contenting themselves that day with a lunch, well known all over Sweden as dopparebröd. It being now dark, the long table was set in the large common room. The whitest linen, the finest plate, plenty of fresh white bread, and two or three home-made cheeses, baskets of cake, and large decanters containing sweet ale, ornamented the table. In front of the seats of husband and wife was placed a large home-made tallow candle with as many branches as there were members of the family. Other candles were placed in candle-sticks or chandeliers, so that there was an abundance of light, in commemoration of the Great Light which came into the world on that eve. There was also a Christmas tree decorated with ribbons, flowers, confectionery and burning tapers. The lighting of the candles was the signal for all to come to the feast. That evening at least - 7 - there was no distinction as to persons. The lowest servant-boy had his seat, and received the same attention as the children or members of the family. When all were seated a Christmas prayer was offered by the head of the family, after which a hymn was sung, in which all joined; then were brought in from the kitchen great dishes of "Lut Fisk," served with drawn butter and mustard sauce; after that a roast of beef or pork, and at last the Yule-mush. About the time that this was finished, some one who had quietly stepped outside returned in the disguise of Santa Claus, and threw baskets full of Christmas presents on the floor. The children and younger servants made a scramble for these, amid shouts of hilarious joy and distributed them according to the directions written on each bundle. No one was forgotten. Then at the table followed cakes with sweet wine or punch, and nuts and apples, all of which was enjoyed hugely and deliberately, so that it was often ten o'clock before the tables were cleared. The remainder of the evening was spent in quiet amusements , such as telling stories about princes and princesses, giants and trolls, conundrums, tricks with cards, etc., and seldom did the happy circle break up until nearly mid-night.

Christmas day was considered a very holy day. There were no visits made, no work done except of the greatest necessity, such as feeding the animals and keeping up the fires; no cooking was done on that day, but meals were served mostly cold from the delicious head cheese, pork roast and other delicacies, which had been prepared beforehand. The greatest event of all the season, and in fact of the whole year, was the early service (ottesång) in the parish church, at five o'clock on Christmas morning. Hundreds of candles were lighted in chandeliers and candlesticks. The altar was covered with gold embroidered cloth; the floor was strewn with fresh twigs of juniper, and soon the people began to - 8 - assemble. They came from every house and hamlet, in sleighs with tinkling bells, on horseback, and on foot along every road and winding pathway, usually in groups, swelling as the parties and the roads intersected, many carrying lanterns or burning pine-knots to light the way. Everywhere the greeting, "Happy Christmas" was heard, but all with joyful solemnity. Outside the church the burning torches were thrown in a pile which formed a blaze that could be seen a long distance off. The church was soon crowded; then the solemn tones of the organ burst forth; the organist led in the beautiful hymn, "Var hälsad sköna morgon stund" (Be greeted joyful morning hour), in which every member of the congregation joined, until the temple was filled with their united voices so that the walls almost shook. And when the minister ascended the pulpit, clad in his surplice and black cape, he had before him a most devout congregation. Of course the sermon was about the Messiah, who was born in the stable, and placed in the manger at Bethlehem. The next service was at ten o'clock, and the rest of the day was spent quietly at home by everybody.

On the next day, called Second Day Christmas, the previous solemnity was discarded, and the time for visiting and social enjoyments commenced.

The one permanent virtue most conspicuous during the whole Christmas season, which in those days extended way into the month of January, was hospitality, and next to that, or linked with it, charity. It seemed that the heart of every one expanded until it took in every fellow creature high and low, and even the brute animals. Many and many were the loaves of bread, grain and meal thrown out purposely for the birds or stray dogs that might be hungry, and many of the farmers followed the beautiful Norwegian custom of placing sheaves of oats and barley on the roof of their barns that the poor birds might also enjoy Christmas.
- 9 -
But there were also other ennobling influences which surrounded and emanated from our home, and I recollect most vividly those connected with nature. The house was surrounded by a large beautiful garden, with choice flowers and fruit, fine grass plats and luxuriant trees, the branches of which were alive with singing birds, the most noted among these being the nightingale, which every summer filled the garden with sweet melody.

Of the incidents of my childhood I will mention a few, which have left the most vivid impression on my mind:

Once my parents took me along to see the king, who was to pass by on the highway a short distance from our home. The people from the country around had congregated by thousands to see his majesty. Most of them, however, did not get a chance to see anything but a large number of carriages each of which was drawn by four or six horses, and postillions and servants in splendid liveries. In the midst of this confusion I, however, succeeded in catching a glimpse of King Oscar I, as he passed by. In my childish mind I had fancied that the king and his family and all others in authority were the peculiar and elect people of the Almighty, but after this event which produced a very decided impression on me, I began to entertain serious doubts as to the correctness of my views on this matter.

At another time I went with my mother to the city of Kristianstad to hear the Rev. Doctor P. Fjellstedt, who had just returned from a missionary tour in India. I can never forget how eloquently he described the Hindoos, and the Brahmin idolatry, all of which aroused in me an eager longing to visit the wonderful country and learn to know its peculiar people. But little did I then dream that I was to go there thirty-six years later as the representative of the greatest country of the world.

At one time I went in company with my mother to the - 10 - Danish capital, Copenhagen, we being among the first Swedish families that traveled by rail, for we took the railroad from Copenhagen to Roskilde, the same being finished several years before any railroads were built in Sweden.

In the summer of 1847, shortly after my confirmation, I was properly supplied with wardrobe and other necessaries, and saying good-bye to the happy and peaceful home of my childhood, I left for the city of Kristianstad to enter the Latin school. In kissing me goodbye my mother urged on me the precious words, which she had inherited from her mother: "Do right and fear nothing."

When I entered this school I was fourteen years and a-half old, tall of stature and well developed for my age, and, like other country children, somewhat awkward in dress and behavior.

My schoolmates welcomed me by giving me a nick-name, and trying to pick a quarrel with me, which they also succeeded in doing, and before the end of the first day a drawn battle had been fought, after which they never troubled me again. The principal study in this school was Latin, early and late, to which was soon added German, and at the close of the second year, Greek, French, history, geography, and other common branches. I made rapid progress, was awarded a prize at my first examination, and finished the work of two classes in two years, only about half the usual time.

During those two years, and even before that time, I had a peculiar presentiment that I would have to make great mental and physical exertions in the future, and that it was necessary for me to prepare for whatever might happen. Therefore, I often chose the hard floor for my bed and a book for a pillow. At times I would take long walks without eating and drinking, and let my roommates strike my chest with their fists until it was swollen and inflamed. I even - 11 - tried how long I could go without food, and still not lose my mental and physical vigor.

When I was sixteen years old, an event took place which had a decisive influence on my whole life.

A captain of the army boarded at my father's home, and was regarded as a member of the family. Among his acquaintances was a young man of my own age, who also had the same christian name as I. One day this young man came to see the captain, and as he approached the house my mother and sister observing him, both exclaimed at the same time, "There is Hans!" He heard this, and was greatly surprised that they knew him, while the fact was that they mistook him for me. At that time I was in the city, but the next day this second Hans visited me, and told me of the incident. If there is such a thing as affinity between men, it certainly existed between him and me; we felt ourselves irresistibly drawn towards each other, and from that day we have been more than brothers, and nothing but death can separate us. We are of the same size, complexion and age. He had already served a short time as cadet in the artillery, but had been compelled to resign on account of poor health. Now he had recovered and entered service again as a volunteer in the infantry. The events of my life are so closely interwoven with this man and his life, that the reader will often hear of him in these pages. Right here I wish to state, that a more faithful friend and a more noble character cannot be found; he has always been a help and a comfort to me in the many and strange vicissitudes which we have shared together. His name is Hans Eustrom, better known in Minnesota as Captain Eustrom.

The first Danish-German war broke out about this time, and I, with many other youths, felt a hearty sympathy for the Danes. The Swedish government resolved to send troops to help their neighbors, and a few regiments marching through - 12 - our city fanned our youthful enthusiasm into flame. Finally, a detachment of the artillery, quartered in the city, was ordered to leave for the seat of war, and now I could no longer restrain myself, but besieged my parents to let me join that part of the army which was going to the battlefield, and to clinch the argument I was cruel enough to send word to my distressed mother that if she would not consent I would run away from home and join the army anyway. This last argument made her yield, and in the fall of 1849 I became an artillery cadet, being then in my seventeenth year. But although I won this victory over my mother, whose greatest desire was that I should become a clergyman, she in turn gained a victory over me by persuading the surgeon of the batallion, who was also our family physician, to declare me sick and send me to the hospital, although I had only a slight cold; thus my plan to go with the army to Schleswig-Holstein was frustrated. This did not make much difference, however, as the war was virtually closed before our troops arrived at the place of destination, and my time could now be more profitably employed in learning the duties of a soldier, and in taking a course of mathematics and other practical branches at the regimental school.

I remained in the army a year and a-half, during which time I received excellent instruction in gymnastics, fencing and riding, besides the regular military drill. Two winters were thus devoted to conscientious and thorough work at the military school.

Knowing that the chances for advancement in the Swedish army during times of peace were at this time very slim for young men not favored with titles of nobility, and being also tired of the monotonous garrison life, my friend Eustrom and myself soon resolved to leave the service and try our luck in a country where inherited names and titles were not the necessary conditions of success.
- 13 -
At that time America was little known in our part of the country, only a few persons having emigrated from the whole district. But we knew that it was a new country, inhabited by a free and independent people, that it had a liberal government and great natural resources, and these inducements were sufficient for us. My parents readily consented to my emigration, and, having made the necessary preparations, my father took my friend Eustrom and myself down to the coast with his own horses, in the first part of May, 1851. It was a memorable evening, and I shall never forget the last farewell to my home, in driving out from the court into the village street, how I stood up in the wagon, turned towards the dear home and waved my hat with a hopeful hurrah to the "folks I left behind." A couple of days' journey brought us to a little seaport, where we took leave of my father and boarded a small schooner for the city of Gothenburg.

At that time there were no ocean steamers and no emigrant agents; but we soon found a sailing vessel bound for America on which we embarked as passengers, furnishing our own bedding, provisions and other necessaries, which our mothers had supplied in great abundance. About one hundred and fifty emigrants from different parts of Sweden were on board the brig Ambrosius.

In the middle of May she weighed anchor and glided out of the harbor on her long voyage across the ocean to distant Boston.

We gazed back at the vanishing shores of the dear fatherland with feelings of affection, but did not regret the step we had taken, and our bosoms heaved with boundless hope. At the age of eighteen, the strong, healthy youth takes a bright and hopeful view of life, and so did we. Many and beautiful were the air-castles we built as we stood on deck, with our eyes turned towards the promised land of the nineteenth century. To some of these castles our lives have given reality, others are still floating before us.

- 14 -

CHAPTER II.

Arrival at Boston—Adventures between Boston and New York—Buffalo—An Asylum—Return to New York—A Voyage—On the Farm in New Hampshire.

The good brig Ambrosius landed us in Boston on June 29, 1851, but during the voyage about one-half of the passengers were attacked by small-pox and had to be quarantined outside the harbor. My good friend and I were fortunate enough to escape this plague; but instead of this I was taken sick with the ague on our arrival at Boston.

Now, then, we were in America! The new, unknown country lay before us, and it seemed the more strange as we did not understand a word of the English language. For at that time the schools of Sweden paid no attention to English, so that although I had studied four languages, English, the most important of all tongues, was entirely unknown to me.

The first few weeks of our stay in Boston passed quietly and quickly, but the ague grew worse and my purse was getting empty. My friend, however, had more money than I, and as long as he had a dollar left he divided it equally between us. I cannot resist the temptation to relate a serio-comical escapade of this period, one that to many will recall similar occurences in their own experience as immigrants ignorant of the language of the country.

In Gothenburg we had become acquainted with a bright young man from Vexiö, Janne Tenggren by name, who had also served in the army. When we met him he had already - 15 - bought a ticket on a sailing vessel bound for New York, so that we could not make the voyage together. But we agreed to hunt each other up after our arrival in America. We left Sweden about the same time with the understanding that if we arrived first we should meet him in New York, and if he arrived first he should go to Boston to meet us there.

About a week after our arrival in Boston, we heard that the vessel on which he had embarked had arrived, and I immediately left for New York to fulfill our promise. But, unfortunately, I found he had already gone west, so I bought a return ticket to Boston the same day. The journey was by steamboat to Fall River, thence by rail to Boston. We left New York in the evening. I remained on the deck, and went to sleep about ten o'clock on some wooden boxes. About eleven o'clock I awoke, saw the steamer laying to and, supposing we were at Fall River, hurried off and followed the largest crowd, expecting thus to get to the railroad depot. Striking no depot, however, I returned to the harbor, only to find the steamer gone, and everybody but myself had vanished from the pier.

There I stood, in the middle of the night, without money, ignorant of the language, and not even knowing where I was! Tired and discouraged I finally threw myself down on a wooden box on the sidewalk, and went to sleep. About five o'clock in the morning a big policeman aroused me by poking at me with his club. This respectable incarnation of social order evidently took me for a tramp or a madman, and as he could not obtain any intelligible information from me in any language known to him, he took me to a small shoe store kept by a German.

Fortunately, my acquaintance with the German language was sufficient to enable me to explain myself, and I soon found that I had left the steamer several hours too early; that the name of this place was New London, that another - 16 - steamer would come past at the same time the next night, so that all I had to do was to wait for that steamer and go to Boston on the same ticket.

I spent the day in seeing the city and chatting with my friend, the shoe maker, and in the evening returned to the wharf to watch for the Boston steamer.

This being my ague day, I had violent attacks of ague and fever, so that I was again forced to lie down to rest on the same wooden box, and again went to sleep. After a while I was aroused by the noise of the approaching steamer; rushed on board in company with some other passengers, and considered myself very fortunate when reflecting that I would surely be in Boston the next morning. I had made myself familiar with the surroundings during the day, and when the steamer started, I noticed that it directed its course towards New York, instead of Boston. I had no money to pay my fare to New York, could neither borrow nor beg, and so I crawled down in a little hole in the fore part of the steamer, where the tackles and ropes were kept, thus, fortunately, escaping the notice of the ticket collector.

The next evening I again embarked for Boston and finally arrived safely at my destination.

We stayed in Boston several weeks, and during that time my ague caused a heavy drain on our small treasury. We had no definite plan, did not know what to do, and as we had never been used to any kind of hard work, matters began to assume a serious aspect, especially in regard to myself. But then, as now, the hope of many a young man was the Great West which, at that time, was comparatively little known even in Boston. Toward the close of the month of July we, therefore, went to Buffalo, which was as far as our money would carry us. Here we put up at a cheap boarding house kept by a Norwegian by name of Larson, with whom we stopped while trying to get work. But having learned no trade and being unused to manual labor, we soon found that it was impossible to get a job in the city; so we left our baggage at the boarding house and started on foot for a country place named Hamburg, some ten miles distant, where we learned that two of our late companions across the ocean had found employment. On the road to Hamburg, about dusk, we reached a small house by the wayside, where we asked for food and shelter. I was so exhausted that my friend had to support me in order to reach the house. We found it occupied by a Swedish family, which had just sat down to a bountiful supper. Telling them our condition, we were roughly told to clear out; in Sweden, they said, they had had enough of gentlemen and would have nothing to do with them here.

We retraced our steps with sad hearts until a short distance beyond the house we found an isolated barn partly filled with hay. *There* was no one to object, so we took possession and made it our temporary home. I am glad to say that during a long life among all classes of people, from the rudest barbarians to the rulers of nations, that family of my own countrymen were the only people who made me nearly lose faith in the nobler attributes of man. I have an excuse, however, for this conduct in the fact that in the mother-country, which they had left a year before, they had probably been abused and exasperated on account of the foolish class distinction then existing there. They evidently belonged to that class of tenants who were treated almost like slaves. The following day we found our late companions a mile from our barn, both working for a farmer at $15.00 per month, which was then considered big wages. They were older men and accustomed to hard labor, so that their situation was comparatively easy. They received us kindly and procured work for Eustrom with the same farmer, while I, still suffering with the ague, could not then attempt to work, and therefore returned to my castle in the meadow, (the hay-barn). There I remained about a week living on berries which I found in the neighboring woods and a slice of bread and butter, which Eustrom brought me in the evening, when with blistered hands and sore back, he called to comfort me and help build better air castles for the future.

A council was finally held among us four, and it was decided to send me back to Buffalo with a farmer who was going there the following morning. One of the men Mr. Abraham Sandberg on parting gave me a silver dollar, with the injunction to give it to someone who might need it worse than I, whenever I could do so. I have never met Abraham since; but I have regarded it as a sacred duty to comply with his request, and, in case these lines should come before his eyes I wish to let him know that my debt has been honestly paid.

On reaching the old boarding house in Buffalo the landlord promised that he would send me to a hospital where I could receive proper treatment and care. I made up a little bundle of necessary underwear, and in an hour a driver appeared at the door; I was lifted into the cart and off we went through the muddy streets to the outskirts of the city, where I was duly delivered at a large building which I supposed to be the hospital. It was near evening, and I was brought into a large dining-room, with a hundred others or more, served with supper, corn mush and molasses water, after which I was shown to a bed in a large room among many others. I suffered with fever, and for the first time in my life with loneliness. Exhausted nature finally took out its due, and I slept soundly until awakened in the morning by a loud sound of a gong. As soon as dressed I walked out in the yard, or lawn, back of the building. On one side was a high plank fence, behind which I heard some strange sounds. I found a knot-hole, and, peeping through this, I observed another lawn, on which were many people. They were strange looking; I never saw any like them before. Some were swinging, some dancing, others shouting, singing and weeping and behaving in a most out-of-the-way manner. I wondered and wondered, and finally it dawned upon me that it must be a lunatic asylum. It was, in fact, as I since learned, the county poor farm, where one part was used for the lunatics and the other for paupers like myself. Has it come to this? I asked myself; is this the goal of all my ambition and hopes? Going back to the room, where I had slept, I stealthily took my little bundle, slipped out through a side door into a back yard, found a gate open and was soon in the street. I started on a run with all the power in me, as if pursued by all the furies of paupers and lunatics, never stopping until I was near the old boarding house, where I was taken in exhausted and in deep despair. I would have killed the landlord for deceiving me if I had been able to do so. One good thing resulted from the sad experience of that day: the mental shock on discovering where I was, cured me for the time being of the ague.

The next day my friend returned from Hamburg, where he could no longer get any employment on account of his blistered hands, and poor health in general. We now put our wise heads together and agreed that we had already had enough of the West for the time being. Having plenty of good clothes, bedding, revolvers and other knick-knacks, we sold to our landlord whatever we could spare, in order to raise money enough to pay our way back to Boston.

During our stay in Buffalo, our renowned countrywoman, Jenny Lind, happened to give a concert there. We were standing on the street where we could see the people crowd into the theatre, but that was all we could afford, and we never heard her sing. Our host advised us to go and ask her for help; but our pride forbade it.

At this time the Swedes were so little known, and Jenny Lind, on the other hand, so renowned in America, that the Swedes were frequently called "Jenny Lind men," this designation being often applied to myself.

Having purchased tickets for Albany, we returned East in the month of August. I still remember how we rode all night in a crowded second-class car, listening to the noisy merry-making of our fellow-passengers; but we understood very little of it, for up to this time we had lived exclusively among our own countrymen, and learned only a few English words—a mistake, by the way, which thousands of immigrants have made and are still making.

Arriving at Albany, we sat down by an old stone wall near the railroad depot, to talk over our affairs. Fate had been against us while we remained together, and we probably depended too much upon each other. Accordingly, we decided to part for some time and try our luck separately; and if one of us met with success he would, of course, soon be able to find a position for the other. We decided by drawing lots that Eustrom should go to Boston and I to New York. When we had bought our tickets there remained one dollar, which we divided, and we left for our respective places of destination the same evening.

Our landlord in Buffalo had given us the address of a sailors' boarding-house in New York, which was also kept by a Norwegian by the same name of Larson. So when I left the Hudson River steamer early the next morning, I paid my half-dollar to a drayman, who took me to said boarding house. I found Mr. Larson to be a kind, good-natured man, told him my difficulties right out, and asked him to let me stop at his house until I could find something to do. He agreed to this, and for a week or so I tried my best to get work. But, when asked what kind of work I could do, I was compelled to answer that I had learned no trade, but - 21 - that I would gladly try to learn anything and do anything whatever, even sweep the streets, if necessary. As a result of my protracted sickness, I was so weak and exhausted that nobody thought I would be able even to earn my bread. As to easy or intellectual work, I had no earthly chance, as long as I did not know the English language. Finally Mr. Larson took me to a ship-owner's office. I still remember that a Norwegian captain was cruel enough to remark in my hearing, that he did not intend to take any half-dead corpses along with him to sea.

After two weeks of fruitless efforts to get work for me, my host finally declared that he could not very well keep me any longer, because his accommodations were crowded with paying customers; nevertheless, he allowed me to sleep in the attic free of charge, while I had to procure my food as best I could, which I also did for another two weeks. Being a convalescent, I had a ravenous appetite, and, indeed, I found how hard it is to obtain food without having anything to pay for it. Of the few articles of clothing which I brought with me from Buffalo, I had to sacrifice one after another for subsistence. When all other means were exhausted, I was compelled to go to the kitchen-doors and tell my desperate and unfortunate condition by signs, and more than one kind-hearted cook gave me a solid meal.

Tramps! In our day there is a great deal of talk about tramps, and it has become customary, to brand as a tramp, any poor wandering laborer who seeks work. There are undoubtedly many who justly deserve this title; but I think there are tramps who are not to blame for their deplorable condition, and who deserve encouragement and friendly assistance, for I have been one of them myself, without any fault or neglect on my part. It always provokes me to hear a young or inexperienced person use the expression "tramp" so thoughtlessly, and in such a sweeping manner. Long ago - 22 - I made up my mind that no tramp should ever leave my door without such aid as my resources would allow. It is better to give to a thousand undeserving, than to let one unfortunate but deserving suffer.

My good host, like his Buffalo namesake, finally contrived to get rid of me by representing me as a sailor, and hiring me to the captain of the bark "Catherine," a coasting vessel bound for Charleston, S. C., telling me that I was to serve as cabin boy. My wages were to be five dollars a month, of which he received seven dollars and a-half in advance, so that I could pay my debts and buy a sailor's suit of clothes.

On the second day of our voyage we encountered a storm. I was on deck with the sailors and the captain stood on the quarter-deck. We were coursing against the wind and were just going to turn when the captain called on me to untie some ropes. Understanding very little English, and being no sailor, I naturally knew nothing about the names of the different ropes, and I grabbed one after another, but invariably missed the right one. The captain was swearing with might and main in English. Seeing that I did not understand him he suddenly roared out angrily the name of the rope in good Swedish and added: "Do you understand me now, you confounded blockhead!" Turning to him, cap in hand, I answered: "No, captain, I do not know the name of a single rope." "And still," he continued "you have followed the sea three years, what a dunce you are." I answered: "Indeed Mr. Captain, I have never been a sailor, and will never be worth anything at sea. But I am willing and anxious to do all you ask if within my power." The captain, whose name was Wilson, was a Swedish American and, although somewhat gruff, he was in fact one of the noblest men who ever commanded a ship. He immediately saw how the matter stood; the boarding house man had - 23 - cheated both him and me and from that hour Captain Wilson became my friend and benefactor.

Afterwards I found out of the whole crew, which numbered twenty-six men, nine-tenths were Scandinavians, but they always used the English language while on board the ship. Captain Wilson told me to see him in his cabin as soon as the work was performed. Here he asked me about my circumstances, and I told him the short story of my life, which elicited his sympathy to such an extent that he even asked me to pardon his rude behavior toward me. He assigned me to a place to sleep in the cabin; told the officers not to give me any orders as he was going to do that himself, and treated me with the utmost kindness and consideration in every respect.

After this I was excused from all work properly belonging to a sailor, but kept the cabin in order, and helped the steward in waiting at the table, and the officers with their calculations. During my spare hours I read and conversed with the captain and his two mates, one of whom was a Dane and the other an Irishman, both splendid fellows. The first mate was preparing the second mate for a captain's examination, and I, having recently taken a course in mathematics, at a military school, was able to assist them in their studies.

On the table in the cabin was a large English Bible, with which I spent many happy hours, and by which I learned the English language. At first I used to pick out chapters of the New Testament, which I knew almost by heart, so that I could understand them without a dictionary or an interpreter. After my first conversation with the captain I did not speak another word in the Swedish language during the voyage, and when I returned to Boston, three months afterwards, it seemed to me that I could talk and read English about as well as Swedish.

- 24 -

I made two trips with the captain from New York to Charleston and back again. At the wharf of Charleston, I was, for the first time in my life, brought face to face with American Negro slavery in its most odious aspect. Crowds of Negroes were running along the pier pulling long ropes, by means of which the ships were loaded and unloaded. Each gang of Negroes was under the charge of a brutal overseer, riding on a mule, and brandishing a long cowhide whip, which he applied vigorously to the backs of the half-naked Negroes. During the night they were kept penned up in sheds, which had been erected for that purpose near the wharf. They were treated like cattle, in every respect. This sight influenced me in later life to become a Republican in politics.

After our second return to New York, Capt. Wilson assumed the command of one of the first clipper ships which carried passengers to California in those days. This was at the most stirring time of the gold fever, and the captain kindly offered to take me along and let me stay out there, an offer which thousands would have accepted. But I was never smitten with the gold fever, and, having a distaste for the sea, I said good-bye to the kind captain, never to see him again. My wages were to have been only five dollars a month, but he generously paid me eight dollars, so that I had earned enough money to pay my way to Boston, whence my friend Eustrom had written me and urged me to come.

I arrived in Boston about the middle of December, and, when I returned to the old boarding house, I spoke English so well that my acquaintances hardly believed it possible that I could be the same person. Mr. Eustrom was now working as wood polisher. He had made many friends and lived happily and contented on $4 a week. By strict economy these wages sufficed for board, lodging, and clothes. - 25 - It happened to be an unfavorable time of the year when I arrived, however, and many men who had been employed during the summer were now discharged at the approach of winter. Mr. Eustrom's employer had a good friend in New Hampshire, an old Swedish sailor, Anderson by name, who was farming up there. He promised to let me come and live with him and do whatever chores I could until something might turn up the next spring.

A few days afterwards I went by rail to Contocook where I was met by Mr. Anderson, who took me out to his hospitable home a couple of miles from the town. This Anderson was a remarkable man. Having no education to speak of, he was a better judge of human nature and practical affairs of life than any other man I ever met. He was pleased with me, and said he wished I would sit down in the evening and tell him about Sweden, and explain to him what I had learned at school. Poor Anderson! He had one fault, rum got the better of him, and it was cheap in New England at that time, only sixteen cents a gallon. He bought a barrel of it at a time, and did not taste water as long as the rum lasted.

The day after my arrival he asked me if I would like to go with him into the woods to help cut some logs. Of course I would, and we took our axes and started off. It was a very cold December day, and I had thin clothes and no mittens. Mr. Anderson went to cut down a tree, and I commenced to work at one which was already felled. This was the first time I swung an axe in earnest, and after a short while I felt that my hands were getting cold. But I made up my mind not to stop until the log was finished. By holding the axe handle very tight it stopped the circulation of the blood through my fingers, and when I finally stopped and dropped the axe I could not move my fingers, for eight of them were frozen stiff. Mr. Anderson now took off his cap, filled it with snow, put my hands into the snow, and thus we ran to the - 26 - house as fast as our legs would carry us. The doctor tried his very best; but, nevertheless, in a few days the flesh and the nails began to peel off, and two doctors decided to amputate all the fingers on my right hand. Fortunately I did not give my consent, but told them that I would rather die of gangrene than live without hands, for my future depended exclusively on them.

My friend Eustrom, having heard of my misfortune, soon came to visit me, and brought with him an old Irish woman who was something of a doctor, and cured my hands by means of a very simple plaster which she prepared herself. But I was forced into complete inactivity for more than three months, during which time I was entirely helpless, and had to be washed, dressed, and fed like an infant. But, as to me, the old proverb has always proved true: "When things are at the worst they'll mend." There were men and women in my accidental home who willingly tended to me in my trouble. May God bless them for it! In the latter part of March, Mr. Anderson, who had always treated me with the greatest kindness, quite unexpectedly told me that I was now able to work again and could try to get a place with some other family in the neighborhood, because he could not keep me any longer.

Our nearest neighbor was a genuine Yankee, Daniel Dustin by name. He was very rich, well read, liberal minded, respectable and honest, but so *close* that he would scarcely let his own family have enough food to eat, and his wife was even more stingy. Mr. Dustin agreed to let me work for my board until spring, and then he would give me five dollars a month, which offer I cheerfully accepted. He immediately took me out into the woods to chop wood for the summer, and he was to haul it home. The new, tender muscles and nails on my fingers made wood chopping very painful to me, and I could feel every blow of the axe through - 27 - my entire body. Never has any man worked so hard for me, when I afterwards hired help for good wages, as I worked for my board here; and, by the way, this board consisted chiefly of potatoes and corn meal cake. When the spring work commenced I got five dollars a month, and had to get up at five o'clock in the morning to do the chores, and then work in the field from seven in the morning until dark.

In the beginning of June I got a letter from my parents, stating that my father and brother were going to leave for New York immediately, and they asked me to meet them there and go West with them. I had never complained in my letters to my parents, but, on the other hand, I had not advised them to come to America, either. They had been advised to do so by some of my fellow-passengers on the "Ambrosius," who went to Illinois, and were highly pleased with their prospects. So I went to Boston again. My father's voyage had been delayed, and I had to wait for him over a month, during which time I got sick, and would have been in a sorry plight, indeed, if it had not been for my friend Eustrom, who now felt like a rich man, with his six dollars a week. A couple of years later he became the partner of his employer.

- 28 -

CHAPTER III.

The Arrival of my Father and Brother—Journey to Illinois—Work on a Railroad—The Ague—Doctor Ober—Religious Impressions—The Arrival of my Mother, Sister and her Husband—A Burning Railroad Train—We go to Minnesota—Our Experience as Wood Choppers and Pioneers.

Finally my father and brother arrived, and again I turned my course westwards in company with them and their friends. We traveled by rail to Buffalo and across the lake to Toledo, thence by rail again to Chicago. In the summer of 1852 there were no railroads west of Chicago, and our company had to take passage on a canal-boat drawn by horses to La Salle, and from this place we rode in farmers wagons to Andover and Galesburg. The country around there was as yet only in the first stages of development; there was very little money in circulation, and no demand for farm products. The immigrants suffered a great deal from fever and other climatic diseases.

My brother who was nearly sixteen years old soon obtained steady work from an American farmer, while my father and I had to do different kinds of work, such as building fences, stacking grain, etc. The only pay we could get was checks on some store. I remember what an abundance of provisions there was in that locality, and nobody seemed to be in need.

A farmer near Galesburg, for whom I worked a week, had so many hens and chickens and eggs, that when people came out from town to buy eggs, they were told to pay ten cents, - 29 - go out to the barn and fill their baskets with freshly-laid eggs, no matter how big the basket. Beef and pork had scarcely any value, and anybody could go into a cornfield that fall and gather a crop on half shares.

There was much religious interest among the Swedes in Illinois at that time. The Methodists and Lutherans were already building churches, and held services side by side in many of the towns and settlements, although they numbered only a few families yet. I remember distinctly one Sunday attending service in a Methodist church listening to an eloquent preacher, taking for his text "The Broad and the Narrow Ways." He depicted both in glowing language, and wound up with the following words, pronounced in a broad (Swedish) dialect: "My dear brethren, I have now shown you the two ways, and you may take which ever you like; that is all the same to me."

My father had taken with him only just enough money to pay his way, although he had by no means exhausted his resources in Sweden, for he had prudently decided to spend at least a year in seeing the country and making himself familiar with its institutions, customs, manner of tilling the soil, etc. At this time he was a strong man, at the age of fifty. In order to obtain steady work, we two, and a few others of our company, hired a man in Galesburg to take us to Rock River, where a bridge for the Chicago & Rock Island Railroad was being built. We all got work, and had to take hold of the spade and the shovel. The wages in those days for railroad laborers were from seventy-five cents to one dollar per day. I received only seventy-five cents, out of which my board was to be paid, which, however, was very cheap, one dollar and a half per week only. A Swede by the name of Hoffman kept a boarding house for thirty-four of us, and all would have been well except for the ague. No man remained there many days without getting the "shakes;" I - 30 - and my father got them the second day. The lower part of the shanty in which we boarded was used for dining-room and kitchen, the upper for sleeping on the floor. The shanty was as shaky as the ague, which came regularly every other day. Fate had so arranged it that seventeen of us had the chills one day, and seventeen the next day. Hoffman and his wife fortunately also had the chills alternate days, so that there was always one to attend to the cooking.

Some may doubt it, but it is a solemn fact, that when seventeen ate dinner below, the shaking of those upstairs sometimes shook the house until we could hear the plates rattling on the table.

During my healthy days I stood on the bottom of Rock River from seven o'clock in the morning until seven at night, throwing wet sand with a shovel onto a platform above, from which it was again thrown to another, and from there to terra firma. The most disagreeable part of the business was that one-quarter of each shovel-full came back on the head of the operator.

After a couple of weeks the company's paymaster came along, and upon settling my board bill and deducting for the shaking days, I made the discovery that I was able to earn only fifteen cents net per week in building railroad bridges.

Being half dead by this time from over work and sickness, we decided to see if we could strike an easier job, and, if possible, a better climate. We happened to meet a farmer by the name of Peterson, with whom we rode to a place near Moline, where my father tended to me during my illness. When he was not occupied with this he chopped cord wood from dry old trees. I also tried to assist him in this, but found my strength gone.

Among the Swedes living in Moline at that time was a tailor, Johnson by name, a good kind-hearted man who, together with his wife, was always ready to aid his needy - 31 - countrymen and get something to do for such as could work. I went to him one day to ask for advice or assistance, just as a great many had done before me. I was so weak and sickly that they had to assist me in getting into the house, but they received me as if I had been their own son, and, after a short rest, Mr. Johnson took me to one Dr. Ober, who carefully investigated my mental as well as my physical condition, and told me that such hard work as I had been doing would kill me, and that I ought to rest and take it easy. He was one of those magnanimous, noble men who are to be met with in all climes and walks of life, but who are easily recognized because they are so few. As I have said before, I have been very fortunate in getting acquainted with the best men and women of different classes and nations with which I have come in contact. While we were sitting in his reception room the doctor suddenly left us and went into his private room. In a short time he returned accompanied by his wife, a lady whose silvery locks and benignantly sympathizing looks made her seem more beautiful to me than a madonna. Having simply taken a hasty look at me, the doctor and his wife again withdrew, and when they returned he offered to let me stay with them like a member of the family in order that he might try to restore my health; he also allowed me to avail myself of his library and to attend school, the only condition being that I should do chores around the house and take care of the horses.

I moved the same day, got a pleasant room and a snug bed, good, substantial food, and, above all, good and friendly treatment, so that from the time I came there until the day I left, I felt as if I had been a child of the house. Dr. Ober, who was a religious man, belonged to the Baptist Church, and as I now lived under its beneficent influence, and also became acquainted with the Swedish Baptist Pastor, Rev. G. Palmquist, and a few others who constituted - 32 - the nucleus of the First Swedish Baptist Church of America. I became a member of their society before spring and would probably have continued a member of this denomination, if circumstances which were beyond my control, had not brought me to other fields of action and other surroundings.

This winter passed in a very pleasant manner. In the afternoon I attended an English school, and in the evening I gave instructions in English to other young men and women. The friendship of Dr. Ober and his wife never failed, and many years afterwards I was a welcome guest at their home in La Crosse, Wis., to which place they had moved from Moline. Both of them now slumber under the sod, but their many good deeds shall live for ever.

My father was much pleased with the great west, and he wrote back to the rest of our family in Sweden to come to this country the next summer, and in May I started to meet them in Boston. As there were no railroads to Moline, I took a steamboat to Galena, and thence the stage-coach to Freeport, and from there to Chicago by rail.

The vessel carrying my mother and the party with her was three months on the ocean, and there was great scarcity of provisions on board. The ship at last arrived, in the month of July, and a couple of days later the whole party, consisting of about two hundred, took the train for the west, I volunteering as their guide and interpreter. All went well until about one hundred miles east of Chicago, when the baggage car attached to our train in front caught fire. It was thought best to try to reach a station, and the burning train sped on at the rate of sixty miles an hour. The scene was a frightful one, the cars crammed full of frightened emigrants, the flames hissing like serpents from car to car, windows cracking, people screaming, and women fainting, all at the same time looking to me, who was not yet twenty years of age, for protection and deliverance.
- 33 -
As soon as possible I placed reliable men as guards at the doors to prevent the people from rushing out and crowding each other off the platform. The train did not reach the station but had to be stopped on the open prairie, where we all were helped out of the cars with no accident of any kind except every particle of baggage, saving only what the passengers had in their seats with them, was burnt. In due time another train brought us to Chicago, where the railroad company immediately offered to pay all losses as soon as lists of the property destroyed could be made out and properly verified. I undertook to do all that work without the aid of consul, lawyer or clerk, collecting nearly twenty thousand dollars, for old trunks, spinning-wheels, copper kettles, etc. Having lost nothing myself, I of course received nothing, and as the Company did not consider it their duty to pay me for my trouble, one of the emigrants suggested that they should chip in to compensate me for the valuable services I had rendered. Accordingly the hat was passed, the collection realizing the magnificent sum of two dollars and sixty cents, which was paid me for being their in-

terpreter during the long journey and for collecting that large sum of money without litigation or delay. No lawyer, consul or agent would have been satisfied with less than five hundred dollars, but I can truthfully say that I never raised a word of complaint, but freely forgave the people on account of their ignorance. Many of them I also served afterwards on the way to Moline and Minnesota. In due time our party arrived in Moline, where my parents bought a small piece of property with the money brought from Sweden.

Minnesota was then a territory but little known; yet we had heard of its beautiful lakes, forests, prairies and salubrious climate. Quite a number of our company had decided to hunt up a place for a Swedish settlement where land could be had cheap. It was finally agreed that a few of us - 34 - should go to Minnesota and select a suitable place. Being the only one of the party who could speak English, I was naturally appointed its leader. My father also went with us, and so did Mr. Willard and his wife, the whole party taking deck passage on a Mississippi steamer, and arriving at St. Paul in the month of August.

At that time St. Paul was an insignificant town of a few hundred inhabitants. There we found Henry Russell, John Tidlund, and a few other Swedish pioneers. Mr. Willard and I had very little money, and for the few dollars which we did own we bought a little household furniture, and some cooking utensils. We therefore at once sought employment for him, while the rest of our party started off in search of a suitable location for the proposed settlement.

We had been told that there were a number of our countrymen at Chisago Lake and a few near Carver, but that all had settled on timber lands. We also learned that near Red Wing, in Goodhue county, places could be found with both timber and prairie, and an abundance of good water. Having looked over the different localities we finally decided on the present town of Vasa, about twelve miles west of Red Wing. The first claims were taken at Belle Creek, south of White Rock, and afterwards others were taken at a spring now known as Willard Spring, near which the large brick church now stands.

After selecting this land my father returned to Illinois. In company with the other explorers. I went to St. Paul, where a council was held in which all participated, and at which it was decided that three of us, Messrs. Roos, Kempe, and myself, should go to our claims that fall and do as much work as possible, until the others could join us the following spring.

Having made the necessary preparations we three went to Red Wing by steamboat and found a little town with half a - 35 - dozen families, among whom was the Rev. J. W. Hancock, who for several years had been a missionary among the Indians. The other settlers were Wm. Freeborn, Dr. Sweeney, H. L. Bevans, and John Day. Besides these we also met two Swedes, Peter Green, and Nels Nelson, and a Norwegian by the name of Peterson. On the bank of the river the Sioux Indians had a large camp. The country west of Red Wing was then practically a wilderness, and our little party was the first to start in to cultivate the soil and make a permanent settlement.

At Red Wing we supplied ourselves with a tent, a cook stove, a yoke of oxen, carpenter's tools, provisions and other necessaries. Having hired a team of horses, we then packed our goods on a wagon, tied the cattle behind, and started for the new settlement. The first four miles we followed the territorial road; after that we had nothing but Indian trails to guide us. Toward evening we arrived at a grove on Belle Creek, now known as Jemtland. Here the tent was pitched and our evening meal cooked, and only pioneers like ourselves can understand how we relished it after our long day's tramp. The team was taken back the next day, and we were left alone in the wilderness.

After a day's exploration we moved our camp two miles further south, to another point near Belle Creek, where Mr. Roos had taken his claim.

It was now late in September, and our first care was to secure enough hay for the cattle, and in a few days we had a big stack. Having read about prairie fires, we decided to protect our stack by burning away the short stubble around it. But a minute and a half was sufficient to convince us that we had made wrong calculations, for within that time the stack itself was burning with such fury that all the water in Belle Creek could not have put it out. Still, this was not the worst of it. Before we had time to recover from our - 36 - astonishment the fire had spread over the best part of the valley and consumed all the remaining grass, which was pretty dry at that time of the year. Inexperienced as we were, we commenced to run a race with the wind, and tried to stop the fire before reaching another fine patch of grass about a mile to the north; but this attempt was, of course, a complete failure, and we returned to our cheerless tent mourning over this serious misfortune.

The next morning we all started out in different directions to see if any grass was left in Goodhue County, and fortunately we found plenty of it near our first camping-ground. Having put up a second stack of very poor hay, we proceeded to build a rude log house, and had just finished it when my brother-in-law, Mr. Willard, surprised us by appearing in our midst, having left in Red Wing his wife and baby, now Mrs. Zelma Christensen of Rush City, who is, as far as I know, the first child born of Swedish parents in St. Paul. Mr. Willard who was a scholarly gentleman and not accustomed to manual labor, had found it rather hard to work with shovel and pick on the hilly streets of St. Paul, and made up his mind that he would better do that kind of work on a farm. Messers. Roos and Kempe having furnished all the money for the outfit, I really had no share in it, and as we could not expect Mr. Willard and his family to pass the winter in that cabin, I immediately made up my mind to return with him to Red Wing. In an hour we were ready and without waiting for dinner we took the trail back to that place. I remember distinctly how, near the head of the

Spring Creek Valley, we sat down in a little grove to rest and meditate on the future. We were both very hungry, especially Mr. Willard, who had now walked over twenty miles since breakfast. Then espying a tempting squirrel in a tree close by, we tried to kill it with sticks and rocks; but we were poor marksmen, and thus missed a fine squirrel roast.

- 37 -

Tired and very hungry we reached Red Wing late in the afternoon, and soon found my sister, Mrs. Willard, comfortably housed with one of the families there. Her cheerful and hopeful nature and the beautiful baby on her arm gave us fresh joy and strength to battle with the hardships that were in store for us. Mr. Willard and his wife had taken along what furniture they owned, a few eatables and five dollars and fifty cents in cash, which was all that we possessed of the goods of this world. But who cares for money at that age? Mr. Willard was twenty-five years old, my sister twenty-three, and I twenty, all hale and hearty, and never for a moment doubting our success, no matter what we should undertake.

Our first work was wood chopping, for which we were less fit than almost anything else. We had to go to a place about three miles above Red Wing, where a man had made a contract to bank up fifteen hundred cords of wood for the Mississippi steamers. There was an old wood chopper's cabin which we repaired by thatching it with hay and earth, putting in a door, a small window, and a few rough planks for a floor. In a few days we were duly installed, baby and all, in the little hut which was only twelve by sixteen feet, but to us as dear as a palace to a king.

We began to chop wood at once. The trees were tall, soft maples and ash, and our pay was fifty-five cents a cord for soft and sixty-five cents for hard wood. At first both of us could not chop over a cord a day together; but within a week we could chop a cord apiece, and before the winter was over we often chopped three cords together in a day. After a few days we were joined by four Norwegian wood choppers for whom we put up a new cabin to sleep in; but my sister cooked for us all, and the others paid for their board to Mr. Willard and myself, who had all things in common. Those four men were better workmen than we, and one of them, Albert - 38 - Olson, often chopped three cords a day. They were quiet, industrious, and generous fellows, so that we soon became attached to each other, and we were all very fond of the little Zelma. My sister managed our household affairs so well and kept the little house so neat and tidy that when spring came we were all loth to leave.

The weather being fine and the sleighing good in the beginning of January, we hired John Day to take us with his team to our claims while there was yet snow, so that we might chop and haul out logs for the house which Mr. Willard and I intended to put up in the spring. My sister remained in the cabin, but Albert went with us for the sake of company. We put some lumber on the sled, and provided ourselves with hay and food enough to last a few days, and plenty of quilts and blankets for our bedding. John Day, who was an old frontiersman with an instinct almost like that of an Indian, guided us safely to Willard Spring. A few hundred yards below this, in a deep ravine, we stopped near some sheltering trees, built a roaring camp-fire, and made ourselves as comfortable as possible. Having supped and smoked our evening pipe, we made our beds by putting a few boards on the snow, and the hay and blankets on top of those. Then all four of us nestled down under the blankets and went to sleep.

During the night the thermometer fell down to forty degrees below zero, as we learned afterwards. If we had suspected this and kept our fire burning there would, of course, have been no danger. But being very comfortable early in the night and soon asleep, we were unconscious of danger until aroused by an intense pain caused by the cold, and then we were already so benumbed and chilled that we lacked energy to get up or even move. We found, on comparing notes afterwards, that each one of us had experienced the same sensations, namely, first an acute pain as if pricked with needles in every fibre, then a deep mental tranquillity which - 39 - was only slightly disturbed by a faint conception of something wrong, and by a desire to get up, but without sufficient energy to do so. This feeling gradually subsided into one of quiet rest and satisfaction, until consciousness ceased altogether, and, as far as pain was concerned, all was over with us.

At this stage an accident occurred which saved our lives. Mr. Day, who lay on the outside to the right, had evidently held his arm up against his breast to keep the blankets close to his body. His will-force being gone, his arm relaxed and fell into the snow. As the bare hand came in contact with the snow the circulation of the blood was accelerated, and this was accompanied by such intense pain that he was aroused and jumped to his feet.

Thus we were saved. It took a good while before we could use our limbs sufficiently to build a fire again, and during this time we suffered much more than before. From that experience I am satisfied that those who freeze to death do not suffer much, because they gradually sink into a stupor which blunts the sensibilities long before life is extinct.

It was about four o'clock when we got up. Of course we did not lie down again that morning, nor did we attempt to haul any timber, but started in a bee line across the prairie for the ravine where Mr. Willard and I had seen the tempting squirrel a few months before. We soon found that going over the wild, trackless prairie against the wind, with the thermometer forty degrees below zero was a struggle for life, and in order to keep warm we took turns to walk or run behind the sleigh. In taking his turn Mr. Willard suddenly sat down in the snow and would not stir. We returned to him, and it required all our power of persuasion to make him take his seat in the sleigh again. He felt very comfortable he said, and would soon catch up with - 40 - us again if we only would let him alone. If we had followed his advice, he would never have left his cold seat again. After a drive of eight miles we arrived at a house on Spring Creek, near Red Wing, where we found a warm room and a good shed for the horses. After an hour's rest we continued the journey, and safely reached our little home in the woods before dark. I do not know that I ever appreciated a home more than I did that rude cabin when again comfortably seated by its warm and cheerful fire-place.

A few weeks later I had an opportunity to visit St. Paul, and while there attended the wedding of a young Norwegian farmer from Carver County and a girl just arrived from Sweden. The ceremony was performed by the Rev. Nilsson, a Baptist minister, who had been banished from Sweden on account of proselyting. Among the guests was Mr. John Swainsson, who since became well known among the Swedes of Minnesota, and who died in St. Paul a short time ago. I also made the acquaintance of one Jacob Falstrom, who had lived forty years among the Indians and devoted most of that time to missionary work among them. He was a remarkable man, and was well known among the Hudson Bay employees and other early settlers of the Northwest. As a boy he had deserted from a Swedish vessel in Quebec and made his way through the wilderness, seeking shelter among the Indians; and, by marrying an Indian girl, he had become almost identified with them. I think he told me that he had not heard a word spoken in his native tongue in thirty-five years, and that he had almost forgotten it when he met the first Swedish settlers in the St. Croix valley. His children are now living there, while he has passed away to the unknown land beyond, honored and respected by all who knew him, Indians as well as white men.

On my return from St. Paul I stopped at the cabin of Mr. - 41 - Peter Green, at Spring Creek, near Red Wing. The only domestic animals he had was a litter of pigs, and as Mr. Willard and I intended to settle on our land in the spring I thought it might be well to start in with a couple of pigs. Accordingly, I got two pigs from Mr. Green, put them in a bag which I shouldered, and left for our cabin in the woods. According to my calculations, the distance I had to walk ought not to be over three miles, and in order to be sure of not getting lost I followed the Cannon river at the mouth of which our cabin stood. I walked on the ice where the snow was about a foot deep, and, if I had known of the meandering course of the river, I would never have undertaken to carry that burden such a distance. From nine in the morning until it was almost dark I trudged along with my burden on my back, prompted to the greatest exertion by the grunting of the pigs, and feeling my back uncomfortably warm. These were the first domestic animals I ever owned, and I think I well earned my title to them by carrying them along the windings of the river at least ten miles. Both I and the pigs were well received when we reached the cabin. We made a pig pen by digging a hole in the ground and covering it with poles and brush, and fed them on the refuse from the table. Before we were ready to move one of them died, while the other, after being brought to our new farm, ungratefully ran away, and was most likely eaten up by the wolves, which perhaps was just as agreeable to him as to be eaten by us.

While living in this camp we saw more Indians than white men. A band of Sioux Indians camped near us for several weeks. They were very friendly, and never molested us. The men brought us venison and fresh fish, which they caught in great quantities by spearing them through the ice. We gave them bread and coffee, and sometimes invited one or two to dinner after we were through. Their women would - 42 - stay for hours with my sister and help her take care of the baby. Indeed they were so fond of the white-haired child that they would sometimes run a race in vying with each other to get the first chance to fondle her. Sometimes we visited them in their tents in the evening and smoked Kinikinick with them. Several of their dead reposed in the young trees near our cabin. When somebody died it was their custom to stretch the dead body on poles which were tied to young trees high enough to be out of the reach of wild beasts, then cover it with blankets, and finally leave some corn and venison and a jar of water close by. At some subsequent visit to the neighborhood they would gather the bones and bury them at some regular burial-ground, usually on a high hill or bluff.

MOUNTAIN CHIEF.

Once we saw a regular war dance in Red Wing. A few Sioux had killed two Chippewas and brought back their scalps stretched on a frame of young saplings. At a given - 43 - hour the whole band assembled, and, amid the most fantastic gestures, jumping, singing, yelling, beating of tom-toms and jingling of bells, gave a performance which in lurid savageness excelled anything I ever saw. The same Indians again became our neighbors for a short time on Belle Creek the following winter, and we rather liked them, and they us. But eight years later they took part in the terrible massacre of the white settlers in Western Minnesota, and thirty-nine of their men were hanged on one gallows at Mankato in the fall of 1862 and the rest transported beyond our borders.

Thus our first winter in Minnesota passed without further incidents, until the beginning of March, when the weather turned so mild that we were afraid the ice on the Mississippi might break up, and we therefore hurried back to Red Wing. By our wood chopping and Mrs. Willard's cooking enough money had been earned to buy the most necessary articles for our new home. When we had procured everything and taken a few days' rest, we again hired Mr. John Day to take us out to our land with his team. Hundreds of thousands of immigrants have had the same experience, and can realize how we felt on that fine March morning, starting from Red Wing with a wagon loaded with some boards on the bottom, a cook stove and utensils, doors, windows, a keg of nails, saws, spades, a small supply of provisions, a bedstead or two with bedding, a few trunks, and a little box containing our spotted pig, Mrs. Willard in the seat with the driver, her baby in her arms, her husband and myself taking turns as guides, John Day shouting to his horses, laughing and joking; all of us full of hope, strength and determination to overcome all obstacles and conquer the wildness. The snow was now nearly gone, and the air was spring-like.

After a twelve miles' heavy pull we arrived at our destination, and made a temporary tent of sticks and blankets, very much after the Indian fashion. Two of the Norwegians had - 44 - accompanied us to help build our cabin. Mr. Day stopped a couple of days hauling building material, and before night the second day the rear part of our cabin was under roof. After a few days the Norwegians left us, and Mr. Willard and myself had to finish the main part of the building which was also made of round logs. For many a year this rude log cabin was the centre of attraction, and a hospitable stopping place for nearly all the settlers of Vasa.

In the month of April cold weather set in again, and it was very late in the season when steamboat navigation was opened on the Mississippi. At that time all provisions had to be shipped from Galena or Dubuque, and it happened that the winter's supplies in Red Wing were so nearly gone that not a particle of flour or meat could be bought after the first of April. Our supplies were soon exhausted, and for about two weeks our little family had only a peck of potatoes, a small panful of flour, and a gallon of beans to live on, part of which was a present from Messrs. Roos and Kempe, who had remained all winter on their claims, three miles south of us. They had been struggling against great odds, and had been compelled to live on half rations for a considerable length of time. Even their oxen had been reduced almost to the point of starvation, their only feed being over-ripe hay in small quantities.

We would certainly have starved if it had not been for my shot-gun, with which I went down into the woods of Belle Creek every morning at daybreak, generally returning with pheasants, squirrels or other small game. One Sunday the weather was so disagreeable and rough that I did not succeed in my hunting, but in feeding the team back of the kitchen some oats had been spilt, and a flock of blackbirds came and fed on them. Through an opening between the logs of the kitchen I shot several dozen of these birds, which, by the way, are not ordinarily very toothsome. But, being - 45 - a splendid cook, my sister made them into a stew, thickened with a few mashed beans and a handful of flour—in our estimation the mess turned out to be a dinner fit for kings.

Our supplies being nearly exhausted, I started for Red Wing the next morning, partly to save the remaining handful of provisions for my sister and her husband, partly in hopes of obtaining fresh supplies from a steamboat which was expected about that time. Three days afterwards the steamer arrived. As soon as practicable the boxes were brought to the store of H. L. Bevans. I secured a smoked ham, thirty pounds of flour, a gallon of molasses, some coffee, salt and sugar, strapped it all (weighing almost seventy pounds) on my back, and started toward evening for our cabin in the wilderness. I had to walk about fourteen miles along the Indian trail, but in spite of the heavy burden I made that distance in a short time, knowing that the dear ones at home were threatened by hunger; perhaps the howling of the prairie wolves near my path also had something to do with the speed. There are events in the life of every person which stand out like mile-stones along the road, and so attract the attention of the traveler on life's journey that they always remain vivid pictures in his memory. My arrival at our cabin that evening was one of those events in our humble life. I will not attempt to describe the joy which my burden brought to all of us, especially to the young mother with the little babe at her breast.

- 46 -

CHAPTER IV.

Future Hopes—Farm Life—Norwegian Pioneers—The Condition of the Immigrant at the Beginning of the Fifties—Religious Meetings—The Growth of the Settlement—Vasa Township Organized—A Lutheran Church Established—My Wedding—Speculation—The Crisis of 1857—Study of Law in Red Wing—I am admitted to the Bar and elected County Auditor—Politics in 1860—War is Imminent.

We had now commenced a new career, located on our farm claims in the boundless West, with no end to the prospects and possibilities before us. We felt that independence and freedom which are only attained and appreciated in the western wilds of America.

From the Mississippi river and almost to the Pacific Ocean, was a verdant field for the industry, energy and enterprise of the settler. To be sure, our means and resources were small, but somehow we felt that by hard work and good conduct we would some day attain the comfort, independence and position for which our souls thirsted. We did not sit down and wait for gold mines to open up before us, or for roasted pigs to come running by our cabin, but with axe and spade went quietly to work, to do our little part in the building up of new empires.

OUR WAGON.

In the beginning of May, my father came from Illinois and brought us a pair of steers and a milch cow; this made us - 47 - rich. We made a wagon with wheels of blocks sawed off an oak log; we also bought a plow, and, joining with our neighbors of Belle Creek, had a breaking team of two pair of oxen. That breaking team and that truck wagon, with myself always as the chief ox driver, did all the breaking, and all the hauling and carting of lumber, provisions, building-material and other goods, for all the settlers in that neighborhood during the first season.

Soon others of our party from last year joined us. Some letters which I wrote in *Hemlandet* describing the country around us, attracted much attention and brought settlers from different parts of the west, and while the Swedes were pouring into our place, then known as "Mattson's Settlement," (now well known under the name of Vasa), our friends, the Norwegians, had started a prosperous settlement a few miles to the south, many of them coming overland from Wisconsin, bringing cattle, implements and other valuables of which the Swedes, being mostly poor new-comers, were destitute. Many immigrants of both nationalities came as deck passengers on the Mississippi steamers to Red Wing.

There was cholera at St. Louis that summer, and I remember how a steamer landed a large party of Norwegian immigrants, nearly all down with cholera. Mr. Willard and myself happened to be in Red Wing at the time, and the American families, considering these Norwegian cholera patients our countrymen, hastily turned them over to our care. We nursed them as best we could, but many died in spite of all our efforts, and as we closed their eyes, and laid them in the silent grave under the bluffs, it never occurred to us that they were anything but our countrymen and brothers.

From these small beginnings of the Swedish and Norwegian settlers in Goodhue county, in the years of 1853 and 1854, have sprung results which are not only grand but - 48 - glorious to contemplate. Looking back to those days I see the little cabin, often with a sod roof, single room used for domestic purposes, sometimes crowded almost to suffocation by hospitable entertainments to new-comers; or the poor immigrant on the levee at Red Wing, just landed from a steamer, in his short jacket and other outlandish costume, perhaps seated on a wooden box, with his wife and a large group of children around him, and wondering how he shall be able to raise enough means to get himself ten or twenty miles into the country, or to redeem the bedding and other household goods which he has perchance left in Milwaukee as a pledge for his railroad and steam-boat ticket. And I see him trudging along over the trackless prairie, searching for a piece of land containing if possible prairie, water and a - 49 - little timber, on which to build a home. Poor, bewildered, ignorant, and odd looking, he had been an object of pity and derision all the way from Gothenburg or Christiania to the little cabin of some country-man of his, where he found rest and shelter until he could build one of his own.

OUR FIRST HOME.

Those who have not experienced frontier life, will naturally wonder how it was possible for people so poor as a majority of the old settlers were, to procure the necessaries of life, but they should remember that our necessities were few, and our luxuries a great deal less. The bountiful earth soon yielded bread and vegetables; the woods and streams supplied game and fish; and as to shoes and clothing, I and many others have used shoes made of untanned skins, and even of gunny-sacks and old rags. Furthermore, the small merchants at the river or other points, were always willing to supply the Scandinavian emigrants with necessary goods on credit, until better times should come. Our people in this country did certainly earn a name for integrity and honesty among their American neighbors, which has been a greater help to them than money.

Some of the men would go off in search of work, and in due time return with means enough to help the balance of the family.

Frontier settlers are always accommodating and generous. If one had more than he needed, he would invariably share the surplus with his neighbors. The neighbors would all turn in to help a new-comer,—haul his logs, build his house, and do other little services, for him.

The isolated condition and mutual aims and aspirations of the settlers brought them nearer together than in older communities. On Sunday afternoons all would meet at some centrally located place, and spend the day together. A cup of coffee with a couple of slices of bread and butter, would furnish a royal entertainment, and when we got so far - 50 - along that we could afford some pie or cake for dessert, the good house-wives were in a perfect ecstacy. The joys and sorrows of one, were shared by the others, and nowhere in the wide world, except in a military camp, have I witnessed so much genuine cordial friendship and brotherhood as among the frontier settlers in the West.

One fine Sunday morning that summer, all the settlers met under two oak trees on the prairie, near where the present church stands, for the first religious service in the settlement. It had been agreed that some of the men should take turns to read one of Luther's sermons at each of these gatherings, and I was selected as reader the first day. Some prayers were said and Swedish hymns sung, and seldom did a temple contain more devout worshipers than did that little congregation on the prairie.

Before the winter of 1854-55 set in, we had quite a large community in Vasa, and had raised considerable grain, potatoes and other provisions. During that winter the Sioux Indians again became our neighbors, and frequently supplied us with venison in exchange for bread and coffee. The following spring and summer the settlers increased still faster, several more oxen and other cattle, with a horse or two, were brought in, and I had no longer the exclusive privilege of hauling goods on the little truck wagon.

That summer I again went to Illinois to meet a large party of newly-arrived emigrants from Sweden, who formed a settlement in Vasa, known as Skåne. The people from different provinces would group themselves together in little neighborhoods, each assuming in common parlance the name of their own province; thus we have Vasa, Skåne, Småland and Jemtland.

About this time a township was formally organized, and, at my suggestion, given the name of Vasa, in commemoration of the great Swedish king. Roads were also - 51 - laid out legally, and a township organization perfected. A school district was formed and soon after an election precinct, and as I was the only person who was master of the English language the duty of attending to all these things devolved upon me. We were particularly fortunate in having many men, not only of good education from the old country, but of excellent character, pluck and energy, men who would have been leaders in their communities if they had remained at home, and who became prominent as soon as they had mastered the English language. This fact, perhaps, gave a higher tone and character to our little community than is common in such cases, and Vasa has since that time furnished many able men in the county offices, in the legislative halls, and in business and educational circles. There can be much refinement and grace even in a log cabin on the wild prairie.

In the beginning of the month of September, 1855, Rev. E. Norelius visited the settlement and organized a Lutheran church.

Thirty-five years have elapsed since that time, and many of those who belonged to the first church at Vasa now rest in mother earth close by the present stately church edifice, which still belongs to the same congregation, and is situated only a short distance from the place where the latter was organized. Rev. Norelius himself lives only a few hundred yards from the church building. Thirty-five years have changed the then cheerful, hopeful young man into a veteran, crowned with honor, and full of wisdom and experience. His beneficent influence on the Swedes of Goodhue county and of the whole Northwest will make his name dear to coming generations of our people.

On November 23d, in the same fall, the first wedding took place in our settlement. The author of these memoirs was joined in matrimony to Miss Cherstin Peterson, from - 52 - Balingslöf, near Kristianstad, whose family had just come to Vasa from Sweden. By this union I found the best and most precious treasure a man can find—a good and dear wife, who has, faithfully shared my fate to this day. Rev. J. W. Hancock, of Red Wing, performed the marriage ceremony. Horses being very scarce among us in those days, the minister had to borrow an Indian pony and ride on horseback twelve miles—from Red Wing to Vasa. On the evening of our wedding day there happened to be a severe snow-storm, through which my young bride was taken from her parents' home to our log house, on a home-made wooden sled, drawn by a pair of oxen and escorted by a number of our young friends, which made this trip of about a quarter of a mile very pleasant, in spite of the oxen and the snow-storm.

The next winter was very severe, and many of our neighbors suffered greatly from colds and even frozen limbs. But there was an abundance of provisions, and, as far as I can remember, no one was in actual need after the first winter.

In the spring of 1856 several newcomers arrived in our colony. That year marked the climax of the mad land speculation in the Northwest. Cities and towns were staked out and named, advertised and sold everywhere in the state, and people seemed to be perfectly wild, everybody expecting to get rich in a short time without working. The value of real estate rose enormously, and money was loaned at three, four, and even five per cent. a month. Fortunately, very few of the settlers in our neighborhood were seized by this mad fury of speculation. I, however, became a victim. I bought several pieces of land, and sold some of them very profitably, and mortgaged others at an impossible rate of interest. And, the world becoming too narrow for me on the farm, I availed myself of the first opportunity to trade away my land for some property in Red Wing, which was a booming little town at that time. We moved from the plain log cabin on the old - 53 - farm into a house in town, where I engaged in a successful mercantile business. But speculation was in the air, and before the spring of 1857 my entire stock of merchandize was exchanged for town lots in Wasioja and Geneva, two paper cities further west. Meanwhile my friend Mr. Eustrom, with his young wife and baby, had arrived from Boston, and both of us, with our families and a few friends, moved out to Geneva early in the summer, with the intention of building up a city and acquiring riches in a hurry. But at that time the waves of speculation began to subside, and nine-tenths of the cities and towns which were mapped out, and the great enterprises which were inaugurated by enthusiasts like myself suddenly collapsed into a mere nothing. Among these was also Geneva, which is not larger to-day than when we left it, and it was about all I could do to raise enough money to get back to Vasa with my wife. My friend Eustrom pre-empted a claim near Geneva and remained there.

Making an inventory of my property after the return to Vasa in 1857, I found that the principal thing I had was a debt of $2,000, bearing an interest of five per cent. a month. In order to pay this debt we sold everything we had, even our furniture and my wife's gold watch. This was the great crisis of 1857. It stirred up everybody and everything in the country, and it was no wonder that I, being an inexperienced and enthusiastic young man, had to suffer with so many others. But now the question was, what should I do? I could not return to the farm, for I had none; that is, it was encumbered for about twice its value.

In the midst of these difficulties I went to Red Wing one day to consult a prominent lawyer in regard to some business matters. During my conversation with him he said: "You have nothing to do now, you have had enough of speculation, you know the English language, you are tolerably - 54 - well acquainted with our laws, well educated, young and ambitious, why not study law, then? This state and this county is just the place for you to make a splendid beginning in that profession. Come to me, and within a year you can be admitted to the bar, after which you will find it easy to get along."

I returned to Vasa in the evening, and, having consulted my wife, who was visiting her parents, I soon made up my mind. The next day both of us were on the way to Red Wing supplied with clothes, bedding, a few dishes and some provisions, which had been given us by my wife's parents, who also conveyed us to town. In Red Wing we rented a room about sixteen feet square, got a cook stove and a few articles of furniture on credit, and everything was in order for housekeeping and the study of law. I immediately commenced my course of study with that excellent lawyer, Mr. Warren Bristol, who afterwards for many years served as United States Judge in New Mexico, where he recently died.

This life was something new for my young wife, who had grown up in a house of plenty. Now she had to try her hand at managing our household affairs, with the greatest economy, and she accomplished her task so well that no minister of finance could have done better. In fact we were so poor that winter that we could not afford to buy the tallow candles which were necessary for my night studies (kerosene was unknown at that time). But every evening during this trying but happy winter my wife made a lamp by pouring melted lard, which her parents sent us, into a saucer, and putting in a cotton wick, and in my eyes this light was more brilliant than the rays from the golden chandeliers in the palaces of the rich. By this light I studied Blackstone, Kent, and other works on law.

Late in the spring of 1858 a place became vacant in the - 55 - justice of the peace, and I succeeded in getting the appointment to this position, which brought me a couple of dollars now and then, thus improving our financial condition considerably. Early in the summer I was appointed city clerk, with a salary of $12.50 a month, which was quite a fortune for us at that time. After one year's hard study I was admitted to the bar, and my honored teacher accepted me as his partner on good conditions. My profession seemed to be well chosen; I had plenty to do, and met with all the success I could expect.

My first case in the district court was before Judge McMillan, who afterwards became chief justice of our supreme court, and then United States senator. In opening the case I became nervous and excited and would have broken down entirely had it not been for the kindly manner in which the judge overlooked my diffidence, and helped me out of the embarrassment by leading me on and putting the very words in my mouth; this was only natural to his kind heart, and he probably never remembered it, but to me it was an act of great kindness, never to be forgotten, especially not when more than twenty years after the little incident he needed all his friends to rally for his return to the United States senate, his most formidable opponent being the venerable and beloved statesman, Alexander Ramsey.

My law practice lasted only a few months, as I was appointed county auditor to fill a vacancy, and soon afterwards elected to fill the regular term of office, and again re-elected two years later. Before that time no Swedish-American had occupied such responsible civil office in the United States. But I probably made a mistake in accepting this office and thereby turning my back on a profession at which I would undoubtedly have made more easy and rapid progress than by anything else. But for the time being it produced great economical improvements in our private life. Our little - 56 - home, the narrow room which served as bedroom, study, kitchen and parlor, was soon exchanged for a neat little house, and a year later we moved into a larger and more comfortable building, which was our own property.

Meanwhile the settlement at Vasa had prospered, and the population had materially increased. The Scandinavian settlers had scattered over the neighboring towns and counties with marvelous rapidity. The crisis of 1857 had been an excellent lesson to us all, for, although the price of real estate had fallen to about one-fourth of its former value, the people were better off now than formerly, owing to better management and more prudent economy.

The Scandinavians had now commenced to take a lively interest in the political discussions which were agitating the entire country at that time. The all absorbing political question of the day was "slavery" or "no slavery" in the new territories. It is unnecessary to say that the Scandinavians were almost to a man in favor of liberty to all men, and that they consequently joined the Republican party, which had just been organized for the purpose of restricting slavery.

In the winter of 1861, while I was holding the office of auditor the second term, the legislature of Minnesota appointed a committee to revise the tax laws. This committee invited five county auditors, of which number I had the honor to be one, to assist in its work. The tax laws which were formulated by this general committee were in force over twenty years.

It was about this time the great American statesman, W. H. Seward, visited Minnesota. I heard him make his famous speech in St. Paul, in which, with the gift of prophecy, he depicted the future grandeur of the twin cities. I also heard Owen Lovejoy, a member of congress from Illinois, and one of the leading anti-slavery agitators of the times. - 57 -
During the presidential election of 1860 the political excitement ran very high in the whole country. The Southern states had assumed a threatening position, and expressed their intention to secede from the Union if Lincoln was elected president. Throughout the whole country po-

litical clubs were organized. The Democrats formed companies which they called "Little Giants," which was the nickname given to Stephen A. Douglas, their candidate for president.

The Republicans also organized companies which they called "Wide Awakes." I was chosen leader of the Republican company in Red Wing. Political meetings were very frequent during the last few weeks before election, and among the most prominent features of those meetings were processions and parades of the companies, which were uniformed, and carried banners and torches. During the campaign C. C. Andrews and the late Stephen Miller, respective candidates for presidential electors on the Democratic and Republican tickets, held meetings together and jointly debated the important questions of the day, taking of course opposite sides, but within a year both were found as officers in the Union army, gallantly fighting for the same cause.

About this time a company of militia organized in Red Wing, and I was one of the lieutenants, and took active part in its drill and maneuvers. Although none of the men who took part in these movements could foresee or suspect the approach of the awful struggle which was to plunge the country into a deluge of fire and blood, still they all seemed to have a presentiment that critical times were near at hand, and that it was the duty of all true citizens to make ready for them. It is a significant fact that fifty-four men out of our little company of only sixty, within two years became officers or soldiers in the volunteer army of the United States. Although the Scandinavian emigrants had been in the state only a few years, they still seemed to take - 58 - as great an interest in the threatening political difficulties of the times, and were found to be just as willing as their native fellow-citizens to sacrifice their blood and lives for the Union.

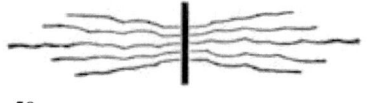

CHAPTER V.

The Beginning of the Civil War—The Scandinavians taking part in it—Appeal in *Hemlandet* to the Scandinavians of Minnesota—Company D. Organized—The Expressions of the Press—The Departure—The March over the Cumberland Mountains—The Fate of the Third Regiment.

Going from the court house on the afternoon of April 12th, 1861, a friend overtook me with the news that the rebels of the South had fired on Fort Sumpter. The news spread rapidly, and caused surprise and intense indignation. In a few days the governor issued a proclamation that one thousand men should be ready to leave our young state for the seat of war; more than a sufficient number of companies were already organized to fill this regiment, and the only question was, who were to have the first chance? This first excitement was so sudden that the Scandinavians, who are more deliberate in such matters, scarcely knew what was going on before the first enlistment was made.

A few months passed, and the battle of Bull Run was fought. It was no longer a mere momentary excitement; it was no longer expected that the Rebellion could be subdued in a single battle or within a few months, but it was generally understood that the war would be long and bitter. Then the Scandinavians of Minnesota began to stir. We had heard that a few Swedes in Illinois, especially Major—afterward General—Stohlbrand and a few others, had entered the army. A few Scandinavians had also enlisted in - 60 - the First and Second regiments; but there was no general rising among them in our state until I published an appeal in the Swedish newspaper *Hemlandet* in Chicago. The following is an extract from that paper:

" To The Scandinavians of Minnesota !

"It is high time for us, as a people, to arise with sword in hand, and fight for our adopted country and for liberty.

"This country is in danger. A gigantic power has arisen against it and at the same time against liberty and democracy, in order to crush them.

"Our state has already furnished two thousand men, and will soon be called upon for as many more to engage in the war. Among the population of the state the Scandinavians number about one-twelfth, a part of its most hardy and enduring people, and ought to furnish at least three or four hundred men for this army. This land which we, as strangers, have made our home, has received us with friendship and hospitality. We enjoy equal privileges with the native born. The path to honor and fortune is alike open to us and them. The law protects and befriends us all alike. We have also sworn allegiance to the same.

"Countrymen, 'Arise to arms; our adopted country calls!' Let us prove ourselves worthy of that land, and of those heroes from whom we descend.

"I hereby offer myself as one of that number, and I am confident that many of you are ready and willing to do likewise. Let each settlement send forth its little squad. Many in this neighborhood are now ready to go. A third regiment will soon be called by the governor of this state. Let us, then, have ready a number of men of the right kind, and offer our services as a part of the same. Let us place ourselves on the side of liberty and truth, not only with words but with strong arms,—with our lives. Then shall our friends in the home of our childhood rejoice over us. Our children and children's children shall hereafter pronounce our names with reverence. We shall ourselves be happy in the consciousness of having performed our duty, and should death on the field of battle be our lot, then shall our parents, wives, children and friends find some consolation in their sorrow in the conviction that they, also, by their noble sacrifices, have contributed to the defense and victory of right, justice, and liberty. And a grateful people shall not withhold from them its sympathy and friendship."

A few days later I left a dear wife, home, and two children, and started for Fort Snelling, but not alone; about seventy Swedes and thirty Norwegians from Red Wing, Vasa, Chisago Lake, Holden, Wanamingo, Stillwater, Albert Lea and other places, went there with me, or joined us in the course of a few days.

MUSTERING VOLUNTEERS.

Meanwhile the third regiment had been called, and one hundred of my companions were mustered in as Company D of that regiment, with myself as their captain, a Norwegian friend, L. K. Aaker, formerly a member of our legislature, as first lieutenant, and my old friend H. Eustrom as second lieutenant. Although Company D was the only military organization in our state consisting exclusively of Scandinavians, there were quite a number of those nationalities in every regiment and company organized afterwards.

I may be excused for saying a few words concerning my old military company. It consisted of the very flower of our young men. It was regarded from the start as a model company, and maintained its rank as such during the whole term of four years' service. Always orderly, sober, obedient and faithful to every duty, the men of Company D, though foreigners by birth, won and always kept the affectionate regard and fullest confidence of their native-born comrades. A large majority of them are resting in the last grand bivouac, many under the genial Southern sun, but no word of reproach or doubt of soldierly honor has ever been heard against any of those living or dead.

About this time a whole regiment of Scandinavians, mostly Norwegians, was organized in Wisconsin,—the Fifteenth Wisconsin Infantry regiment,— which rose to great distinction during its long service. Its brave colonel, Hans Hegg, fell mortally wounded while commanding a brigade on the bloody field at Chickamauga. There were many partially or wholly Swedish companies from Illinois, one of which belonged to the Forty-third Illinois regiment, under the lamented Capt. Arosenius, and came under my command a few years later in Arkansas. There were also many prominent Swedish officers in other regiments, such as Gen. C. J. Stohlbrand, Cols. Vegesack, Malmborg, Steelhammar, Broddy, Elfving, and Brydolf, Capts. Stenbeck, Silversparre, Sparrstrom, Lempke, Chas. Johnson, Erik Johnson, Vanstrum, Lindberg, etc. , and Lieuts. Osborne, Edgren, Liljengren, Johnson, Lindall, Olson, Gustafson, Lundberg, and many others whose names I do not now recall.

In the Goodhue county records for October 15, 1861, is a paragraph which states that, as the county auditor, H. Mattson, has voluntarily gone to the war with a company of soldiers to defend our country, it is resolved that leave of absence shall be extended to him, and that the office of county auditor shall not be declared vacant so long as the deputy performs his duties properly.

The St. Paul *Press* of the same date, has the following: "We congratulate Capt. Mattson and his countrymen for the splendid company of Swedes and Norwegians which he commands. Never was a better company mustered in for service."

In the beginning of November two steamers arrived at Fort Snelling and took the Third regiment on board. We were ordered to join Buell's army in Kentucky. Company E, of our regiment, was also mainly from Goodhue county, and when the steamers arrived at Red Wing, they stopped half an hour to let Companies D and E partake of a bountiful supper, to which they had been invited by their city friends, and to say a last farewell to their families and acquaintances. My wife, with the little children, my sister, father, brother, and other relatives, were gathered in a large room in the hotel opposite the landing. The half hour was soon past, and the bugle sounded "fall in." I pass over the parting scene, leaving it to the imagination of the reader, for I cannot find words to describe it myself. I will only relate one little episode. When the bugle sounded for departure I held my little two-year-old daughter in my arms; her arms were clasped around my neck, and, when I endeavored to set her down, she closed her little fingers so hard together that her uncle had to open them by force before he could take her away from me. When a little child was capable of such feelings, it may be surmised what those felt who were able to comprehend the significance of that moment.

In a few days we were camped on a muddy field in Kentucky, quickly learning the duties of soldier-life, and familiarizing ourselves with the daily routine of an army in the field.

My military career of four years' duration passed without any event of particular interest or importance; it was like that of two million other soldiers—to do their duty faithfully, whatever that duty might be—that was all.

After eight months' service I was promoted to the rank of major in the regiment. At that time we were serving in middle Tennessee. Shortly afterward our regiment, with some three thousand men of the troops, made a forced march across the Cumberland mountains. In order to give the reader an idea of the hardships which the soldiers occasionally had to endure on a march, I shall give a short sketch of this. The detachment broke camp in Murfreesboro in the forenoon of a very hot day toward the close of May, and marched twenty miles before night, which was considered a good distance for the first day. Most of the men suffered from blistered feet, and they were all very tired. We prepared our supper, and had just gone to rest in a large open field and were beginning to fall asleep, when, at ten o'clock in the evening, the signal was given to fall in. In a few minutes the whole force was in line, and silently resumed the march forward. We marched the whole night, the whole of the next day, the following night, and till noon the day after, moving altogether a distance of over eighty miles, over a difficult and partly mountainous country, and stopping only one hour three times a day to cook our coffee and eat, while those who sank down by the roadside entirely exhausted were left until the rear-guard came and picked them up. When we finally arrived at our destination the enemy that we were pursuing had already decamped, and we had to return by the same route over which we had come, though more leisurely. Among the many victims of this march was a bright Norwegian lieutenant of my old company, Hans Johnson, who died shortly after our return to Murfreesboro.

A few days afterward the regiment started on an expedition to the South. During this march I got sick with the fever, and would probably have died at Columbia, Tenn., if my friend Eustrom, who at that time was captain of Company D, had not succeeded in getting me into a rebel family, where I was treated with the greatest care, so that in a few days I was able to go by rail to Minnesota on a twenty days' leave of absence. This took place in the beginning of the month of July, 1862.

Having spent a fortnight in the bosom of my family I returned, with improved health, to resume my command. I arrived at Chicago on a Sunday morning, and, as I had to wait all day for my train, I went to the Swedish church on Superior street. Leaving the church, I heard a news-boy crying, "Extra number of the *Tribune*; great battle at Murfreesboro; Third Minnesota regiment in hot fire!" I bought the paper and hurried to the hotel, where another extra edition was handed me. The Union troops had won a decisive victory at Murfreesboro, and totally routed the forces of Forrest, consisting of eight thousand cavalry. Later in the evening a third extra edition announced that "The Third regiment has been captured by the enemy, and is on the march to the prisons of the South." Only a soldier can imagine my feelings when I received this news. I arrived in Tennessee two days later, only to meet the soldiers returning from the mountains where they had been released on written parole by the enemy. They were sore-footed, exhausted, hungry and wild with anger, and looked more like a lot of ragged beggars than the well-disciplined soldiers they had been a few days before. All the captured officers had been taken to the South, where they were kept in prison several months. Only two of them succeeded in making their escape. One of those was Capt. Eustrom, who, in company with Lieut. Taylor, made his escape from a hospital building, some negroes giving them clothes, and, through almost incredible hardships and dangers, they succeeded in reaching our lines, and I met them two days after my arrival at Nashville.

The capitulation of our splendid regiment was one of the most deplorable events of its kind during the whole war. It was regarded one of the best regiments of volunteers of the Western army. It had defended itself with great valor, and, in fact, defeated the enemy, when for some unaccountable reason, Col. H. C. Lester decided to surrender, and he exerted such a great influence over our officers that seven company commanders went over to his side in the council of war, which he called, while the remaining officers and the soldiers were strongly opposed to the capitulation. When the men finally were ordered to stack arms they did so with tears in their eyes, complaining bitterly because they were not allowed to fight any longer. All the officers who had been in favor of capitulation were afterward dismissed from service in disgrace.

Arriving at Nashville I was immediately ordered to assume command of my own scattered regiment, of the Ninth Michigan Infantry regiment, and of a battery of artillery, which had also capitulated on that fatal Sunday. Having supplied the men with clothing and other necessaries, I took them by steamboats to a camp for prisoners in St. Louis, and returned to Nashville to report the matter in person. On my return to Nashville I was appointed member of a general court martial, and shortly afterwards its president, which position I occupied from July till December, 1862. The sufferings which my friend Captain Eustrom had endured during his flight from the rebels shattered his health so that he was soon forced to retire from service.

About this time the well-known Indian massacre in the western settlements of Minnesota took place. About eight hundred peaceable citizens, mostly women and children, and among those many Scandinavians—were cruelly butchered, and their houses and property burnt and destroyed. The soldiers of the Third regiment had given their parole not to take up arms against the enemy until they were properly exchanged, but, as this did not have anything to do with the Indian war, they were ordered from St. Louis to Minnesota and put under the command of Major Welch, of the Fourth regiment, and soon distinguished themselves by their fine maneuvers and valor in the struggle with the Indians.

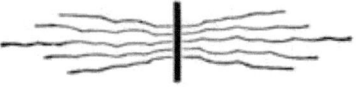

CHAPTER VI.

Events of 1863—The Siege of Vicksburg—Anecdotes about Gens. Logan, Stevenson and Grant—Little Rock Captured—Recruiting at Fort Snelling—The engagement at Fitzhugh's Woods—Pine Bluff—Winter Quarters at Duvall's Bluff—Death of Lincoln—Close of the War—The Third Regiment Disbanded.

In the month of December the officers were exchanged and ordered back to Fort Snelling, to where the enlisted men had also returned from the Indian war. In January, 1863, we again left Minnesota for the South. The whole of this winter and the beginning of spring were devoted to expeditions against guerillas and Confederate recruiting camps in southern Tennessee. Most of this time I commanded the regiment, four companies of which were mounted. We had to procure horses as best we could, here and there through the country. We had many skirmishes with the enemy, and captured a number of prisoners.

In the beginning of June we joined the forces that were besieging Vicksburg under the command of Gen. Grant, and remained there until that city had capitulated. The siege of Vicksburg is so well known from history that I shall make no attempt to describe it here. For five consecutive weeks the cannonading was so incessant that the soldiers became as accustomed to it as the passengers on a steamer to the noise of the propeller, and, when the capitulation finally put an end to all this noise, we found it very difficult to sleep for several nights on account of the unusual silence.

- 69 -

The July number of *Hemlandet*, contained a letter from me, dated Vicksburg, June 24th, from which I make the following extract:

"The army of Gen. Grant is divided into two Grand Divisions, one of which is arranged in a semi-circle toward Vicksburg, only a few hundred yards from the intrenchments of the rebels, the other in a semi-circle turned away from Vicksburg, and fronting the army of Gen. Johnston. We are all protected by strong intrenchments, and always keep over two thousand men as picket guards, and the same number are digging rifle pits and building intrenchments.

"Gen. Logan's Division is close up to the intrenchments of the rebels. The Swedish Maj. Stohlbrand is chief of artillery in Logan's Division, and, has, as such, under his special charge one of the most important positions in the beleaguering army.

"I visited Gen. Logan yesterday, and will relate a little episode concerning this brave commander: When Gen. Logan heard that I was a Swede, and wished to see Maj. Stohlbrand, who had just ridden out to look after his batteries, the general, being always full of fun, assumed a very solemn air, and said: 'Too bad you did not come an hour sooner, for then you could have seen Stohlbrand. There'—and he went to the door of his tent and pointed across the camp ground—'there is the tent of Maj. Stohlbrand. Half an hour ago a bomb exploded from the main fort yonder. Poor Stohlbrand! Only a few remnants were left of the contents of his tent. Poor Stohlbrand! Perhaps you would like to see the remains?'

"Accompanied by Gens. Stevenson, Ransom, and several other officers, I followed Gen. Logan to the tent of Stohlbrand. Then Logan said: 'Out of respect for poor Stohlbrand we have put everything in order again. Here you see his camp stool, there his uniform, and there is his little field cot.' The bed looked as if a dead body was lying on it, covered by a blanket. Logan walked solemnly up to the head of the bed, lifted the blanket, and behold, there was only a bundle of rags! The rest of us, of course, supposed that Stohlbrand was dead, and that his corpse was lying on the bed. This little joke made the humorous Logan laugh so that his whole body shook.

"As to the Swedes in the army, I may mention that, besides our Company D, there are in the same division the company of Capt. Arosenius of the Forty-third Illinois regiment, and that of Capt. Corneliuson of the Twenty-third Wisconsin regiment, and a number of Swedes of the other regiments from Illinois and Wisconsin, and of the Fourth and Fifth Minnesota regiments. Old Company D is a model, as usual,—the best one I have seen yet. Both officers and men are quiet, orderly, cheerful and obedient, always faithful at their post, and ready to go wherever duty calls them. They are loved and respected by all who come in contact with them. When

- 70 -

I feel sad or despondent, all I need do is to walk along the camp street and take a look at some of my old Scandinavians. Their calm and earnest demeanor always makes me glad and proud. I ask for no greater honor than to point them out to some stranger, saying: 'This is my old company.'

"Not these alone, however, but all of my countrymen whom I met in the army have a good name, and are considered most reliable and able soldiers."

I shall now relate a couple of anecdotes from the siege of Vicksburg, which I did not mention in the letter to *Hemlandet*.

GRANT'S HEADQUARTERS.

Outside Gen. Logan's tent stood a big magnolia tree. While laughing at Logan's joke Gen. Stevenson picked up a little stick of wood and whittled on it with his penknife, in genuine Yankee fashion. Accidently he dropped his knife, and, while stooping down to pick it up, a fragment of a shell from the rebel batteries came and went two inches deep into the tree right where his head had been when he was whittling. He coolly remarked, "That piece of iron was not made for me."

One day as I, in company with Lieut. Col. (afterward

- 71 -

Gen.) C. C. Andrews, was visiting Gen. Grant outside of Vicksburg, a wagon drawn by six mules passed close by his headquarters. The driver, an old, rough-looking soldier, stopped, and asked the way to a certain regiment. Gen. Grant's tent stood on a little elevation, at the foot of which were several fresh wagon tracks. A number of officers, including myself, were standing and sitting around the general outside the tent. Gen. Grant, who was dressed in a fatigue suit and slouched hat, without other marks of distinction than three small silver stars, which could scarcely be distinguished on his dusty blouse, went toward the driver and, with the most minute particulars, gave him directions how to drive. While he was talking, we observed that the driver showed signs of deep emotion, and finally he alighted from the mule, which he was riding, stretched out his arms, and, with tears in his eyes, exclaimed: "My God! I believe it is Gen. Grant! General, do you remember Tommy Donald? I was a soldier in your company during the Mexican war!" With touching kindness the great commander-in-chief now took both hands of the ragged soldier in his, and, like old friends who had not met for a long time, they rejoiced in remembering the companionship of fifteen years before.

ARMY WAGON.

When Gen. Grant returned to the tent the conversation turned to the newspaper clamor and general discontent - 72 - because Vicksburg was not yet taken, upon which the general expressed himself in the following words: "I could make another assault and hasten the capture a few days, but will not do it because I *know* positively that within ten days the garrison must surrender anyhow, for I have got them, and will take them all. Let them howl. I don't care. I have got Pemberton tight as wax." Saying which, he closed his right hand and laid it on the little camp table with such force that I noticed the veins filling and turning blue on the back of his hand. These two little incidents give a key to Gen. Grant's whole character, and the secret of his unparalleled success, not only in winning battles, but in bagging the entire opposing force.

A week later Vicksburg fell into our hands. We took thirty-two thousand prisoners, fifteen generals, two thousand other officers, and nearly two hundred cannon.

GENERALS GRANT AND PEMBERTON.

About a week after the surrender of Vicksburg the Third - 73 - regiment was transferred to the Seventh army corps, under the command of Gen. Fred. Steele, and took part in the campaign against Little Rock. In the beginning of September, when we were only ten miles from Little Rock, our regiment enjoyed the distinction of marching at the head of the infantry column. We came upon the Confederate batteries on the west bank of the Arkansas river, where a brisk cannonade was opened. This combat afforded the most beautiful sight imaginable, if carnage and slaughter may be called beautiful. We stood on the east side of the river, the Confederates on the west. The water being very low, a steamer had been grounded about an eighth of a mile above us, and near the steamer the water was so shallow that the cavalry could ford the river; but just in front of the Third regiment the water was so deep that we had to throw a pontoon bridge for the infantry.

Our regiment was stationed in a cornfield near the river bank to cover the march across the bridge, and the soldiers were ordered to lie down on the ground. But we found it very difficult to make them obey, for, in their eagerness to cross the river, they felt more like rushing ahead and shouting for joy. Many shots from the Confederate batteries passed over our heads, so low that the soldiers, in a sporting mood, jumped up and grabbed with their hands in the air, as if trying to catch them. In less than an hour the bridge across the deep channel was ready. A cavalry brigade had meanwhile moved up to the ford above, and now the signal for crossing was given. The Confederates set fire to the steamer, which they were unable to save.

It was about noon on one of those glorious autumn days peculiar to this country, which greatly enhanced the impression of the sublime spectacle then to be seen on the Arkansas river. The burning steamer reddening the atmosphere with brilliant flames of fire, a long line of cavalry fording the - 74 - shallow river in three files, the infantry marching by the flank over the pontoon from which they jumped into the water, forming on double-quick, first companies, then battalion, whereupon they marched cheerily, in knee-deep water, under flying banners and to the beat of regimental music, while the air was filled with shells and balls. Before the infantry had reached the woods where the batteries of the enemy were hidden, the latter was already in retreat, and Little Rock soon fell into our hands.

On our march into the captured city the next morning, the Third regiment was again accorded the place of honor at the head of the army. It was designated to act as provost-guard for the purpose of maintaining order, and the whole regiment was soon quartered in the state capitol. Gen. C. C. Andrews, who held the position of colonel at that time, was appointed post commander at Little Rock, and I, who had been promoted to the rank of lieutenant-colonel soon after the surrender of Vicksburg, took command of the regiment, whereby it became my duty to maintain law and order in the captured city. This was an onerous and difficult task, for it must be remembered that the only executive authority in the southern states during the war was vested in the army, and especially delegated to the provost officers and guards. The third regiment was occupied with this task until the following spring, and performed its duty so well that the governor of Arkansas, in a message, expressed himself regarding it, in the following language:

"During the time of their service in our capital good order has prevailed, and they have commanded the respect of our citizens. When called upon to meet the enemy they have proven themselves equal to any task, and reliable in the hour of imminent danger. Such men are an honor to our government and the cause which they serve. Their state may justly - 75 - feel proud of them, and they will prove themselves to be worthy sons of the same wherever duty calls them."

Toward Christmas I was ordered to Fort Snelling, with a detachment of officers and non-commissioned officers, for the purpose of recruiting our decimated ranks. I remained on this duty till the month of March, and then returned with four hundred recruits. Shortly afterwards the battle of Fitzhugh's Woods, near Augusta, Arkansas, was fought, and the regiment distinguished itself by very gallant conduct. During the stay in Little Rock most of the soldiers had re-enlisted for three years, or until the close of the war, whereby we acquired the title of "Veteran Regiment." But that was not the only distinction which was conferred on our men. A large number of young soldiers had been promoted from the ranks to be officers in several negro regiments, which were organized in Tennessee and Arkansas, and some as officers of new regiments of our own state. Col. Andrews had meanwhile been promoted to the rank of brigadier-general, and, in April, 1864, I was promoted to colonel of the regiment in his place, and was shortly afterward ordered to march with its eight hundred men to Pine Bluff, on the Arkansas river.

From this time until the beginning of August the regiment experienced such hardships and sufferings from diseases and hard service, that it sustained far greater losses from these causes than any other regiment from our state had met with in open battle. Pine Bluff was a veritable pest-hole; the water was of a greenish color, the air full of germs of disease and poisonous vapors. Continually surrounded and threatened by a vigilant enemy, the exhausted and sickly soldiers had to get up at three o'clock every morning for the purpose of working at the entrenchments and strengthening and protecting our position in different ways. Meanwhile the number of those fit for duty was daily decreasing at an appalling rate. The hospitals were overcrowded with patients, and the few men left for duty were continually occupied in caring for the sick and burying the dead, until there were not men enough left to bury their dead comrades, and I was obliged to ask a regiment, which had recently arrived, to help us perform that sad duty.

At this critical moment I received orders from Washington to take six companies to Minnesota, on a six weeks' veteran furlough, to which the regiment was entitled. Those went who were able to. Many died on the way, but those of us who survived until we reached Minnesota were soon restored to usual health and strength, so that we could return in due time and again take part in the campaign in Arkansas. The remaining four companies, which had been furloughed the previous winter, were ordered from Pine Bluff to Duvall's Bluff, on White river, where the whole regiment was reunited under my command in the beginning of October, and remained in winter quarters until the spring of 1865.

Shortly after our return to Arkansas I assumed command of the First Brigade, First Division, Seventh army corps. This brigade consisted of my own regiment, the Twelfth Michigan, the Sixty-first Illinois, and a United States colored regiment. Our prospects for remaining in winter quarters for several months being favorable, many of the higher officers sent for their wives. I did the same, having first erected a comfortable log house for us. My wife and two little children arrived a few days before Christmas, and stayed in the camp the whole winter. No important event took place during the winter, excepting that we were once ordered to make an expedition up White river, with a considerable force of cavalry and infantry, and, after a fatiguing march, succeeded in breaking up a camp of irregular Confederate troops, and taking many prisoners.

I will relate two incidents which took place near Duvall's Bluff, one of a serious, the other of a comic nature.

The first was the shooting of a young soldier of the Twenty-second Ohio regiment, who time and again had deserted his post, and finally joined a band of rebel marauders. It became my sad duty to execute the sentence of death. My brigade formed a hollow square, facing inward, and the doomed man, a strong, handsome youth of twenty years, sat on a coffin in an open ambulance, which was driven slowly along the inside of the square, while a band marched in front of the wagon playing a funeral march. After the completion of this sad march the deserter was placed in the middle of the square, in front of the coffin, with his eyes blind-folded. A detachment of twelve men under a sergeant now fired simultaneously, upon the signal of the provost marshal. Eight rifles were loaded with balls, and the unfortunate young man fell backwards into his coffin and died without a struggle.

SHOOTING A DESERTER.

One day while taking a ride on horseback in company with my wife, who had a fine saddle horse, and had become an expert rider during her long stay in the camp, we galloped mile after mile along the fine plain, outside of the picket-lines where men of my own brigade were on guard, till at last we found ourselves several miles from the place where we had passed through our lines. Returning toward camp, we struck the picket line at a point where a recently arrived regiment was stationed, and where the ground was soft and marshy. Being challenged by the guard I answered who I was, but as he could not plainly distinguish my uniform in the twilight and did not know me personally, he ordered us, with leveled gun, to stand still until he could call the officer of the guard. It was no easy matter to obey his orders, for the horses continually sank down in the soft ground, but finally the officer arrived, and we succeeded in getting to the camp without further trouble. I was not the first officer who thus got into trouble by neglecting to write out a pass for himself.

On a fine April day, which can never be forgotten, the news came that our president, Abraham Lincoln, had been murdered. Stricken with consternation I hurried down to the Third regiment in person to tell the sad news. Never, either before or since, have I witnessed such a scene as the one that followed. Some of the men went completely wild with sorrow, weather-beaten veterans, embracing each other, wept aloud, others swore and cursed. In the prison yard, which was guarded by men belonging to my regiment, a rebel prisoner took off his cap, waived it in the air and cried,

"Hurrah for Booth!" A man by the name of Stark immediately loaded his gun and shot the rebel dead on the spot. Many others, both inside and outside the camp, were shot because they expressed joy at the death of Lincoln. Passions were strong, and all tolerance and patience exhausted among the Union soldiers on that occasion. The main army of the - 79 - Confederates had already surrendered when this calamity occurred, and the war was in fact over. A few days afterward we sent our families home.

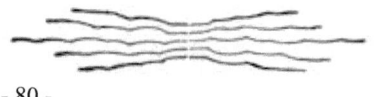

- 80 -

CHAPTER VII.

Reconstruction in the South—Third Regiment Mustered Out—The Farewell Order—Sacrifices and Costs of the War.

A very important work still remained to be accomplished by the union army, namely, the restoration of law and order in the southern states. I had the honor to be entrusted with a portion of that work, an account of which was given in a paper prepared and read by me before the commandery of the military order Loyal Legion, at one of its meetings in St. Paul, in March, 1889, from which I quote as follows:

"After listening to the many interesting addresses on battles and campaigns that have been read before the commandery at our monthly meetings, I fear that you will be disappointed, not only with the subject of this paper, but also with the commonplace incidents which I have to relate, and yet I think that the part taken by the Union army in the so-called reconstruction of civil government in the rebellious states immediately after the war deserves a place in the history of that army and of the war. All the world knows how bravely our soldiers fought, how willingly they endured hardships of the camp and of the wearisome march, how patiently they bore sickness, wounds, and sufferings of every kind, and how faithfully they obeyed the orders of advance to danger and to death. But there is still another trait of their character, perhaps the greatest of them all, that of the good citizen, who was able, as soon as the last smoke of battle had cleared away, to restrain all feelings of enmity - 81 - and revenge, to take the enemy by the hand, to guide, help, and protect him and his in all the rights of citizenship, and it is of that I would relate some facts that came under my own observation and experience.

"Having been stationed at Duvall's Bluff, Arkansas, in command of a brigade, of which my own regiment, the Third Minnesota infantry, formed a part, I received orders from Maj. Gen. J. J. Reynolds, commanding the Department of Arkansas, on the 15th of May, 1865, to establish a military post at Batesville, Arkansas, on the upper White river, and to take command of a district comprising the north-eastern portion of that state. The field organization of the Seventh army corps, to which we belonged, was being broken up. Some of the regiments were sent home to be mustered out of service; others were sent to different points for purposes of occupation. My own regiment and two squadrons of the Ninth Kansas Cavalry were detailed for the work given in my charge.

"On the 18th of May we embarked on steam transports, and reached Batesville on the 20th. A few days later my post headquarters was established at Jacksonport, and the troops were distributed at different points with one or two companies for each, at Batesville, Searcy, Augusta, Powhatan; and the main force at Jacksonport, from which point frequent cavalry patrols were sent to the outlying stations.

"The topography of that country is very irregular and unique. The eastern portion, bordering upon the Mississippi, is flat and marshy, with many lakes and bayous, and has a rich, alluvial soil. The other portion is very broken, with hills and mountain ridges, rocks, caves and beautiful streams, but poor soil. The lowlands had been occupied by wealthy slave owners, whose sympathies were strong for the Southern cause. The highlands were occupied by the poorer class, only a few of whom had owned slaves. Many of this class - 82 - were strong Union men, and soldiers in the Union army. During the great struggle of four years many bloody tragedies had been enacted between the loyal and the rebel residents, and bitter feelings of revenge still rankled in the breasts of the survivors. During the whole period of the war the country had been swept clean, at rapid intervals, by both armies alternately, and each time new atrocities had been perpetrated, and all the worst passions of the people rekindled. It had also been a place of refuge for the worst rebel elements in southern Missouri, when too hardly pressed by our friend Gen. Sanborn [2] and other Union commanders. At the time of our arrival the surviving soldiers from both armies were returning to their homes, also many refugees,—rebels from Texas and Union men from the North,—most of them to find their families destitute and their property destroyed.

"The irregular Confederate troops under Gen. Jeff. Thompson, numbering some eight thousand men, had not yet surrendered, but were scattered over the district in a thoroughly demoralized condition, so that the whole situation was rather peculiar and very bad, and it was a difficult task to prevent fresh outbreaks, and to restore order and get the people started anew in the peaceful avocations of life.

"My instructions were to preserve law and order, to organize and arm companies of home colonists for self-protection, to encourage agriculture and commerce, and to assist the citizens in restoring civil government. The men under my command during the early reconstruction period had certainly no reason to love Arkansas, because they had not only buried their best friends and comrades within its borders, but had themselves for months and months experienced there that dreadful suffering most feared by all soldiers, and for which few receive any credit,—namely, the inglorious privation - 83 - of the silent watch,—in the swamp, in the trenches, in the hospital, on the camp-stretcher, and in the ambulance,—when tired, sore, sick, thirsty, lonely, and seemingly forsaken by God and man, unknown and with praise unsung, with no cheering sound of drum or bugle, no battle flag or cheer in sight or hearing, no voice of comrades or of guns, and no magic touch of elbows or shouts of victory. These men had experienced all that, and had no special reason to sympathize with the inhabitants who had done their full share to bring them into so much misery. And now observe how they treated those inhabitants. Immediately on arriving at Batesville the following order was promulgated, and, by the aid of an old printing press and swift couriers, scattered all over the district:

' Headquarters U. S. Forces ,
' Batesville, Ark. , May 22, 1865.
'General Order No. 1.
'I. It is hereby announced to the people of Batesville and surrounding country that the chief object of the federal occupation of this place is their protection against armed forces, of whatever kind, to give encouragement to agriculture and other peaceful pursuits, and to restore commercial intercourse.

'II. The public safety and mutual interests demand that all persons living within our lines and enjoying the protection of the nation's forces shall declare their obedience to the government.

'III. It is ordered, therefore, that all persons now living or hereafter coming within our picket-lines who have not taken but desire to take the oath of allegiance, with the purpose of restoring and establishing the national authority, shall register their names without delay in the provost marshal's office, where the oath will be administered.

'By order of
' Col. H. Mattson , Commanding.
' P. E. Folsom , Lieutenant and Post Adjutant.'

"On the same day a beginning was made to organize companies of home colonists among the great number of Union refugees who had followed the troops to Batesville. Arms and ammunition were placed in their hands, and the following instruction given:

- 84 -

' Headquarters U. S. Forces ,
' Batesville, Ark. , May 22, 1865.
'*To the members of Companies of Home Colonists:*

'You will, as soon as practicable, depart with your families to your several homes, and there proceed to cultivate the land and secure a crop for the coming year.

'The arms and ammunition with which you have now been furnished by the government of the United States are for the protection of yourselves and families, and for no other purpose.

'The laws of your state guarantee you full redress for private injuries; you will therefore leave all disputes and wrongs to be settled by them and by the military authority of the United States, and it is only against the armed force of marauders that you will resort to the use of these arms; remember, always, that you are not soldiers, but citizens.

'You will promptly report to your own officers and to the military commander of this post any information you may obtain of armed forces of marauders; and in case of emergency you are authorized to act as a military body in pursuing them. The commanding officer will always extend to you aid, both in men and subsistence, so far as lies in his power, but you must, like free and independent citizens, place yourselves, by industrious labor, as soon as possible, beyond the necessity of federal support.

'Let your conduct among your late enemies be such as will elicit their friendship.

'By assisting me to carry out the magnanimous policy of our government you will soon have peace and security restored to your community, and happiness and plenty to yourselves and your families.

'By order of
' Col. H. Mattson , Commanding.
' P. E. Folsom , Lieutenant and Post Adjutant.'

"In a remarkably short time the news of the policy thus announced spread to the most remote parts of the district, and had a very beneficial effect. It inspired hope and confidence everywhere. The disloyal people came out of their hiding places, and, with apparent sincerity and gratitude, took the oath of allegiance, and went to work as good citizens to perform their part in the work of reconstruction. Union men and rebels shock hands over the bloody chasm, and agreed to bury the past and work together for a better future.

- 85 -

"Soon another class of people came in large numbers to seek help and protection from the Union forces. It was the poverty-stricken old men, and the women and children who had lost their natural protectors. It was a sight sad enough to move the stoutest hearts to look at their helplessness and misery, and I never had a more pleasant duty to perform than that of relieving their wants at the expense of our generous government. The department commander had placed a steamboat at my disposal, and given me unlimited power to draw on the commissary stores at Duvall's Bluff. That steamer made regular trips with supplies for all who were actually in need, and most of the applicants returned to their homes with plenty of flour, bacon, salt, seed, corn and other necessaries, with a government mule sometimes thrown in to carry the load home, and there was no distinction made between rebels and Unionists, except that the former were placed on their good behavior as to their future conduct. It was in this work that our soldiers,—officers and men,—showed without exception, that trait of character which entitles them to the name of exemplary citizens as well as exemplary soldiers, which they had previously earned in a service of four years. They never forgot that the conquered inhabitants were our own people, and members of the same great republic.

"After a while our picket lines were withdrawn, and only enough guards posted to take care of the public property. Citizens and soldiers mingled freely in social intercourse, not as conquerors and conquered, but as friends and equals, our men interesting themselves in everything that tended to the welfare of the citizens, often helping them in their work and business, and always treating the helpless with gallantry and tenderness. On the Fourth of July citizens and soldiers, ex-rebels and Union men, to the number of many hundreds, met under the stars and stripes, in a lovely grove, to celebrate - 86 - the day around an old-fashioned barbecue, and, for nearly two days and a night, enjoyed a feast of brotherly love and good will, all proud of the old banner, and happy to be again united as one people.

"During the summer elections were held for town and county officers, and as soon as such officers had qualified, the soldiers, even more readily than the citizens themselves, did all in their power to uphold their authority. In many instances good penmen and accountants among the soldiers gave their services gratuitously to help the newly-elected civil officers start their books and accounts. To the honor of the rebels, especially the returned soldiers, I must say that they behaved in a most exemplary manner, and accepted the situation with good grace and acted most cordially and loyally toward us. The Freedmen's Bureau was not established in that district during my time of command, but I was informed by a friend, Maj. J. M. Bowler, who had command the following winter, that the planters generally yielded to the requirements of that department as soon as it was established; that they made fair contracts with the liberated slaves and strictly and carefully observed them, and were in all respects considerate toward the freedmen generally. Of course, I do not mean to say that all the citizens behaved so well. There were exceptions, even in the first days of reconstruction, and those exceptions were nearly all by the men who had never faced the Union soldiers in open battle, but had either skulked or resorted to guerilla warfare. But I do mean to say that in those early days, before President Johnson had began to show his final hand, the rebels were disposed to accept the situation in a manly and loyal way, and that, if the policy inaugurated by the Union army had been adhered to, the country would probably have been saved from the Ku-Klux and other horrors of a later period.

- 87 -

"One strange fact was deeply impressed upon my mind during the time of my command in Northeastern Arkansas, namely, the genuine regret and sorrow among the returning rebel soldiers over President Lincoln's death. They not only respected him, but actually regarded him as a friend, because they believed him to be kind and just; so that, whatever measures he might have adopted, had he lived, they believed that they could have submitted to them with full confidence that it would be for the best. I can not better illustrate that feeling, as it was daily manifested to me, than by comparing it to the faith and confidence of erring children to an offended but loving father.

"The most noted and influential rebel in the district at that time was, undoubtedly, Gen. Jeff. Thompson. On the 3d of June this noted general arrived at my headquarters at Jacksonport, pursuant to previous arrangements, to surrender his command, consisting of eight thousand officers and men, who began to crowd in on that and the following day in great numbers. They were the hardest looking soldiers I have ever seen. Jeff. Thompson himself was a man of commanding appearance, and a perfect gentleman. In my journal of that day I have described him as follows: 'He is a tall, sinewy, weather-beaten man, a queer looking genius, dressed in a suit of snowy white, from the plume in his hat to the heel of his boot, and with a white sword-belt and white gloves. He is a clever chap, full of fun, telling great yarns, and an incessant talker.' I should judge he was about forty-five years old. On the third day after his arrival the troops had all assembled, and the surrender took place in due form. A staff officer from the Department of Missouri and another from the Department of Arkansas witnessed the proceedings and received the documents. When all was finished, Jeff. Thompson had his men assemble on the levee in front of a steamboat, from the cabin-deck of which he - 88 - delivered his farewell address. I stood by his side while he spoke, and expected every moment to see him pierced by some well-directed bullet from the crowd on shore, but he was allowed to finish his address without interruption, after which the men slunk out of sight, and before evening the whole motley crowd had left the town with the determination, as I verily believe, to follow the good advice of their general. The address deserves a place among our papers, and I will read it, as it appeared a few weeks later in Harper's Magazine, from a *verbatim* report made by one of my officers. He said:

'Many of the eight thousand men I now see around me, very many of you, have been skulking for the last three years in the swamps within a few miles of your own homes,—skulking duty,—and during that time have not seen your own children. I see many faces about me that have not been seen by mortal man for the last three years; and what have you been doing all that time? Why, you have been lying in the swamps until the moss has grown six inches long on your backs, and such men call themselves "chivalrous soldiers." A few weeks ago Gen. Reynolds sent a flag of truce to my headquarters, and I sent out to gather a respectable force to meet those officers, and not one of you responded. A few days later, when Col. Davis and Capt. Bennett, of Gen. Dodge's staff, bore dispatches to me from that general, I attempted again to call about me enough of you to make a respectable show, and how many of these brave men reported at the call? One sore-eyed man with green goggles. But you rally like brave and gallant men around Uncle Sam's commissary stores, and I have now come to surrender you, and hope that you will make better citizens than you have soldiers.

✳ ✳ ✳ ✳ ✳

'Those of you who had arms, with a few exceptions, have left them at home, and those who had government horses have failed to report them here. Now let me say to you, one and all, those of you who have retained your arms, as soon as you get home take them to the nearest military post and deliver them up, or burn them, or get rid of them in some manner, for as sure as there is a God in heaven, if they are found in your houses, just so sure will your houses be burned to the ground; and I hope to God every one of you who keep good arms or military property of any kind in your houses will be hanged; and you will, too.

*****

'But I want you to go home and work hard and take care of your families. - 89 - Work early and late, and get up at night and see if your crops are growing. Above all things avoid political discussions. If any man says "nigger" to you, swear that you never knew or saw one in your life. We have talked about the niggers for forty years, and have been out-talked. We have fought four years for the niggers, and have been d——d badly whipped, and now it is not "your put." The Yankees have won the nigger and will do what they please with him, and you have no say in the matter. If they want him they will take him; and if they say that you must keep him, you have to do it, and no mistake. I tell you that you have no say in the matter, and you oughtn't to have any. Go home and stay there. Don't go anywhere but to mill. Don't go to church, for the minister will put knots and mischief in your heads, and get you into trouble. Be good citizens, and then those of you who have been good, honest and brave soldiers need have nothing to fear; but I warn those of you who have been nothing but sneaking, cowardly jayhawkers, cutthroats and thieves, that a just retribution awaits you, and I hope to God that the federal authorities will hang you, wherever and whenever they find you, and they will do it, sure.

*****

'Do not complain if you are not permitted to have a voice in elections and civil affairs. You have forfeited all such rights, and it now becomes you to submit to such laws and regulations as the federal authorities may deem proper to enact. I believe and know that they will do the best they can for you, especially if you show henceforth that you now desire to merit their confidence by strict obedience to the laws where you may reside.

'We are conquered and subjected; we have no rights, but must accept such privileges and favors as the government may see proper to bestow upon us. Again I say, go home; attend to your business, and try to raise a new generation of boys that shall become better men than you have been.'

"Jeff. Thompson lived many years after that day, a good and loyal citizen. He was a brave and generous man, and had always treated our prisoners with humanity whenever they had fallen into his hands. His advice to his soldiers echoed the sentiments of the better class of the rebels in the district at that time.

"We remained there the whole summer, always impatient to be mustered out and return to our own homes, but never deviating from the orderly and friendly position first taken. Many of the men formed friendships and other connections that have lasted ever since. Some of them returned after - 90 - their muster out, and are still counted among the best citizens of that state; some formed engagements with the country girls, and went back to marry them. One of my young captains, a fine St. Paul boy, brought with the regiment to Minneapolis, as his bride, the most beautiful woman, as well as the most bitter rebel, of that portion of Arkansas, and I am glad to say that, although she soon returned with her gallant husband to her native state, where they still reside, she is now, and has been ever since, as true and loyal to our banner and our cause as any of our Northern wives and mothers.

"I would not have it understood that all our work was so pleasant and peaceful. Sometimes we had to deal with tough cases of both sexes, and then the iron hand of power was freely used to restrain, but seldom to punish. As a relic of old slave times I will relate one incident of many that came under my observation.

"One day a very tidy negro woman came and reported that her late master had recently killed her husband. I sent for the former master. He was a leading physician, a man of fine address and culture, who lived in an elegant mansion near the city. He sat down and told me the story, nearly word for word as the woman did. It was substantially as follows: Tom, the negro, had been his body-servant since both were children, and, since his freedom, still remained in the same service. Tom had a boy about eight years old. This boy had done some mischief, and I (said the doctor) called him in and gave him a good flogging. Tom was outside and heard the boy scream, and after a while he pushed open the door and took the boy from me, telling me that I had whipped him enough. He brought the boy into his own cabin, and then started for town. I took my gun and ran after him. When he saw me coming he started on a run and I shot him, of course. 'Wouldn't you have done the same?' - 91 - he asked me with an injured look. The killing of his negro for such an offence seemed so right and natural to him that he was perfectly astonished when I informed him that he would have to answer to the charge of murder before a military commission at Little Rock, where he was at once sent for trial. What a great change in sentiment a quarter of a century has produced! Our children will never learn to realize what a curse slavery was, even while some of them were in their cradles.

"It has been said that the old soldiers occasionally did a little foraging on their own hook, while in the enemy's country, and I rather think they did; but I wish to state most solemnly, that whatever bad habits the boys might have had in that respect before the surrender of the Confederate army, they reformed at once after that event, most thoroughly and sincerely, and during the whole summer of 1865, although scattered over a wide country, and almost free from military duty and restraint, there was never a complaint made against a man in my command, for depredation of any kind, and I verily believe that the rights of property, even down to the beloved shoat and chicken, were held as sacred by the Union soldiers in our district during that time as those rights are ordinarily held in any well-governed country during times of peace. All things considered I am fully convinced that the excellent conduct of our soldiers in the South during the early days of reconstruction, when the army took a prominent part in that work, did more to establish law and order and to foster friendly and loyal sentiments towards the Union, than all the laws and constitutional amendments enacted for that purpose. Had the great and noble Lincoln lived, or even if President Johnson had remained true to the principles of his early life, and left the Union soldiers at liberty to carry out the firm but humane policy of reconstruction which they inaugurated under the - 92 - inspiration of Grant and Sherman, we would have had not only a united country, but a loyal and law abiding people in the South a quarter of a century ago, because the Union soldier was the best citizen and the best teacher of good citizenship. Armies of other nations have achieved victories as great as ours, other soldiers than ours have been patient, obedient, enduring and brave, but none in the world's history have shown such greatness in civic virtues as the Union soldiers of the war of the Rebellion.

"In the beginning of September, 1865, the regiment was ordered home, and on September 16th it was mustered out at Fort Snelling, Minnesota, on which occasion the following general order was read:

'General Order No. 16.

'*Officers and Men of the Third Minnesota Regiment:*

'After four years of active service this regiment is about to be disbanded. Before another day you will all have received your honorable discharges and be on your way to your quiet, happy homes. The familiar sound of the bugle and drum will no longer be heard among us. The "Stars and Stripes," which we have all learned to love, will no longer wave over our ranks.

'You have toiled, struggled and suffered much during the last four years, yet to those who are now here to enjoy the triumph over our enemies and the peace and prosperity of our country, the reward is ample. I know that we will all regard the acts of those years as the noblest and proudest of our lives. For those, our noble comrades, who have fallen victims in the struggle, let us always, with the most tender affection, cherish their memory.

'You have served your country nobly and faithfully in every field where duty called you, and I am proud to assert that on every occasion and in every locality, from the northwestern frontier, against the savage Indian foes, to the deathly swamps of the Yazoo and Arkansas valleys, against the haughty Southern rebels,—wherever this regiment has been, its rank and file, its bone and sinew, the true representatives of our noble young state, have ever reflected honor and credit on that state.

'As your commanding officer I am greatly indebted to you all, officers and men, for your admirable conduct on all occasions, for your ready obedience of orders, and for your fidelity, patriotism and perseverance in the discharge of all your toilsome duties.
- 93 -
'In bidding you farewell, I give you all my most hearty thanks. May peace, prosperity and happiness ever be your reward.

'For me, the greatest honor,—greater far than I ever expected to achieve,—is the fact of having so long commanded, and at last led home in triumph and peace, the always dear and noble Third Minnesota Regiment.

' H. Mattson ,
'Colonel Commanding Regiment.
' P. E. Folsom , Lieutenant and Adjutant.'"

During this war the Union army had mustered in 2,883,000 men, 400,000 of whom had lost their lives. To this army Minnesota contributed 25,052, or about one-seventh of her entire population. Of this number 2,500 were killed or died of sickness during the war, and it is calculated that 5,000 died since the war on account of wounds and diseases contracted during service. The Third regiment had, during four years' service, a total enrollment of 1,417, of which number there were left only 432 men when we returned in September, 1865. The war cost the Union about two billion, seven hundred million dollars. The sacrifice of gold and blood was not too great. Not only America, but the whole human race has gained more through the victories of our army than can be estimated in gold and blood. And the Scandinavians of the West may justly feel proud of the part they took in this struggle for liberty and human rights.

- 94 -

CHAPTER VIII.

My Reason for Taking Part in the Civil War—The Dignity of Labor—The Firm Mattson & Webster—*Svenska Amerikanaren*, its Program and Reception—The State Emigration Bureau of Minnesota—Its Aim, Plan and Work.

The war which closed with the events narrated in the last chapter was one of the most important of modern times, and proved the greatness and the resources of the American people never properly appreciated before. But it revealed a still greater nobility of character when our immense army, after four years' service, suddenly disbanded, its soldiers quietly and peacefully returning to their common daily toil without the least disorder or disturbance of any kind. The swords were turned into plowshares as quietly and naturally as if they never had been steeped in blood.

For my own part—and that was undoubtedly the case with most of our volunteers—I entered the service because I considered it to be my duty to do my little part in defending the country which had adopted me as a citizen, and not, as many have supposed, on account of ambition or for the sake of gain; in fact, as has been shown already, I resigned a more important and remunerative position in the civil service than the one I first accepted in the army; hence it was quite easy for me to exchange the uniform for the plain garb of the citizen and hang my sword among the reminiscences of the past.
- 95 -
One day shortly after my arrival home, while walking along a street in Red Wing, I noticed a former professor of

a university, who had been a captain in the Sixth regiment working in his shirt sleeves with a plane and helping to build a house. After saluting him I asked how he liked this kind of work, to which he answered that another professor had been appointed in his place while he was in the war, and being through with the service, he neither liked nor could afford to be idle. Having acquired some skill in handling carpenter's tools in his youth, he said he found it easy to get work at two dollars a day, and meanwhile he could be on the lookout for a position as professor of mathematics at some college or university.

Here is the key to the greatness of this country: Labor is respected, while in most other countries it is looked down upon with slight. The former professor and Capt. Wilson was soon thereafter appointed state superintendent of schools, while, if he had remained idle and dependent upon his relatives and friends for assistance, too proud to work, he would most likely have been looking around for something to turn up to this day.

Another little incident, which occurred about this time may interest the Swedish reader. The great Gen. Sherman visited St. Paul, and a banquet was given to him at which I was present. During the conversation I asked about the Swedish Gen. Stohlbrand. "Do you know him?" Gen. Sherman inquired. "Yes, sir; he is my countryman, and we served in the same regiment in Sweden," I said. "Then," said he, "you may be proud of your old comrade, for a braver man and a better artillery officer than Gen. Stohlbrand could not be found in our entire army."

At the same time the general told the following: Stohlbrand had served in his corps for some time with the rank of major, and performed such services as properly belong to a - 96 - colonel or brigadier-general without being promoted according to his merits, because there had been no vacancy in the regiment to which he belonged. Displeased with this, Stohlbrand sent in his resignation, which was accepted, but Sherman had made up his mind not to let him leave the army, and asked him to go by way of Washington on his return home, pretending that he wished to send some important dispatches to President Lincoln. In due time Stohlbrand arrived in Washington and handed a sealed package to President Lincoln in person. Having looked the papers through the president extended his hand exclaiming: "How do you do, General!" Stohlbrand, correcting him, said; "I am no general, I am only a major." "You are mistaken," said Lincoln, "you are a general,"—and he was from that moment. In a few hours he received his commission and returned to the army with a rank three degrees higher than that he held a few days before.

The subject of the conversation thus being Swedish officers, several honorable deeds were told of some of them, among others, how Col. Vegesack, his regiment making a charge with leveled bayonets, and his color-bearer receiving a mortal wound, himself seized the colors and led his regiment to victory.

Soon after the close of the war a well-known lawyer and myself opened a law office in Red Wing, the name of the new firm being Mattson & Webster. I had successfully practiced law but a few months when it was announced that a new Swedish newspaper, to be called *Svenska Amerikanaren*, was to be established in Chicago. This enterprise was backed by a number of prominent Swedes of Illinois, who appointed me editor in chief without my knowledge or solicitation. At that time there was only one Swedish newspaper in this country, viz., *Hemlandet*, which was more of a church than a political paper, hence this was an open and - 97 - large field for me. I accepted the appointment on condition that I should not move to Chicago, but simply help to start the paper and put it on a firm footing, and that I should be allowed to resign in case I found this kind of work unfavorable to my health, which had been very seriously affected by the hardships and sufferings of the war.

On September 18, 1866, the first number of the *Svenska Amerikanaren* was published I quote from the article announcing my having assumed editorial charge of the paper as follows: "It shall be my ambition to so write as to advance the interest of the laboring people of our nationality, and to guide them in becoming good American citizens. I am one of that class myself, and during my residence in the settlements of the West I have learned to know their wants." The paper was very favorably received both in this country and in Sweden, and, under the name of *Svenska Tribunen*, is still exercising a great and good influence among the Swedish Americans.

The following winter (1867) the legislature of Minnesota established a state bureau with the purpose of inducing immigrants to settle in the state, and I was appointed by Gov. W. R. Marshall to be secretary of the board of emigration, with the governor and secretary of state as *ex-officio* members; the Rev. John Ireland, now Catholic Archbishop of Minnesota, was also for a time a member of that board.

The St. Paul *Press* for March 14, 1867, contained the following concerning the new board:

"The state board of emigration, composed of Gov. Marshall, Col. Rogers and Col. Mattson, was organized yesterday, and a general plan of operation agreed upon. We learn that the board concluded that, with the limited means at their disposal, it was not advisable to employ agents to work in Europe, but to use every practicable effort to turn - 98 - immigrants to Minnesota, after their arrival in this country. Efforts will be made to procure the publication of facts in regard to the state, in eastern and European journals; to make arrangements with railroads, more advantageous to emigrants than, heretofore and to afford them through interpreters and otherwise reliable information in regard to the best routes to the state from eastern parts. To give the emigrant a general idea of the characteristics of every locality in Minnesota, it is proposed to procure a map or chart of the state, showing its boundaries, streams, lakes, navigable rivers, timber and prairie sections, etc."

One of my first and most pleasant cuties as secretary of the board was to secure aid for the settlers along the Minnesota river. This locality had suffered from drought the previous year, and the settlers, most of whom were Swedes, Norwegians and Finlanders, were almost entirely destitute, and had no grain left for seed. Having secured an order from the government in Washington for provisions from the commissary department at Fort Ridgely, and being furnished with a letter of credit from our own state, I left for the stricken territory in the beginning of April, passing through the counties of Redwood, Renville, Yellow Medicine and Chippewa. At New Ulm several hundred sacks of flour were purchased, and at Fort Ridgely large quantities of provisions were taken out of the United States military stores. Agents were appointed to distribute these among the people, seed wheat and corn were shipped there from the South, and the settlers were thus relieved.

Soon after my return to St. Paul the board of emigration was again called together, and I was authorized to appoint Swedish, Norwegian and German agents and interpreters to meet our emigrants in New York and Quebec, and be their guides and protectors on the journey through the country to our state. Temporary homes were also secured until the - 99 - commissioners in the service of the board could get work for those who wanted to work out, and direct the rest to the interior of the state, where they could settle on government land or buy cheap land from private parties.

Arrangements were made with newspapers in different languages for publishing articles written by myself and others, which contained descriptions of Minnesota and its resources. Pamphlets and maps with more detailed accounts, were printed in Swedish, Norwegian and German, and distributed in the respective countries, on board the ocean steamers, at the railroad stations and at other convenient places. I was the author of nearly all of this literature, in which great pains were taken to describe everything in detail; how the chests or boxes ought to be made and marked before leaving the old country; what articles ought to be taken along; what kind of provisions were most suitable; what measures ought to be taken with reference to cleanliness and behavior during the long and tedious journey, etc. On my visits among our western farmers years afterwards I have often seen pamphlets in Swedish and Norwegian with my name as author standing in the little bookshelf side by side with the Bible, the prayer-book, the catechism, and a few other reminiscences from the old country. I also spent some time attending to the needs of the emigrants in the sea-ports and in Chicago, made arrangements with railroad companies for securing better accommodations and even free tickets for hundreds of emigrants, who would otherwise have been compelled to part with their companions before reaching their place of destination.

While performing my duty as secretary of the board of emigration I also acted as land agent for one of our greatest railroad companies, whose line went through Wright, Meeker, Kandiyohi, Swift and Stevens counties, and near Lake Ripley, in Meeker county. I purchased some eight - 100 - hundred acres of land for myself, on which I made extensive improvements and spent some time as a farmer.

LAKE RIPLEY.

In the above-named localities there were only a few widely scattered families when I went there in 1867, while it is now one continuous Scandinavian settlement, extending over a territory more than a hundred miles long and dotted over with cities and towns, largely the result of the work of the board of emigration during the years 1867, 1868 and 1869. - 101 - The board of emigration did not show partiality toward any portion of the state, but did all its work with a view to the interest of the whole community. Our efforts, however, in behalf of Minnesota brought on a great deal of envy and ill-will from people in other states who were interested in seeing the Scandinavian emigration turned towards Kansas and other states, and this feeling went so far that a prominent newspaper writer in Kansas accused me of selling my countrymen to a life not much better than slavery in a land of ice, snow and perpetual winter, where, if the poor emigrant did not soon starve to death, he would surely perish with cold. Such was at that time the opinion of many concerning Minnesota. I would be more than human if I did not, in recalling these incidents, point with pride and satisfaction to the condition of the Scandinavians in Minnesota to-day, but will return to this further on.

The position which I held enabled me to be of service to countrymen in more ways than one. Thus the interests of the church were by no means neglected, and I think my readers will excuse me for inserting the following lines from the minutes of the eighth annual council of the Swedish Augustana Synod, held in Berlin, Ill., June 13, 1867:

"Whereas, The same conference reports that Col. Mattson has offered to procure sites for churches, parsonages and burial grounds for Lutheran churches in the new Scandinavian settlements in Western Minnesota,

"Therefore Resolved, That the synod express its thanks to Col. Mattson, and request him to get deeds on said property to be given to the different churches of the Augustana Synod, as soon as they are organized at the different places."

It has always been admitted that during those years the emigrants destined for Minnesota received better care, guidance and protection than was ever accorded to a like class before or after that time. It is also acknowledged that the - 102 - state received great benefits in return by being settled by a superior class of emigrants from the northern countries. As for my own share in that work, although my efforts were sometimes misunderstood and I myself blamed, as any one will be who has to deal with newly-arrived emigrants, I felt much pride and satisfaction in the work, knowing that not only the state, but the emigrants themselves, and even the serving and laboring classes remaining in the old countries, were very greatly benefited thereby. While laboring hard for immigration to Minnesota my chief object was to get the emigrants away from the large cities and make them settle on the unoccupied lands in the northwest, where the climate was suitable to them, and where it was morally certain that every industrious man or family would acquire independence sooner and better than in the crowded cities of the east. I never attempted to induce anyone to immigrate, but tried to reach those only who had already made up their minds to do so, and the only people that I ever induced to leave their mother country were a number of poor servants and tenants among my own or my parents' acquaintances for whom I myself paid partly or wholly the cost of the journey.

- 103 -

CHAPTER IX.

Visit to Sweden in 1868-1869—The Object of my Journey—Experiences and Observations During the Same—Difference Between American and Swedish Customs—My Birth-place—Arrival and Visit There—Visit to Christianstad—Visit to Stockholm—The Swedish Parliament—My Return to America—Reflections on and Impressions of the Condition of the Bureaucracy of Sweden.

For many years I had desired to revisit the home of my childhood, and in December, 1868, saying good-bye to family and friends, I set out alone on my first visit to Sweden, after an absence of nearly eighteen years. The chief object of the journey was recreation and pleasure; the second object to make the resources of Minnesota better known among the farming and laboring classes, who had made up their minds to emigrate. This visit to the fatherland marked an important era in my life. Being only eighteen years old when I first left it, my impressions were vague and imperfect. Nor had I seen much of that beautiful country until my return in 1868. I shall now endeavor to relate some of those impressions and experiences as faithfully as memory permits, and should I have to record some things that will offend certain classes of my countrymen, I do it with no unfriendliness or lack of kindly feeling, but simply in the interest of truth; for after having been a true and loyal American citizen for nearly forty years I still cling to - 104 - Sweden, its people and institutions, with the affection of a child toward its mother.

When I left Sweden in 1851 there were no railroads. On my return the 23d day of December, 1868, via England, Germany and Copenhagen, I landed at Malmö just in time to walk to the railroad station and take the train to Christianstad. The beautiful station with its surroundings, the uniformed and courteous officials in attendance, the well-dressed and comfortable-looking people in the first and second-class waiting room, all made a pleasant impression upon me, which soon was to be disturbed, however, by the following little incident: As I stepped up to the ticket window to buy my ticket I observed a poor working woman at the third-class window with a silver coin in her hand and with tears in her eyes begging the clerk to give her the change and a ticket. I heard her pleading that she had left three little children alone at home, that this was the last train, and if she did not get home with it she would have to walk in the mud after dark. The clerk insultingly refused her, stating that he had no time to bother with her trifles unless she paid the even change; she asked several gentlemen near by to change her money for her, but they all turned away as if fearing contamination by coming in contact with one so poor and lowly. [3] I had only a few large bills, and as the woman was crowded away, the same clerk at the first-class window took one of my bills, and, with a most polite bow, gave me a handful of large and small change. Of course I got the woman her ticket also. This was possibly an exceptional case, but to me it was a striking example of the difference between Swedish and American ways and courtesy. I venture to say that in no railway station or other public place in the whole United States, north or south, east or west, would a poor woman in her circumstances be left - 105 - one minute without a friend and protector. Men of all classes,—from the millionaire to the day-laborer, or even street loafer,—would have vied with each other in trying to be the first to render her assistance.

I passed my old home at Önnestad station after dark, and soon arrived in Christianstad, where four years of my youth had been spent. It was my purpose this time only to pass through the city without looking up any old acquaintances. This was my thirty-sixth birthday, and, thinking of family and friends in my western home, I felt lonely, and repaired to my room at the hotel. I was not left alone very long, however, for the news of my arrival had preceded me by a telegram from Copenhagen, and soon an old schoolmate called, and a few minutes later the editor of the leading newspaper, Karl Möllersvärd, who was exactly of my own age and had been on a short visit to America, and with whom a warm and lasting friendship was soon formed. The stroll through the little city the following morning brought many tender recollections, and I should have enjoyed it more had I not been such an object of attention and curiosity to everybody there.

The advent of the railroad and the leveling of the old fortifications had brought many improvements on the outskirts, but the interior of the town with its little, narrow, but rectangular squares, streets and alleys, and its little one and two-story houses had undergone no change. And yet I could hardly realize that it was the same, because those objects which, to my boyish fancy, had seemed grand and imposing now appeared so diminutive that it was more like a dream than a living reality. This was particularly the case when, at noon, I watched the guard-mount of the artillery at the great square, and saw a large number of finely-uniformed officers, many of them grey with age and service, their breasts covered with decorations and crosses. With their - 106 - sabres dragging and clashing against the pavement, and their spurs rattling, they walked up to the parade line from which they reviewed a couple of dozen soldiers with an air of solemn dignity, which might have done honor to a Grant, a Sherman, or a Sheridan, while reviewing our hundreds of thousands of veterans of a hundred battlefields. Truly, if the army of Sweden is defective in anything it is not in the dignity and style of the officers of the Vendes artillery; but, joking aside, the splendid bearing and discipline of the regiment made a good impression. This regiment has in fact become noted as a training school for young men, who are afterwards employed in the railroad service, and in large establishments where ability, punctuality and practical knowledge are necessary.

Christmas eve found me in Fjelkinge, at the old homestead where my father was born, and where his people had lived for generations. The place was now owned by a cousin of mine, an excellent and very prominent man in his locality. The telegram had not reached this quiet, and, to me, sacred, spot. The astonishment and surprise of my honored cousin and my two aged uncles, who were still living, can more easily be imagined than described, and I was received with cordiality and joy. That night, spent under the roof of my forefathers, surrounded by the old people and the many dear recollections, and by a new generation that had come into being since my last visit there, stands vividly in my memory as one of the most delightful of my life.

Another cousin of mine, a younger brother of Hans Larson, of Fjelkinge, was rector at Trolle-Ljungby, not far from the old homestead. In his church there was to be an early service Christmas morning. We consequently left Fjelkinge very early, and arrived at Ljungby just as the candles were lighted and the service commenced. We entered and sat down in the sacristy just as my cousin had left it to enter the - 107 - pulpit in the church. He did not know that we were there, but we could see him, and hear his words during the solemn "Otte song." On his return with his family to the sacristy after the services, there was another surprise, and such joy as we then experienced does not often fall to the lot of mortal man. He told us that he had just had a dream about me that very night, and his mind was full of anxiety about my safety; but he had not expected to meet me so soon. Between him and me there had been a bond of friendship and brotherhood, even from childhood, which was now renewed, never to be broken again.

I had a third uncle, my father's youngest brother, who lived in Vislöf, three Swedish miles from Fjelkinge. The second day after my arrival he sent his son asking me to come to him immediately, as he had been waiting for me a long time, and I went to his house the same evening. This uncle had been stricken with paralysis two or three years before, and been a bed-ridden invalid ever since, unable to use his limbs, and at times even to speak. His eldest son had gone to Minnesota the previous summer. The evening which I spent at his bedside was a remarkable one. As soon as I approached his bed he partly raised himself to sitting posture and began to speak, which he had not been able to do for a long time. His wife was sick abed in another room, but his youngest son and two daughters were at his bedside with myself. He said he had been wanting to die for a long time, but when he had heard that I was to visit Sweden he wished to live until he could see me again. He asked me to tell all about my father, our family and friends, and his eldest son. Then he asked me to take his family with me to America when he was dead. When he had no more questions to ask or anything to communicate he sent his son for two of the neighbors, said good-bye to all of us with the exclamation: "Thanks for all you have related and promised! - 108 - Now I am ready to die! Farewell! God bless you all!" after which he breathed his last. The following spring his family accompanied me to Minnesota.

I decided to spend New Year's eve with one of my most intimate boyhood friends, Mr. Nils Bengtson, in the little village of Skoglösa, where I was born. Some of the dearest friends of my parents and a number of my childhood acquaintances were present there, and on New Year's day we attended services together in the old church at Önnestad. My presence was expected, and the church was crowded with people who had been friends and neighbors of my parents, or school and playmates of myself. Even the pastor had chosen a text applicable to me: "I think of the bygone days, and of the time that is past." The solemn services made a deep impression on all of us. A day or two later, in company with some friends I visited the little cottage where I was born, and where a number of the neighbors had now gathered to see me. One of my earliest recollections from childhood was the spruce tree, which, as I mentioned in the first chapter, was planted in the little garden by my parents. It was the only tree of its kind for a great distance around. It had grown to be a foot in diameter, was very beautiful, and was the pride not only of the present owner of the little farm, but of the whole neighborhood. After breaking off a sprig or two of the tree to carry back to my parents, we left the place early in the evening for Nils Bengtson's home, which was about half a mile distant, and where I was still a guest.

Early the next morning my host awoke me with the news that the owner of the cottage had arrived before daylight, anxious to communicate a strange accident. Upon being admitted he stated that shortly after I left his house in the evening, a single gust of wind swept by in great force and broke the spruce tree off with a clean cut a few feet from the - 109 - ground. It seemed very strange to us all, and he regarded it as an ill-omen, sold the place shortly afterward, and went with me to America the following spring.

At that time only a few Swedish emigrants had returned from America, and to see a man who had been eighteen years in America, and had been a colonel in the American army must have been a great curiosity, especially to the country people; for wherever it was known that I would pass, people flocked from their houses to the roads and streets in order to catch a glimpse of the returned traveler. So great was their curiosity that on New Year's eve the servant girls of Nils Bengtson at Skoglösa, drew lots as to who should carry in our coffee, and thereby get a chance to take the first look at the American colonel. One of the ladies of the house told me afterwards that when the girl returned to the kitchen she put the tray down with great emphasis and disappointment, exclaiming indignantly: "Oh, pshaw! He looks just like any other man!"

Now followed a season of visits and entertainments in Christianstad and the neighboring country, which I shall ever hold in grateful remembrance. I was received with cordiality everywhere among the common people and the middle classes, while the aristocratic classes looked on with distant coldness, as they always do when a man of the people has succeeded in getting beyond what they would call his legitimate station, and is what we would call, in other words, a self-made man. My plain name and humble ancestry were in their eyes a fault that never could be forgiven. This did not trouble me, however, for I sought no favors, or even recognition from the great, but found plenty of delight in the cordial welcome of the middle classes.

In the month of February I visited Stockholm, in company with my friend Nils Bengtson. It was the first time I had been there, and, like all other travelers, I was charmed with - 110 - the beautiful city, and its gay and festive life. The parliament (Riksdag) was in session, and as a liberal from America I was received with great cordiality by the liberal party. One grand dinner and two evening parties were given by some of its members in my honor, at which some of the most distinguished liberal members of parliament were present. Of course numerous toasts were proposed and speeches made, in one of which I was called upon for my views on the Swedish militia as corresponding largely to the lately disbanded volunteer army of the United States.

There was quite a famine in some of the Swedish provinces that winter, and when the government asked the parliament for an appropriation of several millions for carrying on field maneuvers of the army the coming season, the liberals made a strong opposition, preferring to use the money on some public improvement in the famished provinces. Of course I expressed my sympathy strongly in favor of the volunteer organizations and against the proposed maneuvers of the regulars. A few days afterward my words were quoted in the parliament, and gave rise to a spirited correspondence in one of the Stockholm conservative newspapers.

Returning to Skåne I found myself besieged by people who wished to accompany me back to America in the spring. Having visited my wife's relatives at Ballingslöf, and enjoyed their hospitality, and made some trips to Wermland, Gothenburg, Lund and Copenhagen, I spent the rest of my time with friends in Christianstad, Ljungby and Önnestad.

Having been for many years a Free Mason in America, and advanced to the highest degrees in that order, I was received in great state and full ceremony into the provincial lodge at Christianstad, and on Good Friday, if I remember right, I had the honor of marching in the Masonic procession between the two highest Masons of the province, the aged brothers, Barons Rolamb, wearing their gorgeous uniforms, - 111 - while I was dressed only in a plain black dress suit. The procession marched from the lodge to the chapel, only half a block distant on the same street, but a great crowd had gathered to see the mystic order, and I noticed many manifestations of satisfaction among the masses at the honor bestowed upon me, while I have reason to believe that some of the uniformed brethren silently choked down a grudge over the plain citizen whom the strict rules of the order, for that day at least, had placed in a higher position than most of them could ever hope to attain.

Time passed swiftly, and, as the crowds of intending emigrants were increasing daily, it was found that it would be impossible for one steamer to carry them all, so I went early in April to Helsingborg, where one shipload was started for Minnesota under the leadership of Capt. Lindberg, a veteran from the Anglo-Russian and the American war. A few weeks later I followed across the Atlantic with a party which numbered eight hundred people, and in due time returned to my home in my adopted country.

On the whole that first visit to Sweden was exceedingly pleasant, although there would occasionally come up disagreeable incidents whenever America was the subject of discussion. The laboring and middle classes already at that time had a pretty correct idea of America, and the fate that awaited emigrants there; but the ignorance, prejudice and hatred toward America and everything pertaining to it among the aristocracy, and especially the office holders, was as unpardonable as it was ridiculous. It was claimed by them that all was humbug in America, that it was the paradise of scoundrels, cheats and rascals, and that nothing good could possibly come out of it. They looked upon emigrants almost as criminals, and to contradict them was a sure means of incurring their personal enmity and even insult.

I remember a conversation at an evening party in Näsby - 112 - between a learned doctor and myself. He started with a proposition that it was wrong to leave one's native country, because God has placed us there, and, although the lot of the majority might be very hard, it was still their duty to remain to toil and pray, and even starve, if necessary, because we owed it to the country which had given us birth. In reply I referred to one of the first commandments of the Bible, that men should multiply, go out and fill up the earth; that if it were wrong for Swedes to emigrate, it was equally wrong for the English, the Germans, the Spaniards and even our progenitors, the ancient Arians, and if so, what would the result be? Portions of this bountiful earth would be overcrowded, privation, crime, bloodshed and misery would follow, while other continents would lie idle. If it had been wrong to emigrate, America, which to-day is the larder and granary of the world, would have remained in the possession of a few savages. My argument was of no avail; the doctor, otherwise a kind and humane man, would rather see his poor countrymen subsist on bread made partly out of bark, which hundreds of them actually did at that very time in one of the Swedish provinces, than have them go to America, where millions upon millions of acres of fertile lands only awaited the labor of their strong arms to yield an abundance, not only for themselves, but also for the poor millions of Europe.

Hard as it is for the individual to change habits of long standing, it is still harder for nations and races to free themselves from prejudices centuries old, especially in a small country like Sweden, isolated from the great nations and thoroughfares of the world. The importance of a military officer in Sweden dates from an age when the common soldier was simply an ignorant machine, and the difference between "a faithful servant of the king" and a common mortal was immense. The common mortal of to-day, however, is climbing bravely up towards the - 113 - military demigod. To command a company, or even a regiment, in modern warfare, especially in times of peace, requires but little tact and skill compared with former times, when such commander often had to act independently and at his own risk, whereas now there is scarcely any branch of business which does not require more talent for its proper management than the command of a company or a regiment. It is therefore not on account of superior merits, but on account of old fogy notions and prejudices that the bureaucracy, military and civil, consider themselves to be of such immeasurable importance. My experience in life has taught me that individually men do not count for much in the world; that no man amounts to a great deal by himself; and that the highest as well as the lowest is dependent largely upon his fellows.

What has been said about the military officers applies, in many cases, equally well to the civil officers, or rather, to a class of men holding life tenure offices in the civil service. Just now civil service reform is the question in American politics, and it means that officers in the civil service shall be appointed for life. I have always, for my part, doubted the wisdom of this reform, because I have seen so much evil growing out of that system in Sweden, England and India. To be sure, there would be much good springing from it, but it is very questionable whether the evil results would not be still greater.

We Americans hold that all power of government emanates from the people (as it certainly does with us), and that the officers of the government, from the president down to the village constable, are merely the servants of the people, whose duty it is to enforce the laws and preserve good order. In the other countries named it is still, to a certain extent, supposed that God in his wisdom appoints the ruler, that all power lies in him, and that whatever privileges - 114 - the people receive come as favors from the ruler. The influence and effect of these two ideas are as different in all the ramifications of the system as the ideas themselves are irreconcilable.

In America the humblest citizen goes to a local, state, or United States official with head erect and demands that such and such things be done, according to the law. In the other countries the lowly and even the average individual comes before the magistrate cringing and supplicating for his rights as for a favor. Of course such a false and absurd system, practiced for hundreds of years, can not fail to leave a strong impression both upon the seekers and the granters of such favors.

To me, brought up, ever since my boyhood, under the American system, the importance of the civil officers in Sweden seemed to be greatly at variance with the progress made in the elevation of the people in general. I will only take one example: The provincial governor (Landshöfding) and his immediate subordinates of a little province of the size of half a dozen of our counties, appears with much more pomp and style than any of the governors of our great states; and I have no doubt that such a governor considers his office to be more important than that of the governors of some of our states, each of which has a population larger than that of the smaller kingdoms of Europe.

- 115 -

CHAPTER X.

The Importance of the Scandinavian Element—A Swede Elected Secretary of State in Minnesota—False Rumors of Indian Depredations—The Northern Pacific Railroad is Built—Trip to Philadelphia—The National Convention at Indianapolis—Delegation to Washington—A Swedish Colony in Mississippi Moved to Minnesota—The Second Voyage to Europe.

Politically the Scandinavians in America had exerted no particular influence beyond that they had generally been counted upon as loyal to the Republican party, and a few of them had held county offices and been members of the state legislatures in Wisconsin and Minnesota. The honor of first bringing out a Scandinavian for a state office belongs to F. S. Christensen, a young Dane, who, in the summer of 1869, was editor of *Nordisk Folkeblad* in Rochester, Minn. One day he called on me and asked if I would be candidate for secretary of state, providing the Scandinavians of Minnesota should nominate me, to which I readily assented. A few weeks later a Scandinavian convention was held in Minneapolis and resulted in designating me as their choice for secretary of state. At the Republican state convention held in St. Paul in September that year, I was nominated almost unanimously by the whole Republican party. Being called to the platform after the nomination, I accepted the same in a brief speech, which at the time attracted much attention as echoing the sentiments of our people in the west. - 116 - I therefore regard it of sufficient importance to quote it here:

"*Mr. President and Gentlemen of the Convention:*

"Allow me to tender you my hearty thanks for the honor you have conferred upon me by this nomination. I feel doubly gratified for the very large majority you gave me. The time does not admit of any extensive remarks upon my part, yet so much has been said lately regarding the Scandinavian element, that the subject, perhaps, requires an explanation from me; and, as the chosen representative of the Scandinavian people of this state in the present campaign, I am authorized to express their views, and I do so from a thorough knowledge of them. It is true that we have left our beloved land; we have strewn the last flowers upon the graves of our forefathers, and have come here to stay, come here to live, and come here to die. We are not a clannish people, nor do we desire to build up a Scandinavian nationality in your midst. You have known us here for many years; you have seen us come among you unacquainted with your language and your customs, and yet I know that you will bear me witness how readily and fraternally we have mingled with you, learned your language and adopted your ways, and how naturally our children grow up as Americans, side by side with yours. We have been cordially received in this great west by your own pioneers, and have become prosperous and happy. Yes, we love this great country of freedom, and we wish to be and remain Americans."

Being elected a few weeks later by a large majority, I assumed the duties of secretary of state on the 1st of January, 1870. As secretary of state I was still a member *ex-officio* of the board of emigration, and had charge of all its work and correspondence, which amounted often to a hundred letters a day.

In the month of June following, rumor came to the capitol of a new Indian outbreak on our western frontier. It was said that Indians had come in the night and committed depredations, and quite an alarm was caused all along the frontier; the bloody massacre of 1862 was still fresh in the memories of our people, and while the state authorities did not believe this rumor, we deemed it necessary to take measures at once for pacifying the people by protecting the frontier. Therefore I started out at once with several hundred stand of arms, with ammunition and authority to - 117 - organize the settlers into militia companies and commission officers for the same. Selecting a few friends for company and aids, we went by rail as far as Benson, Swift county, thence by ox teams northward, following the frontier settlements to the northern portion of Otter Tail county. Four companies of militia were organized and officers duly appointed, the last being in Otter Tail county, with a Swedish count, Ragnar Kalling, as captain. This prompt action stopped the panic, and all has been quiet since that time. The rumor of the Indian depredation proved to have originated with some settlers who, in the disguise of Indians, had tried to scare away a Norwegian from a claim which he had taken from another man.

During this year one of the greatest railroad enterprises in the world was commenced, namely, the building of the Northern Pacific, extending from Lake Superior to the Pacific coast, a distance of over two thousand miles. The celebrated financier Jay Cooke, of Philadelphia, who had acquired a great reputation as the financial agent of President Lincoln's administration during the war, was at the head of the enterprise. The Northern Pacific Company had received a government grant of many millions of acres of land along the proposed railroad, and it required millions upon millions of dollars to build the road. One of the important financial questions with Jay Cooke was how to derive a revenue from the sale of lands, and how to get settlers and communities started along the line of the road. So ignorant were the people of this country about the region lying within the limits of the Northern Pacific railroad that it was generally supposed to be either barren or too far north for successful agriculture; yet that very region has since proved to be the greatest wheat producing country in the world. Mr. Cooke himself had been all over it with a small party, under the escort of United States cavalry, on - 118 - an exploring tour, and he was perhaps the only man of that day who foresaw the future greatness of the Northern Pacific region.

Late in the fall of 1870 I received a letter from Mr. Cooke, in Philadelphia, inviting me to come and spend a week with him and talk over the new Northwest. Upon the advice of ex-Gov. Marshall, who had spoken of me to Mr. Cooke, the then Gov. Austin and other prominent men, I repaired to Philadelphia, and spent some days at Mr. Cooke's palatial residence near that city. He had also for guests a delegation of French and German bankers, who had just arrived from Europe. Mr. Cooke impressed me as one of the greatest and noblest men I had ever met. His enthusiasm and eloquent arguments carried everything before him. The millions were raised, largely in Europe, and the road was built, as we all know. The result of my conference with him was my permanent engagement, at a salary more than twice as large as that I had from the state, to repair to Europe in the spring as agent of his enterprise, with headquarters in Sweden, my special duties being to make known in the northern countries of continental Europe the resources of the Northern Pacific, particularly the park region in Minnesota. I was also requested by Mr. Cooke to draw up a general plan on my return home for the disposal of the company's lands, which I did, and that plan was adopted for the guidance of its land and emigration officers and agents.

In the month of December a national convention was held in the city of Indianapolis, Ind., for the purpose of devising measures for the better protection of emigrants on ocean steamers, and while in transit through this country. All the states interested in emigration sent delegates to that convention, and I was one of those representing our state; my knowledge and experience of the subject at issue enabled me - 119 - to take such a part in the proceedings that at the close of the convention, I was appointed one of a committee of five (Gov. McCook, of Colorado, State Treasurer Smith, of Wisconsin, Banker Greenbaum, of Illinois, and a leading newspaper man of Philadelphia, were the other members) to draft a law for the protection of emigrants, and to proceed to Washington and lay the same before the president and congress. There I had an opportunity for the second time to meet Gen. Grant, who was then president. I spent much time with him, and he took a lively interest in the emigration question. The result of our work was the passage by the United States congress of the excellent laws in relation to emigration which still remain in force.

In January, 1871, the state legislature of Minnesota again assembled. The senate then consisted of twenty-two members, and was opened and organized by Lieut. Gov. Yale, and the house of representatives, with forty-seven members by myself as secretary of state.

During that winter I received several touching letters from Swedes located in the state of Mississippi. They were part of a little colony which had gone there the previous year, direct from Sweden. The climate was unsuitable; one-fifth of the people had already died, nearly all the rest were sick, and there was great distress and misery among them. They asked me to get them away into the healthy climate of Minnesota. They were entirely destitute of means, and had to be placed where the men could obtain employment when they should have regained sufficient health and strength.

The Duluth & St. Paul Railroad Company, which was then a part of Jay Cooke's system, upon my request, furnished the necessary means, and sent Mr. F. S. Christensen, heretofore mentioned, to Mississippi to bring the party to St. Paul, which he did under many difficulties, in such satisfactory manner that upon his return he received an appointment - 120 - by the company as local land agent at Rush City, in which position he remained many years. He is now president of the bank at that place, being married as before stated, to my niece, the little Zelma, whom the Indian squaws were so fond of playing with in the old log cabin. The little colony from Mississippi has certainly demonstrated that the northern climate is by far the best for the northern people. They had left Sweden strong, robust and hopeful men and women; after having stayed one year in the South they arrived in Minnesota pale, poor and broken down, lacking strength and energy, and almost without hope.

The railroad company acted most generously towards them. It built them comfortable houses, furnished an abundance of provisions, cooking utensils and other necessaries; they gave the men employment at liberal wages as soon as they were able to work, and yet many of those very people growled and complained because we did not do more for them. I remember distinctly how one of the women, when her share of groceries and provisions arrived, was perfectly indignant because there was only granulated sugar, and she had always been "used to drink coffee with lump sugar in Sweden." This bad trait among newly arrived emigrants from any country is very common, gratitude and contentment being exceptional the first year or two, as all will testify who have had anything to do with them. It really seems that the more that is done for them the less satisfied they are. I am glad to say, however, that after a few years they get over this bad fault, and so did the little party from Mississippi, most of whom have all of late years repented and even apologized for their former folly and ingratitude. They formed the nucleus of the large Swedish settlement west of Rush City, now one of the most prosperous in the state.

After the close of the legislature in the spring of 1871 - 121 - preparations were made for carrying out my agreement with Jay Cooke to go to Europe for an indefinite time. Having been criticised by some of my countrymen, for resigning the office of secretary of state at that time, I owe them the following explanation: First: Personally, I was comparatively poor, and the salary which I received from the government, with the great draw-backs for all sorts of charities and public enterprises, which an official in that position has to meet, was insufficient to support me and my family, and I considered that I had the same rights as any other citizen to better my pecuniary condition, which I did by accepting the offer of Jay Cooke. Secondly: It was of greater importance to the public, and I could render better service to the state at this period of its early development, as agent for a great railroad company, which fact was fully recognized by our leading public men, and it was with their advice and at their earnest request that I took the step. I accordingly tendered my resignation to the governor of our state, but he, out of polite consideration, preferred that I should take a leave of absence until fall, when the people would have an opportunity at the political convention, to designate my successor, and wrote me the following letter:

" State of Minnesota ,

" Executive Department .

"St. Paul, May 25, 1871.

"Col. H. Mattson, Secretary of State:

"Dear Sir: Learning that it is your intention, on taking your departure for Europe, to resign your office of secretary of state, allow me to ask you to reconsider that resolution. You will leave a very competent deputy, perfectly acquainted with all the duties of the office, and in whose integrity, as well as in his honesty, the public have unlimited confidence. Within a few months your successor will be indicated by the delegates chosen by the people, comprising the dominant party of the state, and then he may be appointed, if you are to resign at all, with no uncertainty as to the popular choice of the individual who should fill that important post. For these reasons I hope you will conclude to withhold your resignation, at - 122 - least for the present. I most cordially wish you a pleasant journey to the field of your new labors, great success there, and a safe return to the land you have served and loved so well.

"Very truly yours,
" Horace Austin , Governor."

It is true that even after the state convention the governor did not appoint my successor, but preferred to leave the office nominally in my hands in charge of my very able assistant, the Hon. Pennock Pusey, until the end of the term, so that in fact I did not resign, but kept my office during the whole term for which I had been elected.

In the last week of May I left for Sweden the second time, taking my family with me. The journey passed very pleasantly over England, Germany and Denmark. We arrived in Hamburg in the morning of the day when the Hamburgian troops returned under Prince Carl from the Franco-Prussian war, and made a triumphant entry into the city, being received with the greatest enthusiasm by the whole populace. It was indeed a grand sight, as all these troops marched by our hotel, men and horses literally covered with wreaths, flowers and bouquets, thrown over them by the grateful people. On this journey I carried important business letters from leading railroad men in Minnesota to some capitalists in Holland, who had advanced several million dollars for the construction of railroads in our state. I mention this, because it paved my way to very important business connections with prominent Hollanders a few years afterward.

Shortly before entering upon this journey, a private banking and foreign exchange business was established in St. Paul under the firm name of H. Mattson & Co. My partners were Consul H. Sahlgaard and A. T. Lindholm, who successfully managed the business during my absence. A few years later this affair was merged into the St. Paul Savings Bank, of which Mr. Sahlgaard became the cashier, while Mr. Lindholm and myself both withdrew. The banking firm H. Mattson & Co. was one of the first firms that, as agent for the Cunard Line, introduced the system of prepaid steamship tickets from Europe to America, which has gradually gained the confidence of the people, and developed into a very extensive and important business.

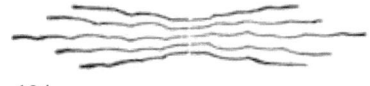

CHAPTER XI.

In Sweden Again—Reception at My Old Home—Visit to Northern Sweden—Field Maneuvers in Sweden—The Opening of Parliament—In Norway—Visit in Stockholm—Royal Palaces—The Göta Canal—A Trip to Finland and Russia—King Oscar II.—A Trip to Dalarne in the Winter.

On June 21, 1871, I landed a second time in my native country at Malmö. As already stated, I was this time accompanied by my wife and children, and intended to remain in Europe several years, which we also did.

At Hessleholm we were met by relatives and friends who conducted us to the old city of Christianstad, where we were to make our home. The early part of the beautiful northern summer we spent in visiting friends and kinsmen. Entertainments, excursions and festivities of all kinds alternated continually. The kindness and hospitality of the people knew no bounds, and no matter how defective some of the old institutions of Sweden may be they are in my opinion more than counterbalanced by the many beautiful and noble traits of character of the people, which we observed everywhere, and which are faithfully stored up in our hearts and minds, so that we always find a great delight in looking back to those days.

Having spent a large portion of the summer in this manner, I started in the month of August on a tour to the northern part of the country, visiting Stockholm, Upsala, Gefle, Hudiksvall, and several other places. This was my first opportunity to see the beautiful scenery of northern Sweden, the fine, quiet bays, the magnificent lakes, the pleasant valleys, the green hills, the mountains dark with pine forests, all of which contribute to make the scenery of Norrland so varied and attractive.

In the fall I returned to southern Sweden, and had an opportunity to witness the field maneuvers of the largest portion of the Swedish army, and also to meet the popular king Charles XV. The maneuvers were very fine, but, in my opinion, the troops could not have endured a long campaign, with its exhaustive marches and hardships. The soldiers complained loudly of fatigue, and quite a number of them were taken sick after the march of only fourteen to eighteen miles, although the weather was fine, cool, and bracing. Compared with our American army during the late war, when marches of twice that distance were quite frequent, the Swedish army was inferior; but these weak points would probably soon be remedied by practice in actual warfare.

After having seen King Charles I was no longer astonished at his great popularity among the people. There was something about him which seemed to electrify and charm everyone who came within the circle of his personal influence. I saw him again the following winter at the opening of parliament in Stockholm. With all due respect for old Swedish customs and manners, I cannot but compare this pageant to a great American circus—minus the menagerie, of course. I would like to describe this serio-comical demonstration for the benefit of my American readers; but I am sorry to say that I can no longer remember the titles of the different officers, heralds, guards, lackeys, pages, etc.,—all of them dressed in the most gorgeous costumes, some of them preceding, others following the king and the royal princes, who were adorned with all the mediæval clap-trap insignia of royalty, and wrapped in huge mantles of gay colors, and with long trains borne by courtiers or pages. We can comprehend the importance of a display of this kind a couple of centuries ago, but it seems to me that the common sense of our times demands its abolishment, and unless I am very much mistaken King Charles himself, who was a practical and sensible man, was of the same opinion.

The same winter I made a visit to Norway, which was repeated the following summer. The social and political conditions of the country reminded me somewhat of America, Norway being ahead of Sweden in that respect, and I am not surprised that the Norwegians are proud of their beautiful country.

One of my most pleasant journeys in Europe was a trip which I took in company with wife and children in the early part of the summer of 1872. On this trip we went through the lovely province of Södermanland, and thence by rail to Stockholm, where we met many old friends and acquaintances. Midsummer-day was celebrated in the circle of a number of happy friends at Hasselbakken, and on the following days we made repeated visits to the enchanting surroundings of the capital. On one of these outings to Drotningholm, a summer palace, we met other American tourists, and I remember distinctly how we all agreed that this was just the locality for some charitable institution, where the unfortunate poor and suffering members of society could be taken care of, as, for instance, a home for old widows, or orphans, or old men who have served their country faithfully in peace or war, but have been reduced to poverty in their old age. As a contrast to Drotningholm we pictured in our minds the Soldiers' Home near Washington, where Abraham Lincoln had a few rooms, and found rest and recreation among trees and flowers, and it seemed to us that some of the country palaces of Sweden might just as well be used for a similar purpose.

- 127 -

Having remained in Stockholm for some time, we directed our course southward, by way of the Göta canal, past Motala, Trollhättan, and Gothenburg. How great, how delightful, how glorious! Dull and coarse must that man or woman be who can make this trip without being proud of the sons of Sweden and their peaceful avocations. In school I had read the history of Sweden, but it treated chiefly of warfare and of the exploits of the kings, only incidentally touching the achievements of peaceful work and the development of social and moral culture, which, in my opinion, are of supreme importance, and deserve the greatest honor. But then, it must be remembered that Swedish history was at that time written with the assumption that royalty and a few warriors are the sun and the stars around which the whole people and the country revolve, and from which they received their light and value. A better time has now dawned on Sweden, and even common people are acknowledged to have a certain inherent worth. Still I am afraid it will take some time before old prejudices can be dispelled.

In the fall of the same year I took a trip through Finland and Russia, having secured a passport issued by Gen. C. C. Andrews, who was then United States minister in Stockholm. I went with the steamer Aura from Stockholm to Åbo, Helsingfors, and Cronstadt. The pine-clad islands and shores of the Bay of Finland afforded a beautiful panorama from the steamer. The sight of Sveaborg made me feel that I was still a Swede in soul and heart, for I was overpowered by a deep sadness when I thought of the heinous treason by which this impregnable fortress was forced to surrender.

I spent several days in St. Petersburg, during which I took in the chief sights of this grand city, such as St. Isaac's church, the monument to Peter the Great, the winter palaces, etc. It happened to be the anniversary of the coronation of the - 128 - Czar, and I had the pleasure of seeing the magnificent military parade arrayed for the occasion. My American passport opened all doors to me wherever I tried to enter, and I was treated with the greatest politeness by military as well as civil authorities. To an uninitiated eye my personal liberty and independence seemed just as great here as in Washington; but that was not the case, for I knew that my every step was being closely watched.

One day my guide conducted me to a place in one of the suburbs, where some hundred prisoners were starting on their long journey to Siberia. He also conducted me to the Church of St. Peter and St. Paul, where the Russian Czars are crowned and buried; and through the fortress and prison, in whose moist, murky dungeons the political prisoners hear the great bell in the steeple striking the hour, and the watchman crying his monotonous, "God save the Czar," while from year to year the victims of despotism suffer and languish, often on a mere suspicion, and without a fair trial, until death finally puts an end to their sufferings. What is the reason that politically Russia has always been on the most friendly terms with the United States? How can liberty and the rankest tyranny have anything to do with each other? This has always been a riddle to me. I despise the friendship of a despotism like that of Russia, where the government orders innocent men and women to be seized in the silence of the night, torn away from their homes and families, incarcerated in dungeons, and subjected to bodily torture and social disgrace simply because they are suspected of having expressed or cherished liberal ideas.

Returning to Sweden by way of Finland I remained a few days at Helsingfors. Having presented my passport to the authorities of the city, the commander of the garrison sent an officer inviting me to visit the barracks and other places of interest. I accepted the invitation and spent two days - 129 - under the guidance of my cicerone. This was of course a rare treat, and it brought me in contact with many prominent citizens and officers. We also took a ride out in the country to see the condition of the peasants. In common with all other Swedes I have always sympathized with unfortunate Finland, in the belief that its people must be very unhappy and yearn for a reunion with Sweden. This proved to be a great misconception. What a peculiar contradiction! The Russian despots treat the Fins with generosity and justice, and as far as I could understand, the people were highly pleased with Russian supremacy, and would not become subjects of Sweden again, even if they could. [4]

The following winter I had the honor of meeting King Oscar, of Sweden, at the funeral solemnities arranged by the grand lodge of Free Masons on the occasion of the death of King Charles XV. I have attended quite a number of official gatherings of different kinds in different countries, and seen persons vested with the highest authority conducting the same, but as to true dignity and lofty majesty, King Oscar excelled them all. When I compare him with the czar of all the Russias, or compare the condition of the Swedes with that of their Russian neighbors, I thank God for my old native land and its noble king.

Of my numerous trips in Sweden I must mention one in particular,—a journey by sleigh,—in company with my old friend Karl Möllersvärd, from Upsala to Gefle, and from Falun south, through Dalarne, past Smedjebacken, and the lakes below this to Vesterås. The beauty of the country of a northern clime does not show itself in its entire splendor until dressed in the garb of winter. The branches of the mighty pines loaded down by the dazzling snow; millions of snow crystals, more beautiful than diamonds, glittering from - 130 - every twig as the sun sends its first morning rays through the forests; the picturesque costumes of the peasantry; the comfortable inns with their fine dishes of northern game; the neat sleighs drawn by small, swift, sure-footed horses; here and there a smelting furnace or a country church,—all these things combined left on my mind a picture of rural life more quiet, happy and beautiful than I had ever seen before.

- 131 -

CHAPTER XII.

Visit in Minnesota and Philadelphia—Conversation with Jay Cooke—The Crisis of 1873—Negotiations in Holland—Draining of a Lake in Skåne—Icelandic Colony in Manitoba—Return to America.

In the spring of 1873 I returned to Minnesota in company with a large number of immigrants. Being anxious to have my children learn the Swedish language, I left my family in Sweden where the children attended school. They spent this summer at Ronneby watering place, where the surroundings are characteristic of the mild and pleasant scenery of southern Sweden.

In traveling from the Atlantic to Minnesota we came by way of the Great Lakes and the Sault St. Marie canal. Having spent a couple of months in Minnesota I returned to Europe again via Philadelphia, New York and Quebec. The reader may remember that the Northern Pacific railroad was building at that time, and that Jay Cooke, by means of his enthusiasm and great popularity, had succeeded in raising large sums of money for this stupendous enterprise. The Union Pacific railroad, south of us, was already in operation, and its owners, fearing the competition of the new road, had resorted to all conceivable schemes to undermine the confidence of the public in the Northern Pacific road and its promoters. Many of those who had furnished money began to feel uneasy, but Jay Cooke went ahead, full of hope and confidence in its final success. Just as I called at his private - 132 - office in Philadelphia in August, one of his bookkeepers handed him a card from a prominent moneyed man in Philadelphia who wished to see him, and the following conversation took place between the two:

"What can I do for you, my friend?" Jay Cooke said.

"We begin," said the capitalist, "to lose confidence in your railroad schemes. I have bought $20,000 worth of bonds, but I am getting a little afraid, and came to ask your advice."

"My dear sir, the Northern Pacific Railroad bonds are just as safe as United States bonds."

"If this is your conviction, will you please exchange them for my bonds?"

"Certainly. Here; give this"—he handed him a slip of paper with a few lines on it—"to my cashier, and he will give you United States bonds in exchange."

The gentleman withdrew perfectly satisfied, and Jay Cooke turned to me with the following explanation: "I have seen the Northern Pacific country; that's the reason I am so confident in the success of this railroad enterprise. If we only succeed in accomplishing the work, I shall certainly prove that I was right; but if we fail, our antagonists will get a grist to their mill. But, whatever the result may be, no one shall have a right to say that I did not stake my fortune on my conviction."

The same day I left Philadelphia for Europe, but I had scarcely reached Sweden when the great crisis came. Jay Cooke, whose fortune was estimated at twenty million dollars, was a ruined man. The work on the Northern Pacific railroad was suddenly stopped, and the obligations of the company depreciated to almost nothing. We all remember the terrible crisis that followed. Thousands of people were ruined, and the whole country suffered one of the most disastrous financial crises of modern times. My own loss was - 133 - a very hard blow to me, not merely because I lost my position, but because my property in Minnesota, which consisted exclusively of real estate, stock and farm products, lost its value. This catastrophe was chiefly due to business jealousy, and there was no real cause for the panic, which was also clearly proven afterward. The Northern Pacific railroad has now been completed, and has proven to possess all the merits which Jay Cooke claimed for it. Its obligations are again above par. Jay Cooke has paid every dollar of his debt, with interest, and again lives in affluence and luxury, respected and honored by the whole country.

Returning to Sweden I passed through Holland, which country I had visited a couple of times before, as already mentioned. I carried important business letters from the leading men of the St. Paul & Pacific Railroad Company, now known as the Great Northern Railroad Company. Dutch capitalists had advanced the money—about twenty million dollars—for building this road. The company had received very extensive land grants from the United States government; but during the first few years after the construction of the road to Breckenridge the country through which it passed was so sparsely settled that the traffic of the road was insufficient to pay its running expenses, hence their stocks and obligations depreciated very much in value. But the American railroad officials with whom I had been connected in the capacity of land agent were firmly convinced that if this road could be extended about thirty miles to the Northern Pacific railroad, and a little more time allowed for the settlement of the country along the line, the enterprise would pay a handsome dividend. It was my task to explain this to the Dutch capitalists, and persuade them to advance another $150,000—a mere trifle compared with what they had invested already—to build said extension, which was to pass through a perfectly level country. The president of the - 134 - company, George L. Becker, and its land commissioner, Herman E. Trott, had previously visited Holland on the same business. But all our representations were in vain. The Dutch were stubborn, and would not give out another dollar. "It is of no use," they said, "to throw away a small sum of good money after a large sum of bad money, for it is all lost, anyway." The crisis of 1873 aggravated the situation still more, for this company, and its bonds were continually depreciating. The St. Paul & Pacific railroad had pledged itself to accept its own bonds at par in payment for its land, and as I and others had sold hundreds of thousands of acres of this land to new settlers on credit, I tried, and also succeeded, in perfecting an arrangement with the Hollanders, by which the new settlers who had purchased land on credit, were allowed to buy on time the bonds of the company, at about twenty-five per cent. of their face value, and apply the same, without discount, on their debts for the land, a method of liquidation that was highly advantageous to the settlers. As soon as this was found out in Minnesota, bankers and other capitalists sent agents to Holland to make similar arrangements, and, in the course of the next three years, a brisk business was done in exchanging those bonds for land, by which thousands of settlers saved large sums of money, and a number of bankers and agents made small fortunes. If I had returned to Minnesota immediately I could have realized a very handsome profit by this arrangement; but I had made agreements which compelled me to stay in Sweden some length of time, and I left this business in the hands of my former partner, Consul Sahlgaard, and the St. Paul Savings Bank. But they did not grasp the importance of this matter until it was too late, and the lion's share of the profits went to new parties; who thus reaped the benefit of my plans, as is often the case under such circumstances.

- 135 -

As in the case of the Northern Pacific Railroad, the subsequent success of the St. Paul & Pacific Railroad proved that Messrs. Becker, Trott, and myself were right, and if the Dutch bondholders had followed our advice they would not only have saved their twenty million dollars, but also made as much more. The bonds continued to depreciate to almost nothing until the company was declared insolvent, a receiver appointed, and very expensive legal measures were resorted to, until finally the Dutch became disgusted with the whole matter and transferred all their interests to an American syndicate headed by J. J. Hill, of St. Paul, at present the well-known Minnesota railroad king. The sum paid was a mere trifle. Hill's syndicate procured money for building the connecting link and completing the system. The syndicate made twenty million dollars by this transaction, and, within five years after the Dutch had sold their bonds for a mere bagatelle and the company had changed its name to the St. Paul, Minneapolis & Manitoba, practically the same bonds were sold on the exchange in Amsterdam for one hundred and fifty cents on the dollar.

The only profit I derived from my connection with this business was that I gained the respect and confidence of the Dutch capitalists, who very soon understood that they would have been all right if they had followed my advice. Therefore, when another Dutch company, known as the Minnesota Land Company, shortly afterward was brought to the verge of ruin by mismanagement, the affairs of this company were intrusted to my hands, and when the Maxwell Land Grant Company of New Mexico, which also consisted of Dutch capitalists, got into similar trouble they appointed me American manager of the affairs of that company, to which I shall refer further on.

Soon after my return to Sweden in the fall of 1873 I became interested in an important business enterprise near - 136 - my old home. A few years before this a number of Englishmen had organized a stock company for the purpose of draining a big swamp, and a lake called Hammarsjö, in the vicinity of Christianstad. After expending a large sum of money the company failed to accomplish the undertaking. An officer in the Danish army, Captain M. Rovsing, who had had experience in that kind of work, in company with myself bought all the privileges and rights as well as the plant and material of the English company, and the work was completed under the supervision of Captain Rovsing in the latter part of 1875. This Captain Rovsing was not only a firstclass engineer, but also an able and good man in other respects. I cannot tell whether it is luck or something else, but it is certain that I have always had the good fortune to enter into close business connections, and to form ties of intimate friendship, with persons distinguished by the highest sense of honor and integrity, and of those acquaintances Captain Rovsing occupies one of the foremost places.

During a part of this time I also contributed some time and work toward colonizing the province of Manitoba, and thereby gave an impetus to the establishment of the first Icelandic colony in the Northwest.

In the spring of 1874 we moved to Gothenburg, where we stayed until the work at Hammersjö was completed, and in January, 1876, we said good-bye to Sweden, and arrived in America after a stormy voyage of nineteen days across the Atlantic. For sixteen days the storm was so violent that the life-boats and everything which was loose on the deck was swept away by the waves, and the officers serving during the night had to lash themselves to the rigging by ropes, not daring to rely on their hands and feet.

It is strange how easily people in the course of time get used even to the most unpleasant circumstances. This was illustrated in a striking manner by the few cabin passengers who sat packed together in the cabin during this storm. After a couple of weeks we got so used to it that we finally found our voyage quite endurable. Still we were very glad when the beautiful steamer Circassian of the Allan Line brought us safely to shore in Portland, Me. A few days more on rail, and we were again safe and sound in our dear Minnesota.

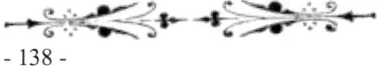

CHAPTER XIII.

Grasshopper Ravages in Minnesota—The Presidential Election—Chosen Presidential Elector—Minnesota *Stats Tidning*—*Svenska Tribunen* in Chicago—Farm in Northwestern Minnesota—Journalistic Work.

"The world do move" nowadays, and most emphatically so in the great American Northwest. An absence of four years is almost enough to bury one out of sight, at least that is what I found on returning to Minnesota. The crisis of 1873 had left my finances in anything but a flourishing condition, to which was added the ravages of the grasshoppers, which caused considerable losses to me on my farm at Litchfield, that being about the only property I then owned.

My attention was soon drawn from these private reverses to public affairs. The first steps toward re-entering the field of politics was my nomination for presidential elector by the Republican state convention, held at St. Paul in the summer of 1876. At the request of the Republican state central committee, I took an active part in the campaign that followed, as in fact I had done at every previous election since my residence in this state, but this time I spent the whole autumn in making a thorough political canvass through most of the Scandinavian settlements in the state. During that canvass it was my good fortune for a long time to be associated with the late William Windom, then a United States senator, and afterward twice secretary of the treasury.

Mr. Windom was at that time in the very prime of his noble manhood; his fine mental and physical endowments made him an object of love and veneration among the people. Though a man of the purest character and exemplary life, he was a pleasant, boon companion, fond of a joke and a good story, liberal and charitable in his judgment of others, easy and polite in his manners, open-hearted and kind toward all. He was a large, broad-shouldered man, weighing over two hundred pounds, with a high forehead, dark eyes, and smoothly shaved face. As a speaker he was earnest, though quiet, fluent and humorous. He never used tobacco or spirits in any form. We traveled together in all sorts of conveyances, and held meetings in country stores and school houses; ate and slept in the lowly cabins of the farmers, but everywhere Mr. Windom felt at home, and made every body else feel at ease also. I was afterward with him often and in many places,—from the executive mansion in Washington to the frontier cabin in the west,—and for the last time in New York city, when he went there in August, 1890, to save the nation from a financial crisis, but never did I notice any difference in his conduct toward the humblest laborer or the highest in power. In sorrow and adversity he was a tender friend; in manners he was a Chesterfield; in the senate a Roman, and in the treasury department a Hamilton. By his death the nation, the state of Minnesota, and his numerous friends, among whom for many years I had the honor to be counted, sustained a heavy loss.

Soon after the close of the campaign I commenced to publish a Swedish weekly newspaper called *Minnesota Stats Tidning*, in Minneapolis, to which place I had just removed with my family, and continued as its chief editor until the summer of 1881.

In 1877 friends in Chicago and myself started another Swedish weekly, called *Svenska Tribunen*, in that city, and for some time I had the actual management of both papers, dividing my time between Minneapolis and Chicago. My aim in this journalistic work was mainly to instruct and educate my countrymen in such matters as might promote their well-being and make them good American citizens. The *Stats Tidning*, or at least a part of it, gradually became a kind of catechism on law and political economy, containing information under the heading "Questions and Answers." This was intended especially for the Swedish farmers in the state. If a farmer was in doubt as to his legal rights in the case of a road, a fence, the draining of a marsh, or wished to know how to cure a sick horse or other animal, or how he could get money sent from Sweden, or if he wished advice or information on any other question relating to everyday life, especially if he got into trouble of some kind, he would write to the *Stats Tidning* for the desired information. Such letters were then printed in condensed form and followed by short, clear, pointed answers, and, so far, I have not heard of a single person being misled by those answers. On the other hand, I know that the public, and more especially the newcomers, reaped very great benefits from them. Few persons have any idea of how irksome and laborious this kind of journalism is, and at times I was on the point of giving it up in despair. As an example I will relate one little incident connected with this work. A farmer in a neighboring county had, through ignorance of the homestead law, met with difficulties in securing title to his claim. As usual he wrote to the *Stats Tidning*, and received the desired information just in time to save his property, which was worth over $1,000. On a visit to Minneapolis a short time afterward his feeling of gratitude directed him to the office of the paper to express his thanks. In a conversation with him I found that he had never subscribed for the paper himself, but was in the habit of going to his neighbor every Saturday afternoon to read it. I asked if it would not be well for *him* to subscribe for it also; it might happen to contain useful information in the future, and he could afford to pay for it. To this he answered: "No, I cannot do that, for I have not much time to read, and if I want to read I have some back numbers of a church paper, from Sweden, and should I want to read answers to any questions I can borrow a copy of your paper from my neighbor." So highly did this good and pious farmer, from a financial point of view, appreciate information which had saved him his home. In my opinion such people do not deserve reproach, but sympathy on account of their gross ignorance. It is also a fact, that, during all this time, the income received from the paper did not cover its expenses, and if it had not been for other resources the enterprise would have failed even at the very climax of its popularity.

After five years of untiring journalistic work I was only too glad of an opportunity to sell the paper in the spring of 1881 to a publishing company, which soon moved the plant to St. Paul. My former associates, Messrs. Lunnow and Soderstrom, soon after commenced the publication of a new Swedish weekly, called *Svenska Folkets Tidning*, which has now a larger circulation than any other Swedish paper in our state. Having sold my share in the *Svenska Tribunen* in Chicago a few years before, and thus being no longer connected with any newspapers, I found more time to devote to my wheat farm in the Red River valley.

FARM IN THE RED RIVER VALLEY.

CHAPTER XIV.

I am Appointed Consul-General to India—Assassination of Garfield—Departure for India—My Stay in Chicago and Washington—Paris and Versailles—Rome—Naples—Pompeii—From Naples to Alexandria—Interesting Acquaintances on the Voyage—The First Impressions in Egypt.

In the morning papers of July 2, 1881, a telegram from Washington announced that President Garfield had appointed me consul-general to India, in the cabinet meeting of the previous evening. The same telegram also announced that the president had left Washington for New England, where he intended to spend his summer vacation in the country. It was with mingled feelings of satisfaction and misgiving that I faced the opportunity to satisfy my longing to see the wonderful Orient, especially India, in which country the missionary Dr. Fjellstedt had aroused my childish interest, as stated in the beginning of these reminiscences. After consulting wife and children concerning this, to us, important news, I walked down town, receiving congratulations from friends and acquaintances on the way, and, arriving at one of the newspaper offices, I found a large crowd of people eagerly reading on a bulletin-board a dispatch to the effect that President Garfield had been shot by Guiteau. The news caused an excitement and consternation almost as intense as that produced by the assassination of Lincoln. Telegrams were received from Washington continually, and outside the newspaper offices were placed bulletins describing the condition of the wounded president, who was very popular with the American people. The last telegram of that day announced that he was very low, and would probably die before morning. The next morning the dispatches announced that the president was still living, and that on the previous evening, believing that he had only a few more hours to live, he had caused to be made out my own and four other commissions and had signed them with his dying hand. I feel justified in narrating this in detail, inasmuch as I am in possession of the document which contains the last official signature of our second martyred president, and which is a very dear treasure to me. Believing that it will interest the reader to see the last signature of President Garfield, I submit a photographic fac-simile of the same.

James A. Garfield.

GARFIELD'S SIGNATURE.

I had only one month to prepare for the journey, and on account of the long and expensive voyage, it was decided, in family council, that I should go alone, leaving wife and children in Minneapolis. It was also understood that I would only be absent about one year, for it was hardly to be expected that a person of my age could stand the dangerous climate of India much longer.

The 17th of August, 1881, was an important day for our little family, for on that day I left my home for a journey of thirteen thousand miles,—to distant Calcutta, the capital of India. Passing through Chicago on the following day, a number of my Swedish friends at that place had arranged a splendid banquet in my honor. About sixty of us spent a most delightful evening around the bountiful table; but what I prized more highly than anything else were the friendly and cordial feelings which were expressed in speech and song.

In Washington I spent a few days in order to receive the last instructions from the state department. Hon. W. Windom, who was secretary of the treasury under the administration of Garfield, accompanied me to the White house, where the president was yet hovering between life and death. We were not admitted to the inner room, which was separated from the front room only by draperies. I can vividly recall the picture of the president's noble wife as she stepped out to us, and, with an expression of the deepest suffering, affection and hope in her face, told us that the patient had taken a few spoonfuls of broth, and that he now felt much better, and would soon recover. Thus life and hope often build air-castles which are destined to be torn down again by the cruel hand of fate.

When the steamer touched the coast of Ireland the first news which the eager passengers received was that the president was still living and had been taken to a place on the coast. The voyage across the Atlantic from New York to Liverpool was a pleasure trip in every respect, and was favored by the most delightful weather. On board the White Star Line steamer Celtic,—a veritable palace of its kind,—the passenger had all he could wish, as far as solidity, speed, reliability, order, comfort, and good treatment are concerned. On September 9th I arrived in Paris. It seemed to me as if it had been only a couple of days since I was sitting in the midst of that happy company of friends in Chicago, whose tender and cordial farewell still sounded as an echo in my ears—or maybe in my heart. Nevertheless I was already in the grand and happy capital of the third French republic.

I had time and opportunity to stay a few days in the large cities through which I passed, each one of which left a particular impression on my mind, and, although they are similar in most respects, each of them has its peculiarities, especially with regard to the character, temperament and customs of the people. I cannot refrain from describing a few of them. Washington did not seem to be itself when I passed through it, a cloud of sadness and mourning brooding over it on account of the critical condition of the president. Boston is prim and stiff, and seems like a place of learning. New York is a turmoil of pleasure and business. "Hurry up" seems to be written in every face; "tumble harum-scarum in the ever-changing panorama of the world!" Liverpool is a good deal like New York, but on a smaller scale. London is the stiff colossus of Europe. Amsterdam and Rotterdam bear the stamp of thrift, cleanliness, earnestness, and comfort. Antwerp and Brussels that of joyous abandonment. Paris includes everything which is worth seeing in the others, and shows everything in gayer colors and to greater perfection.

I remained only four days in the city on the Seine, and the impressions of such a short stay are naturally fleeting and probably even unreliable. Paris has its imposing monuments from the days of Louis XIV. and the two Napoleons, which glorify the exploits of war; it has its beautiful churches, palaces and museums like other great cities; but in my eyes the greatness of Paris is to be found in her boulevards and public promenades. I also made a visit to Versailles, the wonderful city of palaces, and spent a day among the great monuments of grandeur and royalty, misery and tyranny. As works of art they are grand and beautiful, but their historical significance produce varied feelings. In the French capital everything seemed to indicate comfort and satisfaction. The workman of Paris is a gentleman in the best sense of the word. He feels free, independent, and proud in the consciousness that he is a part of the state. Soldiers were no longer to be seen in the city; they being garrisoned at Versailles and other neighboring cities; still there has never before been such a feeling of profound peace and security in France. Liberty is a great educator. The style, name, and other indications of the empire are passing away, and the republic has put its stamp on Paris. The commune is no longer feared, for the state is no longer an enemy of the people, but a protector of its rights and liberty. Fortunate Paris! Happy France!

But I must hurry on, in order to reach the end of my long journey. On the 13th of September I saw the majestic Alps with their snow-clad summits, which seemed to touch the very vault of heaven. The same day I passed through the tunnel at Mont Cenis, and arrived the following day at Rome, via Turin and Florence. And is this great and glorious Rome? Yes! These walls, ruins, palaces, and Sabine hills,—aye, the very air I breathe,—all this belongs to the eternal city. From the window of my room in Hotel Malori I can read the signs,— "Via di Capo le Care," "Via Gregoriana," etc., and among these an index pointing to the Rome and Tivoli street-car line. Indeed, I have seen the great city of Rome, with its churches, statues, paintings, and ancient ruins and catacombs; the little monument to the Swedish Queen Christina in the St. Peter's church; the triumphal arch which commemorates the destruction of Jerusalem, and the temple of Vesta where the ancient vestal virgins guarded the sacred fire. Two thousand years thus passed in review before my eyes in a few days.

ROME.

From Rome I proceeded to Naples. This city is built on the most beautiful bay in the world, and has a population of six hundred thousand inhabitants. It is built in the form of an amphitheatre, with a steep decline toward the water In the south we see the island of Capri, fifteen miles distant, and on the east coast the volcano Vesuvius, which, by its threatening clouds of smoke, seems to obscure the eastern part of beautiful Naples, although it lies fourteen miles distant from the city. Long before the time of Christ the bay looked about the same as it does now. The chief cities around it at that time were Naples, Herculaneum and Pompeii. Mount Vesuvius, however, did not look as it does now, but rose as a green hill, called "La Somma," and served as a summer resort for many wealthy Roman patricians. The city of Pompeii had about forty thousand inhabitants. On August 23, A.D. 79, terrific rumblings were heard from the interior of La Somma, the summit of which suddenly burst open, and a pillar of ashes, steam, and red-hot rocks shot up through the opening to a great height, and fell, scattering itself over the surrounding country, while streams of melted lava rolled down the hill-sides and buried Herculaneum and everything in it under a layer of ashes and lava to the depth of eighty feet. Toward night the eruptions increased in force, and before morning Pompeii and some smaller towns were also buried under the glowing rivers of volcanic rocks, ashes and mud.

The remarkable history of this place absorbed my mind as I passed through the two thousand years-old streets of Pompeii, which, in the course of this century have again been brought to light by the removal of the petrified ashes and other volcanic matter. The ancient city now looks a good deal as it did eighteen hundred years ago. It is situated on a round knoll, and measures three miles in circumference. The houses are built of stone, and only one story high, with roofs of brick and floors of cut stone, just as the modern houses in that vicinity are built to-day. Every house has an open court in the center, and all aisles and - 150 - doors lead to this. Glass windows were not used, but the rooms received light from the open court, which could be covered by canvass as a protection against the sun and rain. I measured the streets. They proved to be twelve feet wide, with a four-foot-wide sidewalk on either side. The paving consisted of boulders, with a flat surface about twenty inches in diameter, and contained deep grooves made by the chariot wheels. The houses were standing in their original condition, with fresco paintings on the walls and statues in their proper niches. The temples with their sacrificial altars, the theatres, the court, the council-house, and all other public buildings were adorned with marble pillars and choice works of sculpture. I saw a barber-shop with chairs, niches for the soap and mugs, and the waiting sofa. In a baker's house I saw the oven, the dough-trough, scales, and petrified loaves of bread. In a butcher shop were a saw, a knife, and other tools. There were also furniture, vessels for cooking, bowls, grain, pieces of rope, and plaster of Paris casts of the human bodies which had been found, generally prostrate, with the face pressed against the ground. There lies a cast of a man with a pleasant smile on his lips; he must have passed unconsciously from sleep to death. But it is fruitless to try and describe this remarkable place which has no parallel on the face of the earth. I heard the Swedish language spoken in this city of the dead, and had the pleasure of making the acquaintance of Alderman Törnquist and wife, from Wimmerby, and a Doctor Viden and his daughter, from Hernösand. Thus the living meet among the dead, representatives of the new times stand face to face with the dead of antiquity, children of the cool North in the sunny South. What a wonderful world this is, to be sure!

The 17th of September I embarked on board the steamer La Seyne, destined for Alexandria in Egypt. The warm, - 151 - Italian noonday sun poured down its dazzling rays; we were surrounded on all sides by ships and steamers carrying the flags of all nations; hundreds of fishing crafts were sailing out of the harbor, and in the distance the mighty volcano Vesuvius towered in imposing majesty above the vine-clad hills. There was a life and a traffic which it is difficult to describe. While La Seyne was lying at anchor for several hours out in the bay, Italian singers in their boats swarmed around the ship and entertained the passengers with music. Other boats contained three or four men each, who begged the passengers to throw coins into the water. As soon as a coin was thrown, down dived one of the men to the bottom, and invariably returned with the coin in his mouth although the water was very deep, perhaps from seventy-five to one hundred feet. The voyage across the Mediterranean was very pleasant, especially in the vicinity of the island of Sicily. The deep blue sky, the orange groves and vineyards on the island, and the neat, white cottages,—all gave an impression of indescribable tranquility and happiness.

On this voyage, which lasted three days, I became acquainted with several interesting persons, among others with a Professor Santamaria, professor in an university in Egypt, and his family, and with a Jesuit priest, Miechen by name. By birth a French nobleman of a very old and rich family, he had been educated for a military life, and had served in the army with distinction, and in the late Franco-German war he had been advanced to the rank of major, although he was only thirty years of age. But suddenly he had been seized with religious enthusiasm, and had given up his illustrious family name, renounced his fortune, his honors, and the brilliant military career which lay open to him, in order to become a priest. After two - 152 - years of theological studies he was ordained a priest, and admitted into the Jesuit order.

He had now been ordered to supply himself with a full set of certain scientific instruments, and with them to repair to Cairo, Egypt, where he would receive further orders. I talked a great deal with this man. He spoke English fluently, and was equally familiar with nearly all the other European languages. He was no fanatic or religious crank, but a polished, cultured gentleman, who had seen and learned to know the world, reaped its honors and tasted its allurements, and he was evidently as liberal and tolerant as myself. And this man went to a field of action of which he had no knowledge whatsoever. Probably an honorable position as professor in a university was awaiting him, or perhaps he would have to go to some isolated mountain to observe a phenomenon of nature in the interest of science, or penetrate a malarious wilderness as missionary among savages, where he would be debarred from all intercourse with civilized people, and deprived of all the comforts and conveniences to which he had been used during his previous life. Still he went willingly and joyfully to his work, completely indifferent as to his fate, thoroughly convinced that he was on the path of duty— to accomplish what God intended he should do. I was on my way to a great country and a court as the representative of one of the greatest nations on earth, but when I walked the deck arm in arm with this humble priest, I felt my inferiority compared with him, and I actually considered his position enviable. On the same voyage I became acquainted with a Danish traveler,—A. d'Irgens-Bergh,—who afterward met me in India, where we visited many places of interest together, and established a friendship which afforded both of us much pleasure.

On the morning of September 21st the coast of Egypt appeared in sight. There is Alexandria, founded by Alexander - 153 - the Great, and formerly renowned for its commerce, and as the centre of learning and culture of the then known world. Even now this city is grand and beautiful, although its beauty and style are different from anything else that I have seen. We often form conceptions of things which we have not seen, but which are interesting to us, and when we afterward find that those conceptions are wrong we feel disappointed. Thus I had always thought of Egypt as a country of a dark tone of color, probably on account of the fertility of the soil of the valley of the Nile, since we Northerners find that fertile soil is dark and poor soil of a lighter color. Therefore I could hardly believe my own eyes when everything I saw on the shore looked white. Not only the houses, palaces, and huts, but even the roads and the fields, all had a white color.

As we neared the harbor, and even before the pilot came on board, we noticed that all the flags were at half-mast. As soon as I landed and had shown my passport to the customs officer an elegant equipage was placed at my disposal under the charge of a dragoman, and we drove to the office of the American consulate, where also the flag was at half-mast. The sad occasion for this soon became apparent. President Garfield had died during my voyage across the Mediterranean, and the whole civilized world was in mourning.

- 154 -

CHAPTER XV.

Alexandria and its Monuments—The Egyptian "Fellahs"—The Mohammedans and Their Religion—The Voyage Through the Suez Canal—The Red Sea—The Indian Ocean—The Arrival at Calcutta.

I was now in Africa and Egypt, among the remnants of ancient glory of which I had read so much, and which I so often had longed to see, in the wonder-land of Egypt, with which every Christian child is made acquainted through the first lessons in Bible history, the country to which Joseph was carried as a slave, and whose actual ruler he finally became by dint of his wisdom and virtue. I was in the Nile valley where Pharaoh built his magazines and stored up grain for the seven years of famine, and whence Moses conducted the children of Israel by means of "a pillar of a cloud and a pillar of fire." In the land of the pyramids everything seemed strange and wonderful, and different from anything I had seen before. The streets crowded with people, the bazaars, the oriental costumes, the Babylonian confusion of all the tongues of the earth,—all this combined made on me an overwhelming impression. Cleopatra's needle; Pompey's pillar; the caravans of camels on their way into the desert; the old graves and catacombs; the palm groves, the oxen turning the old-fashioned water-wheels which carry the water from the Nile for irrigating the fields, just as in the days of Moses,—all this was reproduced in actual, living pictures before my wondering eyes. - 155 - Side by side with these remains of the past we meet with the great European improvements of our days,—the large ships in the harbor, the churches, the schools, the universities, the modern markets for trade and commerce, the splendid hotels and exchanges.

ALEXANDRIA.

I stopped two days in Alexandria. The second day I visited the summer palace of the khedive, or vice-king, on which occasion a funny incident took place. Like every other foreigner coming to Egypt I had bought a sample of the head-gear generally used in that country, consisting of a red cap called "fez," which is made of very thick, soft felt, and fits very closely to the head. With this cap on and wearing a tightly buttoned black coat I rode in the equipage already mentioned to the palace. Ishmael Pasha, the former khedive, who had just abdicated and left the country, had been very popular among his servants and adherents. I was of the same size and build as he, my beard was cut like his, and - 156 - in my red fez I looked so much like him that when our carriage passed through the gateway to the palace some of the servants whispered to each other that Khedive Ishmael had returned, and when the coachman stopped at the entrance I was surrounded by a number of servants who greeted me and evinced the greatest joy. The poor creatures soon discovered their mistake. Their good friend the khedive will never return to Egypt, for England and France will not allow it. He was too sincere a friend of his own people, and too independent in dealing with the shareholders of the Suez canal built during his reign.

Alexandria has a population of two-hundred-fifty thousand. It was founded by Alexander the Great three hundred years before Christ, on account of the great natural advantages of this place as a seaport. At the time of Christ it had about half a million inhabitants. It was repeatedly ravaged by destructive wars, and finally completely pillaged by Caliph Omar, who is also said to have burnt its library, the largest and most valuable collection of books of antiquity, an act by which civilization suffered an irreparable loss, the library containing the only copies of a number of ancient literary works. It is claimed that the caliph gave his generals the following characteristic answer, when asked what was to be done with the library: "If it contains anything contrary to the Koran it is *wrong*; if it contains anything that agrees with the Koran it is *superfluous*; therefore, at all events, it ought to be burnt."

PILLAR OF POMPEII.

The most remarkable of the ancient monuments still remaining in Alexandria is Pompey's pillar, which is a monolithic shaft of polished red granite, seventy-three feet high and twenty-nine feet eight inches in circumference. One of the most interesting objects of a more recent origin was the Café El Paradiso. It consists of an immense restaurant and concert hall, or rather halls, for there are many of them. - 157 - One of these extends over the water, so that when one sits there drinking genuine Mocha coffee and smoking a Turkish nargileh one can hear the beating of the waves and feel the undulations of the azure Mediterranean. I drove out into the country a few miles to see the Egyptian fellahs, or peasants. No—I shall not disgrace the name "peasant" by using it here; for the Egyptian fellah is an ignorant, superstitious, absolutely destitute, and, in every respect, miserable wretch, and is worse off than a slave. Four walls of stones or earth make one or two rooms, with a floor of clay and a roof of straw or sod. A wooden box, a couple of kettles, and some mats made of grass or palm canes, are the only pieces of furniture. A couple of goats, an ass, or, at the very best, a yoke of oxen, are all he possesses in this world. He works hard, and his fare is exceedingly plain. He neither desires nor expects anything better, nothing - 158 - stimulates him to acquire wealth; for that would only give the tax-gatherer a prbook for extra extortions. Miserable Egypt! I have seen much poverty and much misery among men; but of everything I have seen in that line nothing can be compared with the wretched condition of the Egyptian fellah.

FELLAH HUT.

Still these unfortunate people seem to find happiness in their religion. Here some one might object that this is a wretched happiness, because their religion is Mohammedanism or Islamism. Man feels himself drawn to a higher power. No matter what his condition, he longs for a life after this, and searches after an object for his worship, and when he has found this object he will give up his life rather than give up his faith. And still that object for which a person or a nation is willing to sacrifice even life itself is ridiculed and despised by another person and another nation. If the - 159 - ignorant were the only ones who disagree in matters of faith, this condition might be easily explained; even the highest civilization has failed in its attempts to harmonize the different religions, and, in my opinion, this fact ought to make all thinking men tolerant and liberal toward those who hold different religious views. The Mohammedan faith has made a deep and lasting impression on a population scattered over a large part of the surface of our earth, and no one dares deny that its adherents are much more devoted to their religion and much more conscientious in observing its rites than we as Christians are with reference to our religion.

FELLAH WOMAN.

The adherents of Mohammed now number one hundred and thirty millions, and the number is constantly growing. Many believe that this religion gains so many adherents because it is sensual, and allows all kinds of debauchery. But this supposition runs counter to the facts. It is true, that Mohammed allowed a man to have four wives; but it must be remembered that he limited the number to four, and that the number had been unlimited before. The life of an orthodox Musselman is an unbroken chain

of self-denial and self-sacrifice, and, in this respect, we must acknowledge that he is superior to us Christians. His chief article of faith is expressed in this dogma: "There is no - 160 - god but Allah, and Mohammed is his prophet." The leading commandments bearing on the practice of their religion are prayer, ablutions, alms-giving, fasting, and a pilgrimage to Mecca. The use of intoxicating drinks is strictly prohibited, hospitality is recommended, gambling and usury are not allowed. Friday is the Mohammedan's day of rest. Since my first visit in Egypt I have been very closely connected with many Mohammedans, several of whom have been members of my own household, and it affords me great pleasure to testify that, as far as my observations go, they have lived faithfully according to the precepts of their religion. Nay, I am convinced that in most cases they would renounce property, liberty, and even life itself, rather than violate any of the cardinal precepts of the Koran. But as - 161 - to the Egyptian fellah, he has no comfort to renounce, his whole life being made up of continual fasting and abstinence from sheer necessity, so that it is comparatively easy for him to be a good Mohammedan.

IRRIGATION MILL.

Having engaged a berth for the voyage from London to India on the steamer City of Canterbury, which I was to take about this time at the west end of the Suez canal, I could not remain any longer in Egypt, but took the Austrian steamer Apollo to Port Said, at the entrance to the Suez canal. On September 25th, in the evening, I embarked on the City of Canterbury where I made myself comfortable in a fine state-room which had been reserved for me. It takes two days to pass through the Suez canal, which runs through a great sandy plain that was formerly covered by the waters of the Red Sea. Among the many memorable places which were pointed out to us during this passage was also the spot where Moses is said to have conducted the Israelites across the Red Sea. The work on the Suez canal was commenced in 1859 and completed in 1869, and it cost about $95,000,000. The length of the canal is one hundred miles, its width at the surface of the water is three hundred and twenty-eight feet, at the bottom seventy-two feet, and its depth twenty-six feet. To a ship sailing from Sweden or England to Bombay in India, the distance by way of the Suez canal is five thousand miles shorter than by the passage around the Cape of Good Hope.

I recollect an anecdote which dates from the opening of the canal in 1869. On that occasion an irreverent speaker is claimed to have said in toasting De Lesseps, the French engineer who planned and executed the work, that the latter was the only man who had improved upon the work of the creator: He had connected the waters of the Red Sea and those of the Mediterranean. Thus the significance of - 162 - a great work may also find an expression in the garb of a told joke.

Having remained in Suez a short while, the steamer glided out on the Red Sea, keeping close up to the naked coast of Africa. On the second day of our Red Sea voyage we saw Mount Sinai looming up some distance from the coast of Arabia. September is the hottest month of the year in that region, and as we had the wind with us, the customary breeze caused by the motion of the steamer was neutralized, and the heat was terrific. We slept on the deck, and we hailed the morning hour with joy on account of the shower-bath which was afforded when the sailors washed the deck. It is a conundrum to me why this body of water is called the Red Sea, for there is nothing whatever to suggest this color. One day we had a miniature illustration of a sand storm. A strong wind carried the sand from the coast of Africa several miles into the sea and covered the steamer with a layer of fine, white sand, which looked like fresh snow. We also had a chance to see flying fish which flew over the ship, and occasionally fell down on the deck. These fish were small and silver-colored, their fins looking a good deal like the wings of the bat. They can not turn in their course, nor can they fly up and down at pleasure, but only upward and forward in a straight line; and when they fall down on the deck they are just as helpless as any other fish out of water.

Having reached the Indian ocean, the temperature became more pleasant, so that we no longer suffered so much from the heat. At last our splendid steamer plowed its course up the majestic Ganges, the sacred river with its one hundred mouths, on whose peaceful bosom millions and millions of human bodies have been carried to the ocean. For a distance of eighty miles we sailed up this wonderful river, - 163 - and on either side we could see cities, temples, palm groves, and large crowds of people. On October 15th we arrived at Calcutta, where I was received by the American vice-consul, and comfortably quartered in the Great Eastern hotel.

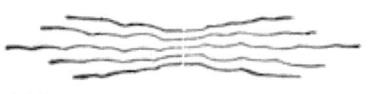

- 164 -

CHAPTER XVI.

India—Its People, Religion, Etc.—The Fertility of the Country—The Climate—The Dwellings—Punkah—Costumes—Calcutta—Dalhousie Square—Life in the Streets.

This is India, the wonderful land of the Hindoos. Africa had appeared strange to us compared with Europe and America; Asia seemed still more so. The Hindoos have a high and very old civilization, but entirely different from that of Europe and America. The country is named after the river Indus. It is hardly equal in area to one-half of the United States, but contains a population of more than two hundred and sixty-nine millions, eighty-one millions of whom are Mohammedans, one hundred and ninety millions Brahmins, two millions Christians, three and a half millions, Buddhists, Parsees or fire-worshipers, two millions Sikhs, and the rest are Jews or adherents of unknown religions. Queen Victoria of England is Empress of India, and the country is ruled in her name by a viceroy. It is divided into three great presidencies, viz., Bengal, Madras, and Bombay, and these are again divided into a number of districts and native principalities. In order to maintain her supremacy in India, England keeps an army of about two hundred thousand regulars, of whom a little over one-third are English and the rest natives; and beside these there is a large militia and police force. Most of the native soldiers hail from the mountain districts. The most prominent of - 165 - them belong to the Sikhs and Gourkas, two Indian nations. The Sikhs are tall, stately fellows, in my opinion ideal soldiers for a standing army. The Gourkas are smaller in stature, but very energetic and hardy; and both are renowned for their courage and endurance. It is said that a Gourka soldier would rather fight than eat, while a Sikh takes the matter more philosophically, and eats first and then fights. All native regiments are commanded by British officers, and a native seldom attains the rank of a commanding officer,—not because he is incapable of performing this duty, but rather because the English do not trust him implicitly.

SIKH CAVALRY MAN.

The bulk of the people belong to the Arian race, as we do; with the exception of the complexion, which is a little darker, their features are the same as ours. Occasionally a Hindoo may have red hair, but never blonde hair and blue eyes. Comparing the higher and the lower classes, the complexion of the former is lighter, and their bodies are better built and statelier than those of the lower or laboring classes, who also have a darker skin. The English language is used at the court and in all official circles, and the men of the higher classes among the natives speak and read English.

The plain of Bengal, in which Calcutta is situated, is triangular in form, each side being about one thousand miles in length. It is bounded by the Bay of Bengal, the Indian ocean, the Bay of Persia, and the Himalaya mountains. The soil is very rich, and, having been cultivated for thousands of years, it still produces two or three fair crops a year without fertilization or proper cultivation. As the Nile in Egypt deposits a rich sediment over its valley, so does the river Ganges carry from the mountains a whitish, slimy silt, which it deposits during its annual overflow in the plains of Bengal. This silt is a great fertilizer, and thus nature supplies what poor husbandry fails to provide.

It is not my intention to give a description of India and its wonderful people, but simply to give some pen pictures of scenes and incidents which came within the range of my observation and experience during the year and a half which I stayed there. I shall therefore ask the reader to follow me on my daily walks of life as well as to some of the fêtes and entertainments where I was a guest, and on my travels through the wonderful country. I had a chance to come in contact with all classes, as the rank to which my official position entitled me not only opened the doors of the palaces and temples to me, but also paved my way to the humblest houses.

STREET IN CALCUTTA.

India has over five hundred cities. Of these Calcutta is the largest, and has a population of about eight hundred thousand. It is called "the city of palaces," but only certain portions of the city deserve that name. Owing to the warm climate, the buildings in India, as in all other warm countries, are low, seldom more than two stories high, and the walls and roofs are very thick. The building material generally consists of brick and cement, the roofs being mostly made of the latter. There are verandas on the sides of the houses, and these, as well as the windows, are protected by heavy Venetian blinds. In the evening the doors and windows are thrown open so as to let in the cool night air, but in the morning they are closely shut, so as to keep as much of it as possible. Inside there are many contrivances for protecting the people against the excessive heat. The most important of these is the punkah, consisting of a wooden framework which is stretched with heavy canvass and is about two and a half feet wide, and from ten to twenty feet long, according to the size of the room. It is suspended from the ceiling, and reaches down to the heads of people sitting on chairs. By means of pulleys this punkah is kept in an oscillating motion by coolies stationed in the back of the house or on the back porch, and it creates such a pleasant breeze that one forgets all about the heat. Every room or office in the houses of Europeans and Americans has its punkah, and even the churches have a great number of them during the hot season. From March till October the punkahs are kept in motion all night over the beds of those who can afford the luxury of four " punkah walla" (pullers); for it always takes two pullers for each punkah in the day-time, and two others at night to relieve each other every hour or two. Servants' wages are very low in India, and as the punkah walla belongs to the lowest grade of servants his wages are only five rupees ($2.50) a month, and he must board himself as do all other servants.

The clothing which people wear also adds largely to their comfort. The cooley, or common laborer, wears a long piece of cloth wrapped around his waist and tucked up so as to resemble a short pair of drawers, and a head gear somewhat resembling a turban; the breast, back, and upper limbs being entirely naked. Both men and women of the better class of natives have loose falling robes of jute, silk or cotton. Europeans generally dress in white linen trousers and jackets, and it is only toward evening when taking a drive near the public parks, or at night while attending parties and receptions, that etiquette compels them to put on the black dress suit. What strikes the newcomer most on his first arrival in India is perhaps the great number of people that he meets and sees. The cities are veritable bee-hives of moving crowds of people, and the bazaars, shops, and dwellings resemble honey-combs, with their many subdivisions, giving each man or group of men the smallest possible space.

TYPES OF THE LOWEST CASTE.

Sitting in my comfortable easy chair

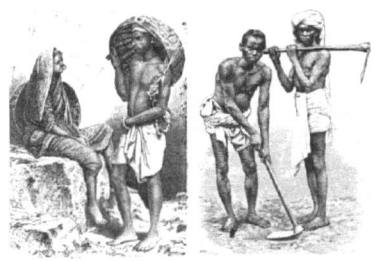

with my eyes closed, thinking of the past, I now see a picture of a spot in Calcutta called "Dalhousie Square," where I loved to walk in the cool evening shades. I wish I were an artist and could paint the picture on canvas for my readers; but since I am not I will try to describe it with the pen. Dalhousie square is about twice the size of our ordinary city parks; it is laid out in walks, flower beds and grass plots, and planted with flowers, shrubs and trees of almost every imaginable kind; it is a perfect gem of a little park. It is surrounded by a high iron railing, with gates at the four corners, which are open in the day time. On one side of the park are the new government office buildings, while the other sides are lined with ordinary business houses, separated from the park by wide streets. The principal one of these streets leads from the viceroy's palace up to the native part of the city, and is generally frequented by a great number of fine carriages, hacks, palanquin bearers, horsemen, and thousands of pedestrians.

At one corner is a hack stand, with hacks just like our own; but instead of our American hackdriver we find the native Jehu, or coachman, who, while waiting for a customer, sits perched on the seat with his feet drawn up under his body, engaged with needle and thread in sewing a garment - 171 - for himself or his wife, perhaps, or occupying himself with a piece of embroidery or fine crochet work.

In front of yonder fine office building is seated a Durwan (doorkeeper), who is a Brahmin or priest. He sits at that door or gate all day long, and sleeps in front of it at night on his little bed, which resembles a camp cot. Early in the morning he takes up his bed and walks with it to the rear, where stands a little cookhouse in which he prepares his food for the day, consisting chiefly of boiled rice and vegetables. Just now he is reading aloud, and with a singing voice, from the Shastras (the Hindoo Bible) to a crowd of listeners, who eagerly and reverently seize on every word from the holy writings. Just behind me on a green spot in the park a dozen or more Mohammedans lie prostrate, their foreheads touching the ground, repeating their prayers; and if it happens to be at the setting of the sun hundreds of people are seen in the streets, shops, hotel corridors, or wherever they happen to be, turning their faces toward the holy city Mecca, reverently kneeling and saying their evening prayers.

Here on the side-walk, close by me, sits a money-changer and broker. He has a box filled with coins of almost every kind and description; he buys and sells gold and silver of other countries, such as are not current in Calcutta, loans money on jewelry and other valuables, and does a general banking business on a very small scale. There comes a peddler,—more of them. Now they are crowding in by the hundred, selling canes, parasols, embroideries, watches, jewelry, and trinkets of every description, following the foot passengers, running beside the carriages going at full speed, sticking their goods through the windows and imploring the occupants to buy.

Going around to the more quiet side of the square, I find a professional writer squatted on the side-walk. He has a bundle of dry palm leaves, and a customer of the lowest - 172 - Hindoo classes stands before him stating what message he wishes to send to his wife and relatives in the country. With a sharp steel instrument the writer inscribes some strange Bengal letters on the palm leaf, folds it up into a little package which is sent by a traveling neighbor, or, perhaps, by a swift messenger, to the dear one in the humble cottage which stands somewhere out on the plain among the rice fields.

A little further on sits a native barber, also on the side-walk. [5] Instead of a barber's chair he has a common-sized brick. The man who is to be shaved squats down opposite the barber; if the customer is the shorter of the two the brick is put under his feet, but if he is taller the barber puts the brick under his own feet, in order that they may be on a - 173 - perfect level before the operation begins. A Hindoo barber not only shaves and cuts the hair, but also cleans the nails and ears and does other toilet work.

HINDOO BARBER.

There I see two stately men walking arm in arm; they have fine cut, very regular features, and beautiful black hair and beard; their intelligent looks and easy carriage command attention; they wear japanned shoes, snow white trousers, long white linen coats buttoned close to the chin, and high black hats without brim. They are Parsees, descendants of the ancient Persians and fire-worshipers, and probably merchants and men of wealth. And there again I see a group of Asiatic Jews in skull caps and long gowns,—keen, thoughtful and intelligent, without the slightest change in manners, costumes, or features since the days of the Jews of nineteen hundred years ago.

In the crowded street I suddenly hear a shout, and see two men running with staffs in their hands, halooing: "Stand aside, get out of the way, you fellows! The Prince of Travancore is coming! Clear the road, get out of the way!" Close on the heels of the runners is a magnificent carriage drawn by four Arabian steeds. By the side of the driver sits a trumpeter, who occasionally blows in a long horn to make known that the great personage is coming. Inside is the prince, and behind the carriage are four mounted soldiers, his body guard.

Just coming in sight around a street

corner, turning up one of the native streets, is a long line of ox-carts. They are loaded with cotton, jute, hides, indigo, or other native products. They are very light, and are drawn by a pair of Hindoo oxen no larger than a two-year-old heifer of our cattle, but with fine limbs and a high hump over the shoulders. They are yoked far apart, about the same way as in Sweden; but the coolie driver sits close behind them and guides them by a twist of the tail with his hand. Several - 174 - palanquin-bearers are passing the square. The palanquin is a long covered box attached to a long pole and carried by four men, two at each end of the pole, which rests on their shoulders. Inside the palanquin is perhaps a Hindoo merchant going to a bazaar, or a couple of students going to the university, or maybe the wife of some well-to-do native merchant on the way to the home of her parents.

INDIGO CART.

The trees in the park are all full of flowers, like the tulip tree and the chestnut in bloom. Innumerable birds of gay colors flutter among the branches of the trees, and on the roofs of the highest houses we discover a couple of the so-called adjutant birds, a species of stork, which stand like sentinels on guard watching the thousands of ravens that hover over the city ready to dive for any garbage that may be thrown out into the street or alley. Formerly, these were the only scavengers in the cities of India. A - 175 - dozen coolies who are almost naked are seen running among the carriages sprinkling water on the streets from goat skins, to keep the dust down.

There comes a family procession of the lower class with a basket of bananas and wreaths of flowers going to the river Ganges to offer sacrifices and enjoy an evening bath in the open river. Early every morning thousands upon thousands may be seen in the streets bent on a similar errand. Men from Cashmere, Afghanistan, China, Arabia, Thibet, etc., are seen in the throng, dressed in their native costumes. It is a strange and beautiful picture to look at for a little while. I have described only a small portion of it, for fear of tiring the reader.

HINDOO MERCHANTS.

- 176 -

CHAPTER XVII.

The Promenades of the Fashionable World—Maidan—The Viceroy—British Dominions in India.

No European or American walks out doors in India, excepting a promenade early in the morning or late in the evening. They are either carried in palanquins, or, which is more common, they keep a horse and carriage. Observing the good old rule of adopting the custom of the country, I also procured a phaeton and a gray Arab as well as the indispensable Hindoo driver and runner, and I now invite the reader to take a ride with me late in the afternoon, when hundreds of equipages fill the fashionable driveways.

It is five o'clock in the afternoon, and the dim rays of the setting sun allow us to lower the top of the carriage so that we may have an open view all around. But before doing this, we must exchange the white business suit and broad-brimmed Indian hat (which are made of the light pith of an Indian shrub somewhat similar to our elder bush, and covered with a thin layer of cotton) for the conventional black hat and coat, for these people are dreadfully ceremonious. The *chandra* takes his place in the driver's seat, and the *badon* on the steps behind the carriage. They are both dressed in snow-white outer garments, which look a good deal like a common nightgown, and a head dress consisting of ten yards of white muslin, wound several times around the head in the shape of a round turban. The Mohammedan - 177 - coachmen and runners generally wear the colors of their masters in the same manner as other native servants do. In my case, of course, it was the red, white and blue sashes, belts and turbans. The runner has his place on a step behind the carriage, and it is his duty to jump off and run in front to clear the way whenever it may be necessary.

We start from the Great Eastern hotel, where I first resided, down a long street called Chowringhee road, which is two miles long and very broad, and lined on the east side by English residences built of stone. Every mansion stands in a large garden full of tropical trees and plants, and surrounded by a stone wall five feet high. There are wide double gates for carriage drives, and at these gates the durwan (gate or door-keeper) sits the whole day long. On the west side of the street runs a double street-car track, and beyond this is an immense common parade or pleasure ground, the Maidan, which extends to the Hoogley, a branch of the Ganges. On the west side it is bounded by the Strand, and on all other sides by a macadamized road about one hundred and fifty feet wide and planted with large, shady trees on either side. The east side of this road is already described. On the north side, from the river to Chowringhee road, between Eden Garden and the palace, it is called the Esplanade. Another hundred-foot-wide road runs south from the palace, and divides the ground into halves. This is called the Red road because it is macadamized with crushed red brick. From the Red road opposite Fort William another great road runs to Chowringhee road. A great number of foot-paths cross each other in all directions, and in the evening these are crowded with people in oriental costumes going to their homes in the suburbs.

Here and there are statues erected to the honor of prominent English generals and statesmen, and certain parts of the - 178 - grounds are also dotted with small groups of palms and other tropical trees. All these trees and plants are different from those growing in the North. Most of them have very broad and thick leaves, nearly all of them bear beautiful flowers, and many of them fruits. They are green the whole year round. In the north-east corner of the grounds is a garden of about forty acres which is called Eden. It is exceedingly beautiful and contains a great variety of trees and flowers, an Indian pagoda, lakes, canals and bridges, and thousands of birds enjoying an almost undisturbed existence, and singing and twittering among the trees and flowers. Eden Garden is surrounded by a low brick wall with several gates, the widest of which is the one next to the Strand. Inside this gate is a high orchestra stand, and below a square promenade on the fine grass plat. From six to seven o'clock in the evening a military band plays to the fashionable world which gathers here to take an evening walk.

GOVERNMENT HOUSE.

A quarter of a mile below the Eden garden is the historical Fort William, around which Lord Clive and other heroes struggled to found the British Empire of India. Below the - 179 - fort and next to the Strand is the drill-ground, and below this again a large race course. South of Maidan are several suburbs, and beyond these a zoological garden.

Driving past the imposing orange-colored palace of the viceroy, called the government house, which very much resembles our capitol at Washington, but is neither so large nor so elegant, we finally strike the Esplanade, where the Chowringhee road meets the Red road.

We stop a few minutes at the Esplanade to take a look at the gay picture. The Esplanade is crowded with a surging mass of humanity, all going from the river bank to their homes in the Eastern part of the city. It is the sixth day of the new moon, and thousands of men, women and children have been down to the river, washed themselves in its waters, and offered sacrifices consisting of fruits and flowers. The women are dressed in white, red, yellow, green, blue or violet garments. The smallest children sit astride on the left hip of their mothers, the men carry large baskets of fruit, mostly bananas, on their heads for the river-god received only a small portion, and the rest is to be eaten at home. Here and there among the pedestrians is a well-to-do Hindoo who takes his family, consisting of two or three wives and a crowd of children, to the river in an ox-cart. There are hundreds of musicians and peddlers in the throng, and all are joyful and rejoicing. It must be observed that only people of the lower classes take part in such public demonstrations in company with women and children. Fashionable women would never walk beyond the gardens around their own houses and do not appear in company.

Soon carriages are seen passing by in long rows, either down the Red road or to the right along the Esplanade toward the Strand. We follow the latter and arrive at the river bank where thousands of people are yet busy with their sacrifices or trading with peddlers for fancy goods and dainties, while - 180 - others listen to the music from peculiarly constructed flutes and drums, which vie with each other in producing the most ear-rending discord. Elegantly covered carriages swarm in four lines up and down the road. Most of the occupants are Englishmen with their ladies; but you may also see quite a number of Hindoo princes or noblemen with their ladies in oriental costumes, or Parsee merchants in black silk coats and high caps. To the right there is a veritable forest of ship's masts extending along the beach for miles, and to the left some native soldiers are being drilled. We drive down and have a chat with the English officers and stop to see a game of polo played, the native cavalry contesting with their English officers, all displaying a wonderful skill. Every now and then a couple of young Englishmen or officers on horseback meet each other, and yonder are two half-naked Hindoos on a jog-trot carrying a load which looks like a big coffin, but which turns out to be a palanquin occupied by a passenger who, in an inclined position, smokes his cigar and takes as much comfort as he can get in that primitive mode of traveling. But see there! At a given sign hundreds of men arrange themselves in long rows with their faces turned to the west, just as the sun sinks below the horizon; they prostrate themselves with their faces turned toward Mecca, and say their evening prayers. They are Mohammedans.

Returning we stop at the gate to the Eden garden where a large number of equipages have already arrived before us, compelling us to wait for our turn to drive up and get out of the carriage. The garden is now illuminated by thousands of gas and electric lights; men, women and children walk forth and back on the soft grass plats; the military band plays well-known tunes; Chinese, Parsees, Jews, Hindoos and Arabs, in the most varied costumes, mingle with each other and with the Europeans. There are plenty of - 181 - seats for such as wish to sit down and rest; but it is now time for exercise, and they walk in rows of ten or more until the band winds up its program for the evening by playing "God save the Queen." In the midst of a general hurry and confusion we hunt up our carriage which was to stop at a certain spot, and return to the crossroad from which the roads of Maidan as well as the streets in the city may be seen glimmering in the gaslight as far as the eye can reach. When we reach home it is just time to dress for dinner, which generally begins at eight o'clock, lasting two or three hours. As to fashionable life, social pleasure, display of dress and finery, etc., Calcutta excels every other place in the world.

PARSEE FAMILY.

My exequatur not having arrived from London, I had to obtain a special recognition from the viceroy as American consul-general, after which my formal presentation took place. The Marquis of Ripon was viceroy during my stay in India. On presenting my credentials I had a lengthy conversation with him, and learned to admire him from that moment. From my memorandum book written on that day I quote the following:

"Lord Ripon is a plain, manly man, whose character, head, and heart would have made him a great man even if he had been born in obscurity, but now he ranks as one of the highest, and is one of the wealthiest of the English nobles. He said, among other things, to me: 'I like America and her people very much. I was there on a commission which tended to make America and England better friends, and all such efforts are well worthy all men (he referred to the Alabama treaty, in which as Earl de Gray he was one of the commissioners). With American and English ideas of liberty it is hard to understand how to rule India. I would educate the natives,' said he, 'even if I believed that it would be dangerous to English power, because it would be right to do so; but I don't think it is dangerous. India has always had a few very able and highly-educated men, while the millions have been in utter ignorance and superstition, and such a condition is more dangerous to English rule than if all are raised in the scale of knowledge. My only object, and I think England's, in India, is to benefit India. Our schools and railroads are doing away with ignorance, and are fast destroying the *caste* system. Considering the natives as enemies, we must put on a bold front and fear no danger, but be always on the guard.'"

Afterward I became intimately acquainted with this truly noble man, and was proud and happy to be counted by him as one of his very few friends in India who stood by him when the powerful Anglo-Indian bureaucracy turned against him on account of his humane efforts to raise the natives socially and politically. Unfortunately for India, she has not had many British rulers like Lord Ripon, but most of them, in conjunction with the office-holding class, rule India, not for the good of India, but for their own interests.

Our British friends are certainly entitled to credit for the audacious pluck which they showed when a handful of their soldiers and citizens conquered that great country with its innumerable inhabitants. The only thing, however, that made it possible to do so, and which makes it possible to hold India to-day, is the internal strifes, the jealousies and the religious intolerance among the natives themselves. If they were united they could free the country from the foreigners in a month. But why should they? The country is better governed than ever before, and it is gaining fast in progress and prosperity. Still there is a deep hidden feeling of ill-will toward the English, and the time will yet come when a terrible struggle will be fought in India. Perhaps Russia will have a hand in the fight. It will be a bloody, savage war, and will cause Great Britain serious trouble. I said that India is better ruled now than ever before; but that is not saying much, for it ought to be ruled still better and more in the interest of the natives. India has civil service with a vengeance, the office-holding class being even more arrogant, proud and independent than the titled nobility. They rule the country with an iron hand, regard it simply as a field for gathering in enormous salaries, and after twenty-five years' service they return to England with a grand India pension. The English look down upon the lower classes with haughty contempt, chiefly because the latter try to insinuate themselves into favor with the former by means of all kinds of flattery. Nobody is of any account in India unless he is an officer, either civil or military; hence all the best talent is circumscribed within narrow office routine limits, and nothing is left for the peaceful industrial pursuits except what the government may undertake to do, and that is usually confined to railroad and canal improvements. England wants India for a market, therefore nothing is done to encourage manufactures, but rather to cripple them. With the cheapest and most skilled labor in the world, the natives of India are compelled to buy even the cotton garments they wear from England though they raise the cotton themselves, and England is very careful not to establish a protective tariff in India.

CHAPTER XVIII.

An Indian Fête—The Prince of Burdwan—Indian Luxury—The Riches and Romantic Life of an Indian Prince—Poverty and Riches.

I shall now invite my reader to accompany me to the city of Burdwan, which is situated about seventy miles north of Calcutta, for the purpose of attending an Indian fête to which I was invited shortly after my arrival at Calcutta. Burdwan is the name of an old principality (as well as of its capital) situated on the great Indian railway. The principality of Burdwan is now under the English government, but it has its own maharajah, or prince, to whom the English government grants certain rights over the people and property of this principality. The ruling prince during my stay in India was a young man of about twenty-two years. He had a good European education, spoke English well, and had, to a great extent, adopted European manners and customs. His name was Aftab Chand Muhtab Bahadur. In the beginning of December, 1881, he was installed as maharajah of Burdwan by Sir Ashley Eden, at which time he came into actual possession of his inherited rights; and this event was celebrated by great festivities in the palace and city of Burdwan.

The fête which commenced December fifth and closed December tenth was celebrated according to a well-chosen program for each day. About fifty English civil and military officers with their families were invited as guests to the -186- palace. Some of them occupied rooms in the palace, others lived in tents pitched in military order in the palace garden, and about three hundred Indian guests were lodged in private houses in the city. I was the only foreign guest, and was assigned a neat pavilion, built partly over an artificial lake in the garden, and the second place of honor at all ceremonies—an honor which was, of course, due to the republic which I represented.

The palace consisted of several large buildings two or three stories high, and several small pavilions, all in Italian style, situated in a park or garden of some forty acres, and surrounded by a stone wall twelve feet high, with two beautiful porticos. The largest building contained the private apartments of the prince, two large parlors, two dining halls, a ball room, a billiard room, a library, several picture galleries and a large armory,—all of them furnished in the most expensive and magnificent style. The floors and stairways were of Italian marble, and the walls of the large parlors adorned by huge mirrors set in frames inlaid with emeralds, rubies, and other precious stones. Sculptures of marble from Italy, of porphyry and alabaster from Egypt, and porcelain vases from China, etc., adorned the corridors and niches of the halls of the main building.

Another large building was inhabited by the women, among whom the mother of the prince is the mistress; but they themselves, as well as the interior of their palace, remain concealed from the gaze of the guests. Elegant carriages with drivers, servants and grooms in oriental livery, caparisoned horses, saddles and bridles shining with gold and silver trimmings, were day and night at the disposition of the guests, and at his arrival every guest received a small blank book with fifty leaves on which to write his name and the kind of refreshment he wished, and hundreds of servants dressed in white were always ready to fetch it to him in -187- the palace garden, at the race courses, or in the summer houses.

NAUTCH DANCER.

The festivities and merriments were arranged so that every guest had perfect liberty and sufficient time to follow his own taste. The following may serve as an illustration:

On Wednesday, December 7th, at half-past seven o'clock, a high school was inspected, and the governor of Bengal distributed prizes among the scholars; at ten breakfast in the large dining hall; at twelve the instalment of the young prince; at two luncheon; at three the opening of the races; at half-past seven illumination and pyrotechnics; at eight grand dinner; at ten a ball in the palace for the Europeans; and nautch dancing and music by native women in a pavilion in the garden.

One day a canal was opened and dedicated. It was twenty miles long, and built for the purpose of supplying several cities and country districts with an abundance of water. All the streets and roads in and around Burdwan were in a splendid condition, wide and macadamized with crushed brick. From the railroad station to the palace and two -188- miles beyond to two villas, as well as along the principal streets in the city, and along all paths and roads in the palace garden, bamboo poles forty feet long were erected on both sides, and about forty feet apart. These poles were all wrapped in red and white glazed paper, and had flags at the top. The poles were connected by lines along which colored glass lamps were suspended six inches apart, and these were all lighted at six o'clock. I was told that there were over forty thousand such lamps, and that it took five hundred men to fill, light, and attend to them. From nine to twelve o'clock every night an electric light was beaming from one of the palace towers, and Wednesday evening there was a magnificent, display of pyrotechnics around an artificial lake about a mile from the palace. The latter cost about twenty-five thousand dollars. Its effect on men, animals, and the -189- tropical plants was such that a man from the North found it difficult to realize that he was still on this earth of ours, and not far away in the fairy world of fiction.

COLLEGE BUILDING.

Reality is so wonderful in India that I have hardly dared to tell the following without gradually preparing my reader for it. This young prince, whose guest I was and with whom I talked a good deal, is a poor foundling, having been adopted by the old prince, who died childless, and by the consent of the English government he was made his sole heir. His landed estates were so large that he paid two million two hundred thousand dollars to the English government in annual taxes on the income from his lands! How large his total income is, nobody knows. Inside the palace walls, which were protected by a strong body-guard night and day, were deep subterranean vaults with secret entrances, where gold and jewels were concealed in such quantities as may be imagined only when it is remembered that during a period of three hundred years the family has been accustomed to accumulate these treasures by at least three "lacs rupees," or one hundred and sixty thousand dollars, a year. But during the same time millions upon millions of people have starved to death in the principality of Burdwan, and even now it is safe to say that nine-tenths of the people who cultivate the soil and live on the estates of the maharajah and pay him tribute are so poor that they could scarcely sustain their life a single month in case of drought or inundations.

To describe the whole fête would require a whole book, and I therefore select the installation ceremony, which, by the way, was the most important of the festivities. It took place in a small mango forest, about a mile from the palace. A pleasant country road, decorated with banners and spanned by triumphal arches covered with flowers, led to the place. A tent pavilion sixty feet long and forty feet wide was erected about a hundred yards from the road. The tent was supported by forty pillars covered with silver tinsel paper, and the canvas consisted of heavy linen woven in many-colored squares, which were about three feet each way. The sides of the tent were open, and between each of the outer pillars was stationed a Hindoo soldier dressed in shoes, gray stockings, black knee breeches, and a red coat, one half of which was embroidered with gold and silver, while the head was covered by a red turban richly adorned with gold ornaments. These soldiers were gigantic, dark figures, armed with curved sabres and long lances. They stood immovable as statues, and only the rolling of their flashing eye-balls showed that they were living men. At the upper end of the tent was an elevated platform with a gilt chair for the governor, and behind this, chairs for the European ladies. From the platform to the entrance at the opposite end was an aisle, on each side of which were four rows of chairs for the guests, all numbered and placed according to their rank. The aisle and the walk to the country road were covered with expensive Persian rugs, and chamberlains in dazzling costumes conducted the guests from the carriages to the seats assigned to them in the tent. The European officers were seated on the first row to the right, and the Hindoo princes and noblemen on the first row to the left, with the young maharajah next to the platform. The other chairs were occupied by Hindoo and Mohammedan zemindars (proprietors of landed estates), scholars, and dignitaries.

A most splendid display of costumes in satin and velvet in all possible colors and fashions, all of them richly adorned with gold and silver trimming and embroideries, besides glittering necklaces and diamond rings, added brilliantly to the scene. All the natives kept their headdresses on, most of them wearing low turbans of colored or white silk, ornamented with gold, pearls and gems.

Only the prince of Burdwan and the young prince of Kutch Behar were armed, and these only with Damascus cimeters. The prince of Burdwan wore a purple satin garment, red silk shoes and a high cap in the shape of a crown. His breast, neck, headdress and hands glittered with diamonds and rubies. Over this garment he wore a mantle of dark yellow cloth, which was very artistically woven, and cost about ten thousand dollars. Most of the native nobles distinguished themselves by a stately, military bearing, looking both handsome and intelligent. Some of them were very dark, but most had about the same complexion as the Spaniards. Jet black hair and black, flashing eyes were universal, only a single one having dark red hair and beard.

When all had been seated the governor, accompanied by two adjutants and several servants, arrived. A guard of honor, consisting of one hundred Sepoys, was stationed in front of the tent, and saluted the governor by presenting arms, during which the military band played an English national tune. Eight huge elephants were arranged in a row between the road and the tent; these were covered by rich caparisons adorned with heavy gold and silver embroideries, and carrying on their backs small pavilions in which richly dressed drivers walked a few steps back and forth. At the door of the tent the governor was received by eight artistically uniformed aids-de-camp carrying marshal's staffs, silver horns, lances and perfumes.

The act of installation was now in order, and was performed in the following manner: The maharajah stepped up before the governor and received from his hand a parchment roll, by which the queen conferred authority. Having read this in a loud and solemn voice, the governor hung a chain of diamonds and rubies around the neck of the prince, and made a short congratulatory address to him. The minister of finance brought a silver basin filled with Indian gold coins, which he handed to the governor as an emblem of tribute to the English government. The prince now resumed his seat, and two chamberlains brought gold vessels on silver trays containing attar of roses, and two others brought spices in similar receptacles. The attar of roses was sprinkled over the audience, and each one of the native guests received a small quantity of spices wrapped in a palm leaf. Finally the band struck up a march, and the whole retinue returned to the carriages by the road side and drove back to the palace. One of the carriages of the procession was loaded with silver coins, which were thrown right and left to the thousands of poor and beggars, who crowded the road on both sides. In the evening, again, provisions and clothing were distributed to about fifteen thousand poor, who had flocked in from all parts of Burdwan, but who had not been allowed to enter the city.

CHAPTER XIX.

Allahabad—Sacred Places—Kumbh Mela—Pilgrimages—Bathing in the Ganges—Fakirs and Penitents—Sacred

Rites—Superstitions.

Allahabad means the dwelling of God, and the Hindoos regard it as one of the most sacred places of India. It is a city of one hundred and fifty thousand inhabitants, and has a strong fortress with an English garrison. It is the seat of the government of the north-western provinces, and is situated on a point of land between the rivers Ganges and Jumna, on the great Indian railroad, about five hundred and sixty-five miles from Calcutta, and about the same distance from the Bay of Persia.

In a tropical climate where rain seldom falls during nine months of the year, it is quite natural that the people regard streams and rivers as their greatest benefactors, and by means of the vivid imagination of the South this sentiment has occasionally been developed into religious worship and idolatry. In this manner the great Ganges, which flows nearly through the entire length of India, has, since time immemorial, been regarded as sacred, as have also all places where three rivers meet. At Allahabad the Jumna meets the sacred Ganges, thus affording two of the necessary conditions to make the place sacred, and it was easy for the fertile imagination of the Brahmins to create the third, which is said to consist in a spiritual current from above, pouring down continually at the point where the Jumna and the Ganges meet and mingle. It is claimed that this invisible river is very abundant, especially in the month of Magh, from the middle of January to the middle of February, but the most favorable period in this respect is under the astronomical cycle Yuga, which occurs every twelfth year in the month of Magh, and is called "Kumbh." This occurred in 1882, which was therefore a very important year for the Hindoos.

To bathe in the Ganges always means a spiritual purification, and to bathe there where the three rivers meet at Allahabad in the month of Magh is a very sacred rite. Every good Hindoo endeavors, if possible, to bathe at this place at least once during his lifetime; but to bathe there during the Kumbh Mela, or the twelfth year's cycle, is the most sacred act a Hindoo can perform, and such a bath is said to atone for the greatest sins both of the bather and his nearest relatives, be they living or dead. Out of the immense population of India, one hundred and ninety millions profess the above faith. Being a very religious people in their way, and testifying to their faith by their works, it is no great wonder that Allahabad in the course of four weeks was visited by nearly two million pilgrims, who came there only for the purpose of bathing in the sacred river. Partly from curiosity and partly in order to obtain reliable information, I also made a short pilgrimage to this place.

INDIAN CART.

I said that nearly two million people visited Allahabad during the Kumbh Mela, which I attended. They came from all parts of India, men and women, young and old, but especially the old, of all classes from the beggar to the prince, of all castes from the despised coolie to the haughty Brahmin. They came on crowded railroad trains, or on elephants, camels, horses, asses, in ox-carts and in boats on the rivers, but most of them on foot along roads and pathways, across fields and meadows, the living ones carrying the ashes of the cremated bodies of their dead relatives to throw them in the holy river. Many of them had traveled great distances and been on the journey for months. Old men who did not expect to return to their homes, but were in hopes of finding a grave in the sacred waters, and had said good-bye to everything which bound them to life; cripples and invalids expecting to be cured on the banks of the Ganges, congregated in large numbers at this sacred place. Fanatical penitents came crawling on hands and feet; holy Fakirs had measured the way by the length of their own bodies for scores of miles. The penitent Fakir who travels in this manner lies down on the ground with his head toward the place of destination, makes a mark in the ground in front of his head, and crawls forward the length of his body and lies down again with the feet where he had his head before; a new mark, another movement ahead, etc., and so he keeps on, one length of his body at a time, until he reaches the holy river. During this journey the Fakir is surrounded and followed by a large concourse of people who furnish him with food and drink, and regard him as a saint. There are instances of men having traveled over five hundred miles in this manner. Every day and hour the crowd was increased by new arrivals, until the river banks, the fields and roads swarmed with countless masses,—a most wonderful gathering. Thousands of Brahmins offered their services to guide and bless the pilgrims, most always for a valuable consideration; thousands of peddlers sold small idols, flower wreaths, rosaries, and other sacred objects at high prices; others peddled rice, fruit, thin bread and other provisions, and thousands of barbers cut the hair and shaved the temples of the pilgrims. There, in the shade of some mango trees a Hindoo prince had gone into camp with his elephants, horses soldiers and servants, the retinue consisting of about two hundred people; and yonder in the shadeless valley is a camp of a thousand or more Fakirs huddled together. Many are entirely naked, others are protected by a few yards of dirty cotton cloth, most of them sprinkled with ashes or dry clay, their faces streaked in gray, red or yellow colors, and the hair done up in the shape of a chignon and held together with wet clay; but although presenting a picture of dire want in their persons they have in the camp a large herd of costly elephants richly adorned with covers of satin and velvet embroidered in gold, silver, precious stones and gems, proving that their begging has not been in vain.

FAKIRS.

On the river bank is the headquarters of

the pilgrims from one of the Southern provinces, and over yonder that of those from the North or East. Everywhere is heard the noise of trading and bargaining, of greeting and ecstacy, of laughter and astonishment, and of the moaning and cries of the sick and suffering—indeed a regular pandemonium.

The February sun already shone scorchingly hot upon the low, shadeless valley, the thermometer rising to 90°. In the night, however, it was unusually cold for that country, and most of the pilgrims being poor and their clothing and food wretched, dangerous diseases began to break out among the weak and exhausted. The terrible cholera claimed numerous victims every day, many died from weakness and negligence, others again perished through accidents on land and water, for nobody seemed to be very particular about human life, since death just there was considered so very desirable. Along the shores of the river flickered hundreds of fires, at which the remains of the dead are burned to ashes and scattered into the river by the officiating Brahmins, to the infinite edification of the relatives of the dead.

The Hindoos are a very peaceful and loyal people, and willingly submit to order and discipline. Thus designated groups were conducted to the water at certain times and places, which was highly necessary, as otherwise the strong would have trampled down and crushed the weak.

The first ceremony consists in shaving the head, or at - 198 - least the front part of it; the hair which is cut off ought to be offered to the Ganges, but the barber smuggles most of it out of the way, to be sold in more civilized countries. From the barber the pilgrim is turned over to the care of the Brahmin, who leads him down into the river, under the following ceremonies: The Brahmin repeats a Sanscrit formula which is called "Sankalpa," and which states that "the pilgrim N. N. on the day X. of the month Y., and in the year Z., takes his bath in the sacred water for the purpose and intention of cleansing himself from all sins and frailties," after which the pilgrim immerses himself several times under the water and rinses his mouth with a handful of it, after a few minutes returning to the shore where he is at once surrounded by peddlers who offer him flowers, milk and lean cows or goats for sale at an exorbitant price. He always buys the flowers and the milk and offers them to the river, and, if he has sufficient money, he buys a cow or a goat and offers it to the Brahmin; but if his means are too limited the latter must be content with the few coins the pilgrim can spare. Most of them, however, have brought a handsome offering to the Brahmin, because they regard the duty toward him just as important as the duty toward the river god.

Then follows the "Shiadda" ceremony, consisting of an offering of cake, sugar, plums and dainties to the ghosts of their deceased relatives; next a banquet is spread before the Brahmins, the sacred places of the vicinity are visited, offerings are made at most of these, and a present called "vidagi" is made to the Brahmin who has attended to the spiritual wants of the giver.

And now the object of the long and arduous journey is accomplished, the pilgrimage, "tisthayatra," is successfully performed, and the cleansed sinner stands ready to begin a new record of sin. He has been plundered of his last penny, - 199 - and, if he succeeds in reaching his distant home, his neighbors and friends will look up to him as an exceptionally happy being, and his own soul is filled with the hope of temporal and eternal bliss.

Those who have reaped the pecuniary benefits of the pilgrimage are the Brahmins and Fakirs, the former through offerings and the latter through begging. They have filled their coffers and collected large herds of cattle, and now they can lead a gay and happy life until the next Mela, when they will again try to fan the dying embers of enthusiasm into a flame by sending emissaries all over India for the purpose of convincing the credulous populace that it is greatly to be feared that the Ganges will soon lose its power of salvation, and that therefore as many as possible ought to come next time, which may be the last chance.

- 200 -

CHAPTER XX.

Benares, the Holy City of the Hindoos—Its Temples and Worshipers—The Sacred Monkeys.

Returning from Allahabad I visited Benares, the holy city of India and the centre of Hindooism or Brahminism, its religion, art and literature. It is situated on an elevation on the east bank of the Ganges about four hundred and seventy-six miles from Calcutta. Benares is to the Hindoos what Jerusalem was to the Jews, Rome to the mediæval Christians, and what Mecca is to the Mohammedans, and it is visited by thousands of pilgrims and penitents every year. The learned men or Pundits of India have their academies and gatherings there, and many of its princes and nobles have their costly palaces in which they usually spend a few weeks every year.

The whole city seems abandoned to sacrificing priests and idolatry in its most disgusting forms. There are one thousand four hundred temples for idols, and nearly three hundred mosques, besides hundreds of shrines, holy graves, wells, trees and other objects of Hindoo worship. Benares is a very old city; great and renowned when Babylon and Nineveh were competing with each other; when Tyre sent out her colonists; when Athens was in her infancy; before Rome existed, and long before Nebuchadnezzar had carried the Israelites into captivity.

We are accustomed to look at hoary ruins with reverent - 201 - interest, and it is no wonder that the first sight of the historical monuments of Benares made a profound impression on my mind. I felt almost as if transported to a time far back in the misty past, and found it difficult to realize that I walked the same streets, lanes and market places where the Babylonian heralds of war and the ambassadors of Alexander the Great were received by the same people whose - 202 - descendants still inhabit the same city, and have retained the same civilization and the same institutions through all the intervening centuries.

HINDOO TEMPLES.

The sun cast its last rays over the memorable city when I had the pleasure of seeing it for the first time. At a distance of two miles I could see the palaces and temples with their domes, cupolas, and minarets merged into a confused mass, and on the summit of the hill towered the renowned mosque of Emperor Arungzebes with two minarets, the spires of which rise two hundred and fifty feet above the level of the Ganges. It was a beautiful oriental picture, the most beautiful I had yet seen.

The next morning at sunrise a Mohammedan dragoman or interpreter took me down the river in a boat, and in the course of an hour we passed, according to the estimate of the interpreter, over twenty thousand bathing Hindoos. Every two miles are built ghats, or broad flights of steps down to river, some of these being eighty feet high. Along the edge of the water Brahmins are squatting about twenty feet apart under large sun shades made of palm leaves in the form of an umbrella. These Brahmins have a certain inherited right to these little spots where they have thus raised their sun shades for the purpose of collecting an offering from every bather. Men and women bathe side by side. They all go into the water in their thin cotton suits, and everything is conducted with order and decorum.

After the bath flowers are offered to the river, and oils and fruits to the Brahmin.

A short distance above the edge of the water is an open place for the cremation of the bodies of the dead, and on the river close by are scores of boats and barges loaded with wood which is cut into small sticks and is used for the funeral-pyres. We stopped a few minutes here while three corpses were brought on biers. They were covered by a - 203 - white cloth with a red dye-stuff scattered over the chest. The body was first immersed in the river and then placed on its pyre, which was kindled by the nearest relative of the deceased. After the cremation the ashes were scattered on the river by the Brahmin, who, of course, charged a round sum for these highly important services.

We next went up the high steps and visited several temples and other objects of interest of which I shall give a brief description.

The Hindoo temples are not so large as our churches, but only from fifteen to forty feet square, and their style of architecture is frequently very pleasing to the eye. They contain no seats or pulpits, and the ceremonies consist exclusively of offerings, prayers, and signs. People come and go incessantly, there is no silence or devotion, but all is noise and turmoil. The Brahmins glide quietly around everywhere and watch closely so that no one escapes until he or she has parted with as much loose change as possible, and it frequently happens that the Brahmin and the worshiper get into a loud quarrel about the fee which the latter is to pay for the benediction.

We ascended an eight-foot-wide street paved with large flag stones, which were crowded with endless rows of people coming out or going into the temples on either side. To some of these a few steps led downward, to others upward.

In some of the nooks and niches formed by the outer walls of the temple sat peddlers selling ornaments, flowers, fruit, boiled rice, popcorn, confectioneries, and small idols, of stone, porcelain, or metal.

DYING BRAHMIN.

We stepped into the so-called golden temple, dedicated to Bishashar, or Shiva, the most prominent deity of Benares. Like most of the temples it is built of brick, and has a gray coat of plastering on the outside. It has three domes which - 204 - are covered with colored metal, and the interior is divided into three rooms, in each of which is a stone image representing the creative principle. The worshipers throw rice and flowers at these images, and officiating Brahmins continually pour over them water from the Ganges. Within a separate inclosure is a sacred well called "Gyan-Bapi," or the well of knowledge, into which the rice and the flowers from the images are washed by a continual stream of water. Out of this well rises an intolerable stench from the putrefying mass which poisons the air in and around the temple, for it is not permitted to take these offerings out of the well. Around the well is a colonnade of small beautiful pillars, back of which, on the east side, is a seven-foot-high stone statue of a bull consecrated to the god of Mahadeva.

Another temple is divided into stalls

which contain well-fed sacred animals, such as bulls, cows, goats and birds, all of which are objects of worship of the faithful. This temple was kept more clean than the former, but the bellowing of the animals and the jostling and crowding of the worshipers made the visit to those deities intolerable.

One of the finest temples in Benares is called "Durga Kund," and is devoted to the goddess Durga. It is a large - 205 - and beautiful pyramidal structure with a number of towers and steeples of different sizes, and the whole building is adorned with fine works of sculpture, representing the sacred animals of Hindoo mythology. Inside the temple, facing a wide entrance, stands a large stone statue of Durga with the face of an ape, and in front of this is a well into which the faithful throw flowers. But the most interesting feature about this temple is the great number of monkeys which are kept there. A large, square court surrounds the temple, and in this as well as on the steps, floors, pillars, roof and walls, inside and outside of the temple itself and in the neighboring houses, in the trees, on the streets, in the gardens, in short, wherever they can find a footing, there are thousands of gray, yellow, black, white and brown monkeys, with all possible monkey physiognomies and monkey natures, sitting, lying, jumping, hanging and climbing. They are considered sacred and must not be killed, consequently they are increasing so fast that if no interdicts are fulminated - 206 - against them they will soon become the ruling element in Benares. And so assiduously is this temple visited by well-to-do and generous worshipers that both the Brahmins and the monkeys live in affluence and luxury. Incredible as it may seem, I have myself seen one crowd of people after another enter this temple and prostrate themselves in worshiping the living monkeys as well as the ape-faced stone image, and then return home rejoicing because the Brahmins have assured them that their worship and offerings have opened for them the gates of heaven.

MONKEY TEMPLE IN BENARES.

In some temples domestic animals are sacrificed by the servants of the priests, the blood and the meat being distributed among the priests, the intestines and other offal among the poor. In others, butter, oils, sweetmeats and rice are offered by first giving the idols a taste in the same manner as our children feed their dolls, whereupon the rest is consumed by the priests and the people. In several temples are Fakirs or saints sitting in unnatural positions with lean limbs and vacant looks, and these are also objects of the worship and offerings of the people. In other temples are even lewd women, who, by their dancing and singing, act as mediators between the people and their angry gods.

As far as these descriptions go, they may be applied to all temples and ceremonies, and the chief and absolute universal feature is the question of money and other offerings to the Brahmins. All the temples are surrounded with beggars who are as importunate as the Brahmins themselves, and the whole of it makes the European wish to get away from the sacred places of the Orient as soon as possible.

Man Modir, is the name of a remarkable astronomical observatory which towers above the temples on the Ganges, close to the place where the dead bodies are cremated. It was built two hundred years ago by the emperor, Jai Sing, and still remains in well-preserved condition as an evidence - 207 - of the deep astronomical knowledge of the Hindoos at that period. It is a large stone building with a flat roof, on which are constructed astronomical instruments and figures of brick and mortar of gigantic proportions. As examples I shall mention a quadrant which is eleven feet high and nine feet wide in the direction of the meridian, and is made for calculating the altitude of the sun, and another instrument, thirty-six feet long and four and one-half feet high which is used in calculating the altitude and distance of a planet or a star from the meridian.

Descending from the observatory my attention was called to a large crowd of people on a knoll near the river bank. Going over there I found what might be called a religious circus attended by thousands of people, in the midst of which was a group of Fakirs. Most of them were squatting with crossed legs, one arm extended toward the river, and the eyes fixed on a certain spot in the water or on the sky. One was squatting on a plank through which long sharp nails were driven with their points projecting upward over an inch. I counted eight such nails about an inch long under each foot. The nails had not caused bleeding wounds, but simply made deep indentures in the flesh which must have been very painful, at least in the beginning. One Fakir had suspended himself on an eight-foot-tall cross, with the head downward, by tying one of his feet to the top of the cross by a cord. Formerly they used to suspend themselves by a big iron hook penetrating their muscles, thus swinging their bodies back and forth for hours; but this practice is now prohibited by the English government. An acrobatic Fakir was turning sommersets on a grass mat, and was considered very holy because he could twist his limbs as if they had been without bones. Another carried an iron cage which was forged around his neck, and which he had carried thus for years in order to mortify his flesh. A loathsome dwarf, - 208 - kept in an iron cage, was blessing the admiring crowd, several dancing girls gave animation to the scene by singing and dancing, some Brahmins were exhibiting a sacred bull, others sacred monkeys, and liberal offerings were made everywhere by the enraptured pilgrims. Such are the religious ceremonies in the sacred city of India.

FAKIR WITH IRON CAGE.

During my stay in Benares I visited one of the most remarkable - 209 - ruins in the world, situated six miles from the

sacred city. It is the remnants of two large and tall towers built of brick and cut stone, about three thousand years ago. These towers were closely connected with the history of Buddha, one of them, according to tradition, being his dwelling and the other his place of worship. This was formerly the site of a great city, called Sarnath.

TOWER OF SARNATH.

CHAPTER XXI.

Nimtoolaghat—Cremation in India—Parsee Funeral Rites.

India is the only country in the world where the civilization of the East and that of the West are found side by side with equal rights and equal chances of a free and full development. For, although the English have conquered, and at present rule the country, they have respected the peculiar customs and manners of the Hindoos, and guaranteed them liberty to practice the same and to develop their social and religious institutions in so far as they do not conflict with the generally acknowledged principles of humanity.

Accordingly in Calcutta and other cities in India we frequently find a stately Christian church side by side with a Hindoo temple with its officiating priests. On one side of the street we may see a fine European residence filled with guests around the dinner-table, eating, chatting, and toasting just as at home, and on the other a Hindoo villa, where turbaned Brahmins, in a squatting posture, eat their rice or smoke their hokah, while extolling the merits of their juggernaut. At popular meetings and fêtes European lords, bishops, officials, and ladies are often seen engaged in a friendly conversation with Hindoo princes, or learned pundits, Mohammedan warriors, Persian, Armenian or Jewish merchants. On the streets and promenades the European carriage and the Hindoo palanquin are seen side by side; in Calcutta there are scores of high schools and academies on the European plan, and close to these again others where young students in oriental costumes and turbaned heads, squat before a half-naked Brahmin, seeking wisdom and knowledge from the works of the Vedas or Shastras.

It is therefore not surprising that in the very harbor where American and European flags are waving from hundreds of mast-heads lies Nimtoolaghat, a Hindoo place of cremation, from which the whole day long dense clouds of smoke arise, scattering the vapors of burning human bodies. It is a large brick building which is divided into two apartments by a brick wall. The apartment which is next to the street is covered by a roof, but the one next to the harbor is open at the top. The floor is made of clay, excepting the spots under the funeral pyres, where it consists of large flagstones. I have often stood at this place, and it always seemed to me that our cemeteries with their monuments, grass plots, trees, and flowers are dear places which, to some extent, reconcile man to stern death, while here everything seemed dead and hopeless. I will describe for the reader what I saw at one of my visits to this place of desolation. On the flagstones in the roofless apartment were six separate pyres, two of which were already reduced to ashes when I entered, two others were about half consumed by the fire, only a few bones being visible among the fire-brands; but on each of the other two was a naked corpse, the outside of which was scorched by the flames, while blood and water were slowly oozing out of mouth and nostrils, while the burning flesh hissed and sputtered where the heat was most intense, so that the whole presented a shocking sight. A score of half-naked Brahmins were busy around the pyres muttering prayers and making signs over the dead, while the nearest relatives walked around the corpses uttering cries of lamentation. Particularly violent was the grief of a young woman whose mother had just been laid upon the pyre, deep sorrow and heart-rending lamentations testifying to the love she had borne the deceased.

NIMTOOLAGHAT—PLACE OF CREMATION.

Now the fine-split wood is piled up into a new pyre about six feet long, two feet wide, and two and one-half feet high, and four men bring the corpse of a man on a bier. It is covered with a white sheet, which is taken away, so as to leave only a small piece of cloth covering the corpse. This is the body of a Fakir, a stately man with fine features, and past the prime of life. As soon as the body is placed on the pyre, two Brahmins pile fine-split wood around and over it so that only the face is visible. Then comes the eldest son of the deceased and rubbing the face with fresh butter lays several lumps of it on the pyre. He then walks three times around the corpse and lights with a fire-brand a whisk of straw in his father's pyre. The fire spreads rapidly through the dry wood. The melting butter flows through it, the flames roar and crackle, and the dead body makes writhing muscular motions under the influence of the fire, the skin bursting open in several places, and a thin fluid trickling out which adds fuel to the flames. The face shrinks and vanishes under our eyes, an unpleasant smell of burnt flesh permeates the air, and in a little while all is over, and the Brahmins gather the ashes and scatter them on the waters of the sacred Ganges.

Who can wonder that a stranger, witnessing such a ceremony, experiences in his own breast questions and surmises such as these: Is this, then, all? Where is the Fakir who mortified his body by all kinds of torture, who struggled and suffered in order to become acceptable to the gods? Was there nothing more than that shell, consumed before our eyes? Is the man who spent half of his life-time gazing into the boundless realm of space and yearning and longing for the unknown, the infinite, no longer in existence? Was his longing only a mockery, or was it a foreshadowing of that which is to come? What would life be if all terminated in the pyre or in the grave? To what purpose, then, all noble endeavors, whose aim and object only relate to the uncertain future? The deepest premonitions of the human soul, and the most beautiful hopes of the heart, how far are these from the thought that all our feelings, our loftiest ambitions,—in one word the best part of our being,—can be annihilated in a crematory! The Fakir whose body was now reduced to ashes had lived in the faith of his immortality, had worshiped the deities of his people, because he knew no better, but was he on that account less welcome in the everlasting mansions?

Formerly the wife was burned alive on the pyre of her husband, but this practice has been abolished by the English government, although it is still said to be adhered to secretly in the interior of the country. That woman is considered very fortunate who can enjoy the privilege of "sati," that is, be burned alive on the funeral pyre of her husband, for thereby she secures unquestionable happiness in the next world. So strongly can religious enthusiasm, even in our days, influence a sensible and civilized people. We generally suppose cremation in India to be an imposing ceremony, such as a great pyre, intense heat, which keeps a devout congregation at a proper distance, etc. Such is not the case, however; for, leaving out the mourning relatives, it may better be compared with the hilarious soldiers around the camp-fire roasting the booty of a nightly raid,—a shote or a quarter of beef.

An entirely different mode of burial is used among the Parsees, who are descendants of the ancient Persians, and live in the western part of India where they were driven from Iran by the Mohammedans. They profess the religion of Zoroaster and are fire-worshipers. They regard the earth, air, water and fire as sacred objects, but a corpse, on the contrary, as something unclean, and therefore they would not pollute the fire by burning the dead, nor soil the earth or the sea by burying them. In place of this they expose the dead bodies in the open air to be devoured by birds of prey. For this purpose are erected towers of stone, on the top of which are iron grates to put the bodies on. In one of the suburbs of Bombay are three such towers on Malabar hill. They are called "The Towers of Silence." Each of them has only one entrance, and they are about twenty feet high. Large flocks of ravens and vultures surround them sitting on branches of the palm trees in the vicinity. As soon as a corpse is exposed there is a fierce rush for it, and within an hour the birds have consumed everything except, of course, the bones, which drop down into a vault under the tower, or are thrown there by means of tongs held by gloved servants, who afterward clean themselves by bathing and change of clothing.

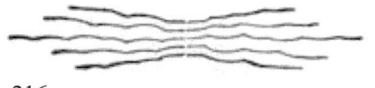

CHAPTER XXII.

Heathenism and Christianity—The Religion of the Hindoos—Caste—The Brahmins—Their Tyranny—Superstition—The Influence of Christianity—Keshub-Chunder-Sen, the Indian Reformer—His faith and Influence.

Having given a sketch of the divine worship, religious rites and sacrificial feasts of the Hindoos, I shall now call the attention of the reader to a brief description of their religion and spiritual culture in general.

"In the hoary past India had mighty religious leaders and authors who laid claim to divine authority. Religious systems were announced, and voluminous, erudite verses were published for the guidance of the people, or rather the Brahmins or priests, which writings are still the Bibles of the Hindoos. The most important of these books are called 'Vedas,' 'Shastras,' and 'Puranas.' The lively imagination of the authors and the religious enthusiasm of the people were not content with a few deities, therefore their number has been increased from time to time, until they now amount to thirty-three million gods and goddesses. The most important of the former are Brahma, Visnu and Shiva, and of the latter Durga, Lakshmi and Saraswati. The former are worshiped as the creating, preserving and destroying powers, and from these three all the others have originated; at first considered as representatives of certain attributes and principals of the three chief deities, but later as independent, individual deities. Many of these gods are represented by images and pictures, which originally the whole people, but at present only the learned, regard merely as representations of certain divine principals and attributes. Later on these were put in the place of the things which they represented, so that the stone image, the river, the tree, or the animal is regarded as the god himself by the ignorant multitude.

"According to the Hindoo doctrine of creation the earth rests on the back of a tortoise, and the human race was originally created members of four different classes or castes. Thus the class or caste distinction of India is closely incorporated with its religion, and shows that the priests have been very shrewd in founding a religious system which secured for themselves not only salvation after death, but, above all, an abundance of the good things of this world. Brahma was from the beginning, and from him emanated Vishnu and Shiva. Thereafter Brahma created first water, then the earth, then from out of his head a man who was the *Brahmin*, and became the chief of the caste of priests, or the highest class. After this he let a *Kshatriya* issue from out of his arms, a *Vaisya* from his loins and a *Sudra* from his feet, and which became respectively the progenitors of the three other castes, the warriors, the craftsmen and merchants, and the common laborers. These castes have gradually been divided into many subdivisions, but the four principal ones still remain with all their rigid distinctions. Through certain misdemeanors, which may be very insignificant, a person belonging to a higher may be degraded to a lower caste, but one of a lower caste can never rise to a higher, not even by the most meritorious achievements."

Of all the cruel chains by which tyrants have fettered men, none has been a more formidable enemy of liberty or a greater impediment to human progress than this dreadful system of caste. It has stifled all noble efforts, all brotherly love and humane feelings; it has plunged the people into superstition, indifference and ignorance; it has doomed ninety-nine hundredths of the myriads of India to the most cruel slavery, in body and in soul; it has placed locks and fetters on the human mind and branded the infant in its mother's womb to infamy and execration; and, the worst of all, it has stifled all incentive to progress and development. It has smothered many noble feelings, and taught men to hate and despise each other; and so strong is the class distinction of this system that a good Hindoo of our day would a thousand times rather die of thirst or hunger than take a glass of water or a piece of bread from a person of a lower caste. Like other evils it has also been a curse to its authors, the Brahmins themselves, by lulling the great majority of them into ignorance and indifference. For why should they take the trouble to study or work when the whole world with its joys, pleasures and honors is open to them anyway? Space does not allow discussing this matter more fully, hence I will simply cite some of the doctrines which the Brahmins claim to have found in the divine books, and which the people still regard as sacred:

"Whoever disturbs a Brahmin during his religious contemplations shall lose his life; if a person of a lower caste sits down on the mat of a Brahmin, his back shall be burned with red-hot irons; if he touches the hair, beard or neck of a Brahmin, the judge shall order both his hands to be cut off; if he listens to evil reports about the Brahmins, molten lead shall be poured into his ears; if he does not arise when a Brahmin approaches, he will be changed into a tree after death; if he casts an angry look at a Brahmin the god Yama shall pluck out his eyes. The Shastras teach that a gift to a Brahmin is of incalculable value to the giver. Whoever gives a Brahmin a cow shall gain a million years of bliss in heaven, and whoever wishes success in anything must fête the Brahmins and wash their feet. Whoever bequeathes land or other valuable property to the Brahmins on his death-bed immediately receives forgiveness of sins and the greatest bliss in heaven. To drink the water in which a Brahmin has washed his feet and to lick the dust from under a Brahmin's feet are works of great merit for the life which is to come. No one but a Brahmin is allowed to give religious instruction, and all offerings to the gods must be brought to the Brahmin, because no ceremony will avail anything unless it is accompanied by an offering to them. Therefore a multitude of ceremonies have been introduced by the Brahmins in order that their coffers may be well filled. I will name a few of those ceremonies which relate to everybody's life and death, and which cannot, therefore, be neglected.

"As soon as a mother knows she has conceived, a Brahmin must be sent for to read certain formulas; when the child is born a Brahmin must be called for the same purpose, also when it is a week, six months, two years and eight years old, and again when the young people are to be married; in all cases of sickness, at the death-bed, at the cremation of the body, and every month the first year after a person's death; and at each one of these visits the Brahmin is entitled to money or other gifts. Also if a family is subject to any misfortune the Brahmin must be called to conjure the evil powers; if a bird of prey alights on the roof, the owner of the house must call a Brahmin to purify the house by his blessing; when he moves into a new house the Brahmin must bless it beforehand; when a man dies on an *unlucky day* his son must pay the Brahmin money to ward off a similar calamity from him; when a well is dug a Brahmin must bless it before its water can be used; during eclipses of the sun and the moon everybody sends gifts to the Brahmins; at every change of the moon the Brahmin is entitled to gifts as well as on forty regular holidays every year; during small-pox or cholera ravages he is called to ward off the plague; the farmer cannot reap his grain, the fisherman cannot go to sea, the merchant cannot make a bargain unless he has bought the blessing of the Brahmin and paid for the same."

And still the Hindoos possess a high culture, and their civilization is one of the oldest in the world. They are endowed with a strong religious feeling. They are profound, peaceful, diligent, economical and law abiding; many of them have become distinguished in learning, art and science; they have been the teachers of the philosophers and scholars of other nations, and for thousands of years they have pondered deeply on questions pertaining to the human soul, immortality and the life to come, and endeavored to satisfy their craving and yearning for a closer union with the infinite by a devotion and self sacrifices which can well be compared with the sufferings of the Christian martyrs. Accordingly if any people could attain a higher development and a happy condition by other means than the influence of the Christian religion, that people ought to be the Hindoos. Yet, after all their struggles, we now find them on a lower level than they were thousands of years ago. What a picture! All these millions of civilized, peaceful, diligent, sensible people bend their knees before thirty-three millions of disgusting images and pictures, and among all this people, in all their thirty thousand cities there was not a hospital for the sick, not an asylum for the blind or deaf, not a home for lepers or insane, not one voice saying to the lowly and the poor: "Thou art my brother."

Then came Buddha, the great reformer, preaching the religion of self denial and human love. The old petrified social fabric and religion were shaken to their foundation, and the system of caste was on the verge of dissolution. Under the first wave of enthusiasm caused by the teachings of Buddha, hospitals for the sick and asylums for the poor were established. Every fifth year the Buddhistic kings gave away their riches, not only to the monks but also to the poor, to the orphans and outcasts, and even asylums for sick animals were established. But Brahminism soon avenged itself by bloody wars, Buddhism was to a large extent driven out of India, and gradually its noble principles were forgotten. Nearly the same condition as that which prevailed before the Buddhistic reformation again prevailed, until the Christian civilization quite recently began to make itself felt through the practical measures introduced by the English government. Woman without liberty, without human worth, and almost without virtue; the countless many oppressed and despised by the privileged few, and not even allowed to read a religious book at the risk of eternal damnation; one of the greatest and mightiest nations on earth, discordant within itself, divided into different hostile classes; the one suspicious, envious, and full of hate toward the other, all of them humiliated, conquered, and ruled by a few strangers,—the English,—whose forefathers were savages a thousand years after the period when the Hindoos possessed the highest civilization of antiquity.

The cause of this deplorable condition is clear enough to those who have grown up under the influence of Christian civilization. With all its studies, all its wisdom, all its genius, and all its religious contemplation, this people have neglected or spurned the simple truths on which the Christian civilization is founded,—love and charity: "Thou shalt love thy neighbor as thyself."— "Inasmuch as ye have done it unto one of the least of these, my brethren, ye have done it unto me,"—these beautiful principles are not found in the Hindoo Bibles, and, consequently, not in their acts and lives.

But a happier day has dawned on India. The star of Bethlehem is seen at the horizon. A new light is kindled which shall soon lead the people out of the ancient darkness to a true and happy condition. And, strange enough, the youngest of the nations,—America,—is foremost in missionary work among the oldest, and next to the Americans are the Scotch, the English, the French, the Germans, the Belgians; and even good old Sweden has one or two mission fields there where the results are as yet rather meager; but in the course of time this work, too, will undoubtedly bear golden fruits, for just as surely as people and races are to continue, just as surely shall the simple doctrine which the great Master taught be spread and accepted among them all, because it is the only one by which the nations can reach their true destiny.

KESHUB-CHUNDER-SEN.

A remarkable attempt at reformation in the spirit of Christianity has been made in our day by a native Hindoo, the late Keshub-Chunder-Sen, the founder of the society, Brahmo Somaj in Calcutta, whose object was to introduce the Christian civilization in all its better forms. One day I went to hear a lecture

by this renowned Hindoo prophet and teacher, which afforded me one of the most pleasant and instructive hours in my life. The great hall contained an audience of nearly three thousand people, consisting chiefly of persons of influence and high rank, among the cultured Hindoos of the capital. The speaker was listened to with the greatest attention and respect, and the impression he made could not but be beneficial and lasting. I sat very close to the speaker, and took pains to notice his ways and manners while speaking to the large audience. His bearing in the pulpit made a remarkable impression, especially when, under the influence of some absorbing and transporting thought, his body was stretched out to its full height, and seemed to grow by the glow of inspiration. He was at that time a man of about forty-five years of age, of robust health, of symmetrical proportions, and with a face which beamed with intelligence and enthusiasm. The fame of this man is not limited to his native land, for even in Great Britain, where he spent several months a few years ago, he is very highly respected by thinking men and women of all classes who are devoted to the progress and improvement of mankind, and in his own country he is almost idolized. His faith, as far as formulated in definite language, coincides with that of the Unitarians of America, although he called it unitrinitarian, *i.e.*, he believed in one God, the Creator of the world and the father of all men; and also in Christ and the Holy Spirit as revelations of the divine, which is one but not as three different persons in the deity. He believed that the propagation of true religion in the world has been greatly impeded by what he called the idolatry which in Christian countries has grown up around the human person of Jesus Christ, manifested as in the flesh, and he begged the missionaries who came to India not to confuse the minds of the Hindoos by any such idea as a deity consisting of three different persons; polytheism had been the curse of India from time immemorial.

Such are the main features of the teaching of this reformer - 224 - which seem to promise a better time for the oppressed people of India. Later I became more intimately acquainted with him, and he had intended to visit America in my company, but was taken sick shortly before I left India, and died a couple of months thereafter.

- 225 -

CHAPTER XXIII.

Steamboating On the Ganges—Life on the River—The Greatest Business Firm in the World—Sceneries—Temples—Serampoor—Boat Races—An Excursion to the Himalayas—Darjieling and Himalaya Railroad—Tea Plantations—Darjieling—Llamas—View from the Mountains.

Having received all its tributaries on its course from the Himalaya Mountains through Central Hindustan, the Ganges has now swelled to such vast proportions that it cannot keep its volume of water within one regular channel through the level, soft soil of the Hindoo Peninsula, but flows into the ocean by several independent channels. One of these which is called the Hoogley, and has been mentioned already, is at Calcutta, about eighty miles from the sea, as broad as the united Missouri and Mississippi at St. Louis, and still the eastern half of it, close to the city, is so crowded with ships, barges and boats for a distance of six miles that it requires great care and skill at the helm to navigate safely.

On Jan. 2, 1882, the Calcutta rowing club had arranged a race between Barrackpoor and Serampoor, to which four hundred guests, including myself had been invited. Two large and ten smaller river steamers, all adorned with flowers and waving flags, lay around the pier between the Hoogley and the Nimtoolaghat waiting for us. Other steamers packed with natives, and Indian river boats with their half-naked rowers, crowded around the little flotilla, partly - 226 - from curiosity, partly in order to sell flowers, garlands and fruits to the guests. On the river bank were thousands of Hindoos and Mohammedans sitting or standing, in white clothes. Here and there was a penitent Fakir, bareheaded, his half-naked body partly covered with ashes, his eyes riveted on a point at the horizon or on the water, without being in the least disturbed by the noise and the festivity. From Nimtoolaghat a dozen small clouds of smoke were seen ascending uniting into one column of smoke, above the roofless building. A number of unkempt, half-naked Brahmins were carrying ashes and bones of cremated bodies from the crematory down to the river. Stately carriages with murky coachmen and fore-runners in white garments arrived in long lines at the pier with the guests of the day. When all were on board, the steamers whistled, the band struck up "God save the Queen," and the little flotilla steamed up the river amid merry chatting and deafening hurrahs.

STEAMER ON THE GANGES.

We first passed hundreds of Indian river boats from twenty-five to seventy-five feet long, with roofs supported by bamboo poles and loaded with grain, cotton, fruit, jute, goats, etc. The crews consisted of men, women and children who live on these river boats for years. They take advantage - 227 - of the tides in going up or down the river, and also use a broad oar in the prow of the boat.

RIVER BOAT.

On the west side of the river lies the manufacturing city Howrah, with the largest railroad depot in India, and dock-yards extending about two miles. On the east bank, a short distance above Calcutta are immense warehouses and hydraulic presses for preparing jute, a kind of hemp. The largest of these employs three thousand workmen day and night, and belongs to a Greek firm, Rally Brothers, who are said to have the greatest mercantile establishment existing. They own branch houses in thirty-six of the largest commercial cities of the world.

TEMPLE ON THE RIVER BANK.
WATER CARRIER.

Amid the happy strains of music we passed up the river. Stately palm trees in small groups rose above the surrounding groves, villages, temples and houses, while the dense foliage of other kinds of trees hung down the river banks wherever they were allowed to grow. Many of these bore flowers resembling tulips, acacias, jasmines, etc. Birds of the most gorgeous colors, but poor songsters, were flitting - 228 - and hopping about among the branches; vast numbers of small, white cows and oxen

were being herded by children on the meadows between the rice fields along the river, and at intervals of about two miles were temples consecrated to Hindoo gods. These temples were of a beautiful style and of perfect symmetry. Toward the river was an open portico. From this a flight of steps led down to the water. This was a Hindoo bathing place, where the holy water was taken. Just then a number of women were seen on the steps fetching water in clay jars, somewhat similar to the one Rebecca used at the well. These jars are carried either on the head or on the left hip. On either side of the portico, but from fifty to a hundred feet to the rear, stood the temples proper, in rows, facing the river, generally six on either side, with an eight to twelve-foot-wide path between each temple. The temples are about sixteen feet square, with a pointed - 229 - roof surmounted by a round cupola. They are made of brick, with a coating of white plaster on the outside; there are no windows, and only one door, opening on the river side. Inside this door is a niche in which the idol is placed. Only the Brahmins are allowed to enter these temples; wherefore the common heathen has to content himself with simply looking at the god from the outside; the Christians also are generally kept at a respectful distance.

Here and there along the banks of the river nestle rustic villages, the houses of which are generally square, and from sixteen to twenty feet on the sides, with pointed thatched roofs. The walls are of bamboo poles, interwoven with grass mats or plastered with mortar. There are no wooden - 230 - floors, no furniture, and the only utensils are a few bowls of clay for cooking, baking vessels of brass, some straw mats spread on the clay floor to sleep on during the night. The country is low and flat, and during the wet season, which lasts from July to October, destructive inundations are quite frequent.

NATIVE HOUSES.

Our steamers soon approached Barrackpoor, a garrisoned city on the east bank of the river. This place, which is one of the summer residences of the viceroy, has a very beautiful park, where there are several samples of the remarkable banyan or sacred fig-tree. From the branches of the tree certain shoots grow downward, and when they reach the ground they strike root and grow into new trunks, so that one and the same tree finally covers a vast space of ground, and looks like a pillared hall. In the park at Barrackpoor may be seen one of these trees, large enough to cover one - 231 - thousand men. On the west side of the river, directly opposite, lies the old city of Serampoor, which formerly belonged to Denmark, but was taken by the English in the beginning of this century, and now has only a few inscriptions and documents which remind us of the Danish period.

BANYAN TREE.

In the river, midway between these cities, a gigantic government barge was anchored. On this occasion it was covered with canvas, and served as a dining

room where a tiffin, or lunch, for four hundred persons was served. Our steamers anchored, and we sat down at the sumptuous tables. A band of forty pieces from a Sepoy regiment garrisoned at Barrackpoor struck up an English march, the champagne bottles popped, and all was life and joy. After lunch we witnessed six different boat races, all between Englishmen, and, the prizes having been awarded, the whole company walked on foot about a mile through a - 232 - fine park to the railway station, whence a special train carried the excursionists back to Calcutta.

After a summer of eight months in the Bengal lowlands with a constant temperature of 90° to 100° Fahrenheit in the shade, fresh breezes and cool air become luxuries more keenly enjoyed than those who live in a more temperate climate can conceive. To benefit by both I made a short journey in October, 1882, to the celebrated Himalaya mountains, among which the city of Darjieling is situated. The train on the Bengal railroad carried us about three hundred miles in a northerly direction through a level lowland teeming with gardens, palm groves and rice fields, to Siligori, at the foot of the mountains, where we arrived in the morning at sunrise. Having enjoyed a good breakfast and a bottle of Norwegian export beer at the railway eating house, we were transferred to a train on the Darjieling & Himalaya railroad to be carried up seven thousand feet high in a distance of forty-two miles.

This mountain railroad is so different from all other railroads that it deserves a special description. It is narrow gauged in the fullest sense of the word, the distance between the rails being only two feet. The cars are very small and low, and the wheels are about twelve inches in diameter. The car is ten feet long and six feet wide, and contains four seats, each of which accommodates four persons; it is open on the sides so that passengers can get on and off easily and have an open view. The locomotive is no larger than the cars, but powerful enough to pull ten or twelve of them up the mountain at the rate of eight or ten miles an hour. Nowhere is the track straight even for a distance of a couple of hundred yards, but it winds right and left in the most fantastic manner, and reminded me strikingly of the lines described in one of the old country dances.

The signal is given, the pigmy locomotive puffs and sputters, - 233 - the train with its load of humanity rolls away up hills and mountains and across awful chasms, up, up, up; hour after hour, with a grade of one to eighteen and twenty-eight, or on an average of twenty-three feet. It winds along the rugged mountain side, over awful chasms, and with such short curves that one's hair stands on end when looking down or up the steep cliffs, the summits of which tower above the clouds. A loose stone rolling down, a broken rail, or a derailment would immediately hurl the iron horse with its cars and human lives thousands of feet down to the bottom of the abyss, and reduce the whole to an unrecognizable wreck. Beautiful trees, grass, flowers, creeping plants adorn hills and vales except in the ravines and cliffs, where foaming creeks and cataracts have torn away the vegetation by tumultuously tossing themselves from rock to rock, from cliff to cliff, from valley to valley, gradually uniting in the rivers that continually feed the mighty Ganges.

The track follows a twenty-five-foot-wide driveway, the most part of which is hewn out of the solid rock, and on this highway may be seen the mountaineers from Nepaul and Thibet driving large numbers of pack animals (ponies and cattle) carrying products of Europe and America into and beyond the mountains to the peoples of northern Asia. Here and there on the green hills are the best tea plantations of India. These long, low, white buildings are the residences and factories of the planters, and close by are the dwellings of the native laborers, consisting of long rows of thatched huts, and in terraces along the steep hills are endless rows of tea bushes, among which laborers dressed in picturesque costumes of gay colors are busy picking tea, advancing in irregular lines—resembling the skirmish lines of an army. This picture is at first seen against the horizon, so far up that the men can scarcely be distinguished from the bushes, - 234 - and a couple of hours later the same picture may be viewed far down in a deep valley.

After awhile at the head of a long valley appear lofty, white objects whose summits rise far up above the mist and the clouds; it is the highest peaks of the Himalaya mountains, from sixty to one hundred miles distant. Thus the journey is continued up the mountains until the train finally stops at Darjieling, which is one of the most noteworthy places in the world. It is a sanitarium, and the summer residence of the government of Bengal, and during the hot season makes a favorite resort for many of the Hindoo nobles and princes as well as Europeans. The city has a few thousand inhabitants, the majority of whom are Thibetan and Nepaul mountaineers. There we see the Christian church, the Mohammedan mosque and the Hindoo temple in close proximity to each other, and on the streets one may often meet - 235 - Catholic monks carrying the crucifix, and Llamas or Thibetan priests in long, brown felt mantles, turning their praying-wheel, which consists of an artistically made machine of silver, in which are engraved the following words: "Rum mahnee padme hang," which means. "Hail thee, jewel and lotus flower," or "Glory to God."

PALACE AND TEMPLE IN THE HIMALAYAS.

Residences, churches, hotels and all public and private buildings lie in a semi-circle on the western slope of one of the mountains, offering a very fine picture. Excellent roads are built in zigzag form up and down over hills and mountains. There are scarcely any carriages but a kind of palanquin called dandies, and small ponies which are so sure-footed that they can climb up and down the mountains like goats. Both men and women ride these or are carried by three strong bearers from Thibet. Darjieling is elevated eight thousand feet above the level of the sea, and at this place black clouds may often be seen sweeping along the western side far below one's feet. The air is so clear, fresh and salubrious that it seems to infuse new strength, vitality and almost new life. It impels either to activity or to sleep; it is impossible to sit still or be mentally inactive. The view of the landscape below is claimed to be the most beautiful in the whole world. Beneath the terraces on which we walk are seen smiling valleys, one below another, away down far into the plains of Bengal, variegated by rivers, forests, cities and many-colored fields, and far away to the distant north against the blue horizon, one great mountain rises above and beyond another, capped with eternal crowns of snow high up among the restless clouds—twenty thousand feet higher than Darjieling, and twenty-nine thousand feet above the sea,—over five miles in height.

The loftiest peaks are Kinchinjunga forty-five miles, and Mount Everest, sixty miles distant from Darjieling. It is claimed that these peaks can be seen for a distance of - 236 - three hundred miles in clear weather. There these mighty giants stand clad in snowy garbs, like sentinels at the portals of infinite space, seemingly belonging more to heaven than to earth. No wonder that the Hindoos look at them with solemn awe, for cold and insensible to beauty and grandeur must he be, who does not at this sight, feel his own littleness and the inconceivable greatness of the creator.

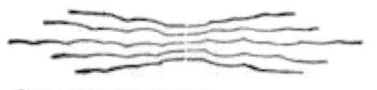

CHAPTER XXIV.

Cholera and other Diseases—The Causes of Cholera—How the Soldiers are Protected Against it—Sudden Deaths—Fevers—The Teraj—Contempt for Death—The Cholera Hospital—The Sisters of Mercy—The Princes Tagore—Hindoo Family Customs—Hindoo Gallantry—A Hindoo Fête.

The cholera has its home proper in India, and breeds in the Bengal lowlands after the rainy season, which closes in the fall. Its ravages are most pronounced in the month of December, but cases are quite frequent the whole year round. During my second year's sojourn in India it was very violent in December, but I would scarcely have known of it at all if my official duties had not made it incumbent on me to report from the board of health of India to that of the United States at Washington. Now and then I was reminded of the existence of the malady by the sudden deaths of my acquaintances. On three different occasions I enjoyed a pleasant evening entertainment in company with a number of friends, one of whom was not only dead, but even buried before the next morning.

Although India is ravaged by different deadly diseases, especially a kind of fever of which people die after one or two days' sickness; still, disease and death are scarcely ever mentioned among Anglo-Indians. They don't like to talk about such unpleasant things. A friend is suddenly and unexpectedly snatched away from social circles, but his death is seldom or never mentioned, just as if a secret and united agreement of taciturnity had been entered into by the survivors. Once I was invited to dine at the table d'hote of the officers at the military station Dum-Dum, a few miles from Calcutta. I drove out there in the evening, and at eight o'clock I had dinner in company with about forty officers, the majority of whom belonged to the Scotch frontier regiment. Col. Chapman, one of the party, was a jolly old Scotch warrior and Lieut.-Col. Hill was my host. After a splendid dinner such as India alone can offer, the company grouped themselves around several whist-tables according to the custom in the higher circles among the English. Col. Chapman was my partner, and we parted company at one o'clock. I accompanied Lieut.-Col. Hill to his villa, and retired for the night. At eight o'clock the next morning he entered my room with the sad news that he was just returning from the funeral of Col. Chapman. The stern old warrior who returned unscathed from twenty battle-fields was attacked by the cholera at two o'clock, died at four o'clock, and was buried at six o'clock. Such is life in India.

At the foot of the Himalayas is a very extensive territory called Teraj. Its soil is very fertile and adapted for tea culture. The whole territory is covered with timber, bushes and other plants, which, with the exception of certain cultivated portions, form an impenetrable jungle, affording a natural resort for tigers, leopards, and other wild beasts. The lofty mountains and the dense jungles shut out the sun, and the whole region is full of poisonous vapors which are never dispelled. It would be almost certain death for an European to live there for any length of time, and it is customary even in passing through the country on the railway train to take double doses of quinine as a precaution. The fever and cholera which are thus generated in the jungles and spread through the rice fields cause terrible ravages, not only among the Europeans, but also among the natives. Medical science has done a great deal to mitigate this evil, and the cholera, at least, has been carefully studied and controlled by the medical department of the Anglo-Indian army, so at present the malady is not feared so much as might be expected. The germs of the disease consist of microbes, which are carried in swarms by the wind. If such a pestiferous current of air strikes a place where soldiers are stationed, they are immediately ordered to break camp, and in a few hours the whole force is marching at a right angle with the wind, and after a day's march and a night's bivouac the physicians are generally able to tell whether the troops are out of the cholera district or not. If not, the march is continued day after day, always at a right angle with that of the preceding day, until the air contains no more cholera microbes.

Old officers of the army told me that they had seen the cholera pass over one part of the camp attacking every fourth man on one side of the camp street without touching a single one on the other. It is claimed that the fear and anxiety caused by this dreadful malady are even more dangerous than the disease itself.

One day while sitting at my breakfast table I received a message from the University hospital that an American sailor was very anxious to see me before he died. I immediately drove over there and was met at the entrance by the president, Dr. J. M. Coates, but when I arrived in the cholera apartment the man had just died. A sister of mercy was present at his death-bed, and had promised to carry his last message to me, which consisted in a greeting of love and a few trinkets to be sent to his mother in the state of Maine. There was a large apartment filled with cholera patients. Many of the native patients were visited by their friends and relatives; for the Hindoos do not entertain any fear of death, but rather court it, believing that a death caused by a contagious disease or a poisonous snake is simply a dispensation of Providence by which they are called away to a better life.

As an illustration of this fact I mention the following incident: One day while I was inspecting an American vessel a Hindoo laborer fell overboard, and a Norwegian sailor plunged into the water and saved him. After being brought safely on the deck the Hindoo became so angry at the Norwegian that he could have killed him, simply because he had prevented his entering paradise. Such occurrences are quite frequent.

I mentioned that I met a sister of mercy at the death-bed of an American cholera patient in the hospital. I cannot neglect this opportunity to express my heartfelt gratitude to these noble women, the modern nuns of the Catholic church. I have seen them in the dens of degradation and wretchedness in the American cities, among the sick, wounded and dying soldiers on the battle-fields of the South; I have seen them in an Arabian sea-port, searching for poverty-stricken travelers, among the cholera patients and among the unfortunate inmates of the prisons of India, always performing the same angelic duty, helping the poor, tending the sick, and comforting the despondent. Of course I am no Catholic, nor is it my intention to defend the Catholic faith; but I wish to acknowledge my appreciation of and pay my respect to the noble work which the priests and nuns of that church are carrying on among the lowly and erring members of our race.

The Hindoos are the most polite and clever people I ever saw. Their manners are exquisitely fine; no rudeness, no profanity, no intemperance is to be found among them, not even among the lowest classes. As has been said already, the higher classes are exceedingly polished and cleanly; all treat their parents and old people with marked respect. I shall narrate a few incidents to illustrate this: Shortly after - 241 - my arrival in Calcutta I became acquainted with the two Princes Tagore, especially the younger of them. They are titled princes, and enormously rich. They have many palaces, hundreds of secretaries, workingmen, servants, and pensioners, and, as is the custom among the Hindoos, whose families are governed according to the principles of patriarchal life, they all live together and get their support from the common property. I visited them several times, but mostly the younger prince who was at that time about forty-five years old, and a great admirer of America. Although a man of that age and rank he never talked in the presence of his elder brother until the latter had by a word or a nod signified that he was allowed to speak. A son is never allowed to talk in the presence of his father until the latter has finished. The eldest member of the family is its highest ruler, and even the Princes Tagore would never take any important steps before obtaining the consent of their aged mother.

Many prominent Hindoos and Mohammedans, some of whom were native rulers, came and visited me, before they invited me to their great fêtes. One of the frequent visitors was Dr. L. N. Maitra, a Brahmin of the highest class, and one of the most intelligent and clever men I met in India. He used to sit with me for hours, telling about the life, history and religion of the Hindoos. Having become acquainted with each other by several months' intercourse, one day he sat a long while at my house as if absorbed in deep - 242 - thought, and when he was ready to leave he asked if I would allow him to recite a Hindoo proverb in Sanskrit. In doing this he proved himself to be a fine elocutionist, and it seemed to me that I had never heard more music in prose, although I could not, of course, understand a single word of it.

DR. MAITRA READING SANSKRIT.

I asked him for a translation, and the next day he sent me one with the assurance that he intended to apply the proverb to me. It reads thus: "Do not enter into a very intimate acquaintance with anybody; but if you do, see that your friend is not a stranger; but if he is a stranger, see to it that he is not an educated man; but if he is educated, never part from him; but if fate compels you to part from him, then try to control that which we cannot control, that is, die, for death alone can make up for the loss of such a good man." I have told this to show not only the Hindoo's conception of the happiness of death, but also his exquisite politeness and delicacy of feeling.

When a Hindoo wishes to pay an elderly man or woman his respect or in some manner honor them, he calls them father - 243 - or mother, or, if they are his equals in age, brother or sister. Even to-day, when my former clerks write to me they call me father, and ask me to remember them to their dear mother, that is, my wife.

MY CHIEF CLERK.

On a few occasions some Hindoo princes and nobles would arrange special entertainments and fêtes for me, or rather in honor of the country represented by me, and on such occasions the invitation was not limited to me, but was extended to my friends also, so that I could take with me of these as many as I pleased.

The Tagore family had a beautiful country house outside the city, where one day shortly after my arrival, a party was given in honor of myself as representing the United States. Among the friends who accompanied me on this occasion was the Danish traveler, D'Irgens-Bergh, whose acquaintance I had made on my journey from Naples to Alexandria. The villa might more correctly have been called a palace, for it was on a grand scale and a perfect gem of architectural beauty. The floors and walls of all apartments were of marble. A beautiful and finely kept park surrounded the palace, and here, on the evening of our visit, hundreds of Chinese lanterns illuminated the spacious grounds. The most brilliant feature of the entertainment was music rendered by a complete orchestra of native musicians who used Hindoo instruments entirely different from ours; but pianos, guitars and other instruments with which we are acquainted, were also used. The younger prince was a great lover of music, and maintained, at his own expense, a conservatory of music and a large orchestra, giving instruction in music free of charge to any young man who was peculiarly gifted in that line. He is also well versed in Sanskrit literature, and has written several scientific works in Sanskrit. Before I left he presented me with one of these works containing his autograph, which is reproduced here as a sample of the hand-writing of an educated Hindoo:

Our refreshments at the fête consisted of dainties prepared by native cooks. Cream, rice, sugar, eggs, fish, flour, and spices were the chief ingredients of the different courses. Champagne and other European drinks were served with the courses, and after the repast we were offered coffee, and the servants brought wash basins and towels. Finally the major domo passed an urn-shaped golden goblet, placed on a gold tray. In this goblet was a fine sponge soaked with attar of roses, which costs about a dollar a drop, and in which the guests dipped the tips of their fingers and moistened their foreheads and clothes. The least contact with this attar causes a fragrance which lasts for months.

Neither on this occasion nor at any other festivity arranged by native Hindoos were any of the women present or visible to us, although we knew they were close enough to see us through windows or gratings. The men themselves assisted in waiting on us, but tasted nothing in our presence. When finally the carriages drove up and the guests parted each one of them received a huge bouquet of beautiful, fragrant flowers.

RAJAH TAGORE.

CHAPTER XXV.

Agriculture, Manufacture and Architecture—Wheat Growing—The Farm Laborer—His Condition, Implements, etc. The Taj-Mahal—Jugglers—Snake Charmers—From My Journal.

A large majority of the Hindoos are agriculturists. The staple crops are wheat, rice, and different species of pease. The wheat production of India exerts a great influence on the grain market of Europe, and is one of the most dangerous competitors to our American wheat. Having been ordered by the United States government to report on the wheat growing of India, I made this a special object of investigation and study, and in December, 1882, sent a report to the government in Washington which is our first reliable information on that subject; it elicited a great deal of attention, and was a source of genuine surprise in this country. I submit a few extracts from this report:

The annual wheat production of India now reaches two hundred and forty million bushels, of which two hundred million may be exported, while the natives make their bread from other kinds of grain. The total area devoted to wheat each year is now a little over twenty million acres, and the best average yield is thirteen and one-half bushels per acre. Wheat growing is now receiving the special attention of the general and local governments, and important works are being made and projected for an extensive system of canal irrigation. One of these, the Sirhind canal in the Punjab, has just been completed; it was built mainly by prison labor, is five hundred and two miles long, and will irrigate seven hundred and eighty thousand acres through two thousand five hundred miles of minor channels.

The wheat is sown in the autumn and harvested in March or April; it is usually sown in drills or rows, weeded like garden stuff, and in quantities not much larger than garden patches in the United States. The agricultural population numbers nearly two hundred millions; it is the aggregate of innumerable little units which, in agriculture, as in everything else in India, brings the country into importance; and this fact is so closely interwoven with the whole social, industrial and legal network of India, that it bears a strong influence even upon the future question of Indian *versus* American wheat.

PLOWING IN INDIA.

The Indian agriculturist,—"Ryot,"—can in no sense be compared to the American farmer, but rather to the late serf of Russia. He is a tenant on hard conditions, and is by custom and bigotry almost a fixture on the spot of land where he was born; his farming is done on a very small scale and according to old methods, to which he clings with re-

ligious veneration; his wants are very few, and he endures poverty and even hunger with patience; he cultivates his patch of five to fifteen acres on shares for the landed proprietor,—"zemindar,"—who holds under rental to the government, and the better half of his gross income generally goes to the zemindar, the priest (Brahmin) and the usurer, in the form of rent, presents, offerings and interest, - 248 - and if he can net ten cents a day by his hard and hopeless labor, that will suffice for the most pressing wants of his household. His home is a mud, or bamboo-hut, his property a pair of small bullocks, a few cows, calves and goats, a wooden cart, and a few brass and earthen pots, in all worth about fifty dollars, and his implements and tools are of the rudest kind, such as his ancestors used a thousand years ago; and yet he is making some progress under British rule, and finds his wants increasing, and at the same time better outlets for his produce and better recompense for his labor, and on the whole, is so independent on ten cents a day, that he will eat or store his wheat rather than sell it below a certain price. Of course he does not employ machinery in farming, but plows his land with a crooked piece of iron-pointed wood, harrows it with an instrument resembling a common ladder laid flat on the ground and dragged by little bullocks crossways over the field; he sows by hand, reaps with a rude sickle, carries the sheaves home on his back or in the bullock cart, threshes them with a wooden club, or lets the cattle tramp out the grain, and cleans it by hand-winnowing.

LABORERS AT THE INDIGO

PRESS.

India of course yields a great number of other kinds of agricultural products, especially the indigo plant, from which - 249 - the renowned dye-stuff is made; rape, mustard and other species of seeds from which oils are pressed, the opium plant, etc.

In the cities and towns the people devote themselves to trades and handicrafts, in some of which they attain greater perfection than any other people. Their beautiful carvings in wood and ivory, their exquisite embroideries, their textiles and yarns exceed everything in that line. But their ability is not due to any genius or ingenuity, but to close observation and patient application. According to their religious tenets the sons must learn the trade of their father, and they begin to work at his side as soon as they can handle a needle, chisel, or other tool, and continue the practice day after day, year after year, until they also in turn, have taught their children and grandchildren the same trade. Certain places are noted for certain industries, as Dakka for its fine muslin; Benares for its embroideries, etc. The muslin weavers of Dakka can with their hands spin and weave fabrics which are almost as fine as cobweb, and a person who is not accustomed to such work would not be able to feel the thread between his fingers; but the sensitiveness of the Hindoo spinner in Dakka has been developed to such an extraordinary degree during a hundred generations that he is able to perform works which would be perfectly impossible for others. I have seen a garment presented to a Hindoo king which was so fine in texture that, although it was a complete suit, it was folded up and safely packed into a mango shell, which is only a little larger than an almond shell, and thus presented. I have in my possession a little box two inches wide and four inches long, made of sandal-wood and adorned with fine carvings; all the edges are inlaid with pieces of ivory, in which are again inlaid more than two thousand separate pieces of different metals so skilfully put - 250 - together that the joints can not be detected even by using a magnifying glass.

In architecture the Hindoos also distinguished themselves centuries ago by the erection of buildings which are still objects of the admiration of the world. One of these master works of architecture is regarded as the most beautiful ever erected by the hands of men. It is the Taj-Mahal at Agra, a mausoleum erected by emperor Shah Jehan over the remains of his wife, Bengos Begum, who died in 1630. "During a period of seventeen years after her death Shah Jehan collected building material of marble and precious stones to be used in the construction of the mausoleum. All parts of India contributed to this, as did the different parts of the Holy Land to the temple of Solomon, and its estimated cost is twenty-five million dollars. It is built in Moorish style, with slender pillars, and its majesty and beauty profoundly impress the beholder. Many buildings in the world excel this - 251 - temple in size, but none can rival it in ideal beauty and finish. It looks more like a temple of thanksgiving and praise than an abode of sorrow, and the spirit of love seems to fill its silent chambers, quickening and warming the cold marble and transforming the whole building into a dream, into a psalm in stone. It is rich in mosaics, and precious stones of different colors assume the shape of fresh vines and living flowers. There it stands in solemn silence on the banks of the Jumna, like an enchanted vision It seemed to grow in magnificent splendor before my eyes as I approached it The airy dome and the white marble pillars glittered in fabulous, mystic beauty, and towered far above the gigantic cypress trees, which stood in rows like sentinels around it. One enters the park in front of the main building through a pillared archway of colossal dimensions, built of red sand-stone and surmounted by twenty-six white cupolas. The height of the arches is one hundred and forty feet.

TAJ-MAHAL.

"Taj-Mahal is erected on a base of red sand-stone nine hundred and sixty-four feet long and three hundred and twenty-nine feet wide, one side of which is washed by the river Jumna, and on each of the four corners is a tower of red sand-stone covered by a white marble kiosk. Two mosques take up the east and west sides. From this ground rises a fine terrace of white marble, three hundred and thirteen feet square, in the center of which is the beautiful main building itself. At each angle is an airy marble spire of exquisite style, surmounted by a noble cupola resting on eight pillars. They are about one hundred and fifty feet high, and a spiral stairway leads to the very top. The ground-plan of Taj-Mahal forms a regular octangle. The four sides on which the entrances are located are each about one hundred and thirty feet long, and turn to the four cardinal points of the compass. The roof is seventy feet above the base. Over each corner is a gorgeous spire, and over the center towers a - 252 - marble dome measuring seventy feet in diameter, and rising to a height of one hundred and twenty feet. It is covered by a gilt vault in the shape of a half-moon about two hundred and sixty feet above the floor. All this is of the finest Jaypoor marble, carefully polished, and still retaining its pure color.

"Notwithstanding the colossal size of Taj-Mahal, every part of it, from the foundation to the dome, is adorned with artistically executed designs, and the whole is as carefully wrought as the finest ebony ornament. Thus the entire Koran is inscribed on it. Even to-day the burial vault of the beautiful queen is filled with the fragrance of roses, jasmines and sandal-wood. The graves of the empress and emperor constitute sarcophagi of the purest marble, covered with elegant inlays of agate, carnelians, lapis lazuli and other precious stones, and surrounded by a six-foot-high gallery in the open net-work of which lilies, roses and other flowers of gems are inlaid. The dome in Taj-Mahal produces an echo which is more pleasant, pure and lasting than any other. A single musical sound produced by the human voice seems to flow or soar up there like a prolonged, pleasant modulation, which dies away so slowly that one seems to hear it after it is silent, just as one seems to see a lark after following it with the eyes after it has disappeared. Twenty thousand workmen were engaged for twenty-two years in erecting this mausoleum."

These recollections from India would be incomplete if I should omit to describe some of the wonderful tricks which I saw performed by Hindoo jugglers. As I was sitting one day in an open place before the hotel in Benares, together with some English army officers, an ordinary looking Hindoo of the lower classes, accompanied by a small boy, appeared before us, and asked permission to show the mango trick. This being granted, the boy scraped up some earth - 253 - on the road before our eyes, and made a little mound of it on the floor of the open veranda in front of the hotel. The magician, who had no other garment on than a loosely wrapped cotton cloth, usually worn by the men, and in his hand a white cloth and a little bag containing a few sticks and other small implements, stooped down beside the little mound of earth, and, with his eyes fixed on us, took a mango kernel about twice the size of a peach stone, which he planted in the little mound. Having smoothed the mound with his hands he recited several prayers and incantations, and made some motions over the mound with a magic wand, carefully assuming an air of expectancy. After a minute or two we saw the mound slowly opening at the top and the tender shoot of a plant coming up through the crack. The Hindoo sat with folded hands, occasionally breathing on the plant, and every now and then he would invoke some invisible being. Meanwhile the plant grew taller and more solid, until it finally assumed the shape of a dwarf tree, which kept growing and sent out branches and leaves. This development took place gradually and slowly, until finally a ripe mango fruit was seen hanging down from one of the branches. During this wonderful performance the magician had only now and then for a moment covered the plant with the cloth in his hand.

At another time, when I was on the deck of a large steamer, a Hindoo accompanied by a little girl asked the passengers to permit him to perform a trick. This being granted, he placed a round wicker basket, resembling a paper wastebasket, on the deck, and the little girl sat down in it so that her head and feet were flush with the edge of the basket, which was thus fairly filled up by the girl. Thereupon the Hindoo put the cover on and took a long, straight, double-edged sword which he ran through the basket in all directions. It was a shocking sight, some of the ladies screamed, - 254 - others fainted. But when he removed the cover from the basket the girl came out alive and without injury. The sword was handed to us for inspection, and I am perfectly sure that it was a straight, solid, honest infantry weapon. During all this time the basket stood on the deck of the ship so that no springs, machinery or other contrivance could be concealed under it.

Snake charmers are very common in India. "When one of these is to perform a trick he asks for a piece of paper, which he puts in the out-stretched hand of the spectator, and begins to play on his flute, and stare with his eyes as if he sees something near the hand. His whole body seems to be changed; writhing like a worm, he continually plays on the instrument and keeps his eyes riveted on the hand. Suddenly he rushes forward and points to the same.

But the spectator sees nothing, and the charmer again plays and contorts his body still more wildly. His arms are bare up to the elbows, and he holds the flute with both hands. Suddenly he throws his flute away, continues his motions and repeats incantations. Again he points to the paper, and while the observer turns his eyes in that direction without seeing anything unusual, the charmer presses his folded hands down on it and pulls out three large cobras, raising their heads and stretching out their poisonous tongues in different directions while he holds them in his hand."

SNAKE CHARMERS.

These and similar tricks are performed daily, yet no one has been able to detect how they are done. The theory of hypnotism has recently been advanced, and it does not seem improbable.

The following extract from my journal may be of interest:

Oct. 8, 1882.—Yesterday I witnessed one of the most important expressions of public opinion ever recorded in Asia, in favor of religious liberty. Three thousand prominent persons, mostly Hindoos and Mohammedans, and a few Christians and Parsees, assembled in the city hall of Calcutta, and brilliant speeches were made eliciting most animated applause from the native non-Christian inhabitants as a protest against the police prosecuting the salvation army, lately arrived in Bombay. What do the American and European Christians think of the necessity for Brahmins, Mohammedans, and Parsees to protest against prosecutions by Christians against Christians?

Darjieling, Oct. 17, 1882.—Here dwells a tribe of mountaineers who are polyandrists, the reverse of polygamists. Each woman has several husbands, who are generally brothers or near relatives. This practice has locally decreased the population, while in all other Hindoo sects it is rapidly increasing.

The English aristocracy is strongly represented here. The summer residence of the Bengal government, which is located here, as well as the excellent sanitarium, attract thousands of travelers. Excursions, dinners, balls and other festivities follow each other in rapid succession. This afternoon I was present at one of these gatherings, and met the Greek merchant Patochi, and made other interesting acquaintances. This evening shall attend a ball given by the governor of Bengal. At all these parties "simkim," or champagne, flows in streams. Life is gay and luxurious among the aristocracy in India.

Nov. 23, 1882.—Was present at a quiet and select entertainment with the king of Kutch Behar, in his palace in Calcutta. His wife is a daughter of the great Hindoo reformer Keshub-Chunder-Sen; she is a well educated, beautiful woman, who, together with her husband, the young and elegant king, defies the Hindoo caste restrictions, and appears publicly in company with other ladies and gentlemen.

Dec. 28, 1882.—Attended the decennial missionary conference; five hundred missionaries from all parts of Asia, Africa and Australia were present, and made it a most interesting religious convention. It was a gathering of highly cultivated, intelligent, courageous men and women, from the gray haired veteran to the young novice fresh from college. The American missionaries took a most prominent part, notable among whom was Dr. Thoburn, since made a bishop in the Methodist church. There were also three Swedes, with whom I formed an acquaintance,—Ungert, Edman and Erikson.

Jan. 18, 1883.—Attended the great state ball in the palace of the viceroy. Fifteen hundred guests were present, and the throng formed a brilliant picture of beauty, fashion and royal splendor. There were many native nobles, princes and rulers, the most prominent ones being the gawkwar (king) of Baroda, and the Kahn of Khelat. Wherever the gawkwar went he was closely followed by half a dozen turbaned attendants and four body guards armed with daggers and cimeters, or Damascus blades. His garment consisted of blue and green plush and satin, and the many-colored turban was almost covered with diamonds. It was claimed that the jewels he wore that evening on his breast and turban had a value of two million dollars.

Feb. 10, 1883.—In spite of all efforts to live quietly I am incessantly drawn into the whirl of social life; yesterday I attended one of the most pleasant festivities of the season. It was a magnificent fête given by the Mohammedan prince Raja Rajendra Naryan Bahadur in his gorgeous palace and parks in Shova Bazar in honor of the British victory in Egypt. Three thousand guests were present. All kinds of amusements were arranged, such as dancing, concerts, a circus with uninterrupted performances, nautches or dances performed by native dancing girls, etc. In different parts of the palace refreshments were served, all in the same grand style as the rest of the entertainment. The parks and gardens were illuminated by thousands of Chinese lanterns and many electric lights.

The following is also taken from my journal:

* * * Received visits from the Reverend Phillips Brooks and Joseph Cook, and from a young Swedish count, Wachtmeister by name, who was on his way through Asia, and also from a young prince from Madagascar, a son of the queen of that country, who, under the guidance of Ludvig Larson, a Norwegian sea captain, made a voyage through the seas of Asia for the purpose of learning practical navigation. The young prince spoke English fluently, and was a very intelligent man.

Attended a great festival at a masonic lodge where about one hundred and fifty members of the order were present, among whom were men of nearly every nationality and religion. The Master's degree was conferred on three brothers who knelt before the same altar. One was a Christian, and took his obligation with the hand on the Bible ; one was a Mohammedan, who took it with the hand on the Koran; the third, a Hindoo, with his hand on the Shastra. The obligation was dictated by an English lord, judge of the supreme court, assisted by the secretary of the Grand Lodge, my friend Rustomji, a Parsee and fire-worshiper. With the religious intolerance in India, where all unite in hating the Christians, it is only among the Free Masons, who know of no nationality, race or other barrier, that such things are possible.

THE GODDESS KALI.

Visited the temple of the goddess Kali in a suburb of Calcutta. Kali is the goddess of hate and vengence, and this temple is one of the most celebrated in India. One hundred and fifty Brahmin priests officiate in the same. The chief priest, Roonish-Chunder-Mokerje, was a young man with liberal education. He had spent several years in American mission schools. His office is held by inheritance. He was a most agreeable companion, well versed in western as well as Sanskrit literature. Once upon telling him that I had an intimate friend in Sweden who was a Christian priest, he gave me some pictures of the goddess Kali and other idols to send him with his compliments. In return, I had the pleasure a few months later to present him with a Swedish Bible, with his name in golden letters on the cover, from my friend, the Swedish minister, which present he cherished very highly. This Bible is now kept in the temple of Kali.

At my request Mokerje prepared a brief extract of the religious doctrine of the Hindoos, which reads as follows: - 258 -

"We believe in heaven and hell as temporary abodes of reward and punishment. When a man dies his good and evil deeds are weighed on the scales. First he goes to heaven to receive his reward, then to hell to suffer in proportion to his sins. When everything is squared up he again returns to the world in the form of another being, the same process is repeated again and again, and he can attain perfect bliss only after he has reached such a stage of development that he can do neither good nor evil deeds, but must lose himself in the contemplation of God until he finally ceases to exist as an individual being, and is reunited with God of whom he really constitutes a part."

ABDUL, MY MOHAMMEDAN SERVANT.

Was invited to the home of Col. Gordon to see some proofs of occultation, which is very wide-spread in India, and witnessed phenomena, which were so strange, that I hesitate to write them down. I saw heavy objects moving in the air through the room above our heads, and a man with the chair on which he sat rising several feet from the floor without the aid of any visible force whatever. I heard a slate pencil, moved by an invisible power, writing on a slate, and read in plain English what was written. I also saw in the same manner a pen writing on paper with ink, and felt with my hand the moisture of the ink. I know not wherein the invisible power consisted which caused these phenomena, but that such a power does exist I know for certain, for in this case, at least, there was no chance for deception.

At the home of the prince Tagore I met the renowned Madame Blavatsky, and many Hindoo theosophists. She is a large, corpulent woman, with intelligent, though rather coarse, features. She believes that she is attended by Kut-Hu-mis-Lal-Sing, a Buddhistic hermit who is claimed to be two thousand years old, and have the power of moving his "astral body" as swiftly as thought to the most distant places. For my part I saw nothing remarkable among the theosophists, but it is a common belief among the - 260 - Hindoos that certain pundits, or learned men, who for years have lived in the mountains as hermits, abstaining from food and all sensual pleasures, thereby attain such a power of mind over matter as to be able to separate the former from the body and let it, untrammeled by the laws of matter, move from place to place, still retaining the same form and ability to speak and act. Whether this is so or not I cannot say, but this I know, that "there are more things in heaven and earth than are dreamed of in our philosophy."

TYPES OF MOHAMMEDAN SERVANTS.
SOBULLA, AN IDIOT.

What luxuries one may enjoy here in the most pleasant company,—a glorious

CHAPTER XXVI.

The Women of India—The Widows—The American Zenana—Prizes Awarded in a Girl's School—Annandabai Joshee—Her Visit to America—Reports to the Government—Departure from India—Burmah—Ceylon—Arabia—Cairo.

From our point of view the social condition of women in India is highly deplorable. The women are not regarded as the equals of men, but rather as an appendix to them. Their religion teaches that they have no acknowledged rights as individuals, and that the only happiness they can attain in this world and in the world to come is to become wives and mothers of men, and that the more a woman sacrifices herself for man the greater will be her reward in the future. If the man to whom she is married dies, the remainder of her life is full of sorrow and suffering, and it is only in the life hereafter that she can expect any happiness, and that by being reunited with him.

This belief gave rise to the so-called "sati," or the custom to burn the wife on her deceased husband's pyre in order that she might *at once* be reunited with him and enjoy salvation through him. "Sati" is now prohibited by the English government, but every widow in India is still doomed to a life of misery and degradation.

When we consider that polygamy is practiced to a very large extent among the rich so that a man is allowed to have any number of wives, and may keep on taking new wives as long as he lives, it may easily be understood what a great number of widows there must be. There is an old man, for example, who dies and leaves many widows of different ages, some of them only ten or twelve years old, none of whom are allowed to marry a second time. They are deprived of all ornaments, and compelled to wear a very coarse, plain dress, to live on the plainest food, and work hard for the man who inherits the property of the deceased husband, and who is generally his brother or his son. This is the reason that rich families have a large number of women in all ranks and conditions, from the mistress of the house, which position is held by the husband's mother, to the humblest servant woman. The education of women is prohibited; hence they are very much like children, playing with their dolls, jewels and other toys, and having no higher idea of life in general than what they have been taught in the nursery. It is rather fortunate, therefore, that these lamentable victims of prejudice live in ignorance, as long as the present condition exists, for otherwise their life would be still more miserable.

In the course of the last few years missionaries from Europe and America have opened schools for the education of girls. The most prominent of these is located in Calcutta, and has many branches in other parts of India. It is called "the American Zenana," or ladies' mission, and during my stay in India it was managed by a Miss Hook, a very estimable lady of Danish descent, the fruits of whose noble work will be of incalculable value to future millions of Hindoo women.

MISSION HOME AND SCHOOL.

At an examination in this school I had the honor of distributing the prizes, consisting of five hundred American dolls sent by Cyrus Field of New York. The recipients were the most dainty and pretty little girls one could see. I wish I could describe this festivity. I sat on the platform in the great hall with Miss Hook to the right, a pundit or learned Brahmin to the left, and surrounded by the American and native teachers and some American tourists. The immense hall might be compared with a beautiful flower terrace alive with different colors, every little girl shining like a pretty flower in her red, green, white, blue or purple dress, her pretty black hair sparkling with gold and silver ornaments or jewels. They were all listening

nature, palatial residences, choice fruits, dishes and wines, pleasures of all kinds, surrounded by a host of servants, who, in snow-white garments and with bare feet, noiselessly and swiftly move about in order to gratify one's desires upon the slightest sign,—and still how I long for the home in the North, with the cool winds and frost and snow which quicken the blood, give appetite, and fill one with a feeling of surging vitality and energy, unknown in the enervating climates of the South.

From my veranda I see a crowd of people on the street who seem to pay homage to some one. It proves to be an idiotic beggar, Sobulla. The Hindoos believe that when a person has lost his reason he is filled with the spirit of God, and hence they always treat the insane with respect and tender care.

This April heat makes it easy to realize the Hindoo proverb, which says: "Never run when you may walk, never walk when you may stand still, never stand when you may sit, never sit when you may lie down."

with close attention until their names were called, when they modestly, their faces beaming with joy, stepped up to receive the pretty dolls sent by the generous American.

At first these schools met with bitter opposition on the part of the better classes of natives, but these prejudices gradually died away, and at present the mission schools are not subject to either persecution or ill-will.

One day in February, 1883, I received a visit at my home by a Brahmin of the highest class, accompanied by his young wife and her little sister. Her name was Annandabai Joshee. Her husband was postmaster in the old Danish city - 264 - Serampoor. He was a highly educated man, about forty years of age, with fine, affable manners. His wife was nineteen years old, and they had been married nine years. With the exception of the queen of Kutch Behar and a few in the Zenana mission, she was the first educated Hindoo woman that I had met. Her husband had given her an excellent education.

ANNANDABAI JOSHEE.

Their errand was to consult me and, if possible, obtain my assistance in a matter of the greatest importance to the women of India. The young woman had reflected somewhat in this manner: "Since I have acquired education, and the same amount of knowledge as a man, why may not other women in India do the same? In America many women are renowned for their great learning, and many of them are doctors of medicine. The women of India are not allowed to be visited by any man except their husband, and as all our physicians are men, who cannot see and carefully examine their female patients, they cannot, of course, prescribe proper treatment for them; hence many women in India must suffer and die without a remedy, which often could be avoided if women studied medicine. If American women can become physicians, then I can, and I have decided to go to America and enter the female medical - 265 - college in Philadelphia and study for the degree of doctor of medicine, and then return to India and do good among my countrywomen, and disprove the false doctrine which keeps Hindoo women in ignorance and degradation." Her husband was very enthusiastic for her plan, and, being rich, was also able to assist her in carrying it out if I would favor it and contribute toward its realization by reason of the influence my official position gave.

A few weeks later, the noble minded little Brahmin woman was on her way across the great ocean to that country where not only man but also woman enjoys a free existence. She carried official letters from me to all American authorities with which she might come in contact, also to the mayor of Philadelphia, and to the state department at Washington. Before leaving Calcutta she delivered an extempore address before a large audience at the University of Serampoor, of which address I have made the following extracts:

"I am asked hundreds of questions about my going to America. I take this opportunity to answer some of them.

"I go to America because I wish to study medicine. I now address the ladies present here, who will be the better judges of the importance of female medical assistance in India. I never consider this subject without being impressed that none of those societies so laudably established in India for the promotion of science and female education have ever thought of sending one of their female members into the more civilized parts of the world to procure thorough medical knowledge, in order to open here a college for the instruction of women in medicine. The want of female physicians in India is keenly felt in every quarter. Ladies, both European and native, are naturally averse to expose themselves in cases of emergency to treatment by doctors of the other sex. There are some female doctors in India - 266 - from Europe and America, who, being foreigners, and different in manners, customs and language, have not been of such use to our women as they might. As it is very natural that Hindoo ladies who love their own country and people should not feel at home with the natives of the other countries, we Indian women absolutely derive no benefit from these foreign ladies. They indeed have the appearance of supplying our need, but the appearance is delusive. In my humble opinion there is a growing need for Hindoo lady doctors in India, and I volunteer to qualify myself for one.

"Are there no means to study in India? I do not mean to say there are *no* means, but the difficulties are many and great. There is one college at Madras, and midwifery classes are open in all the presidencies; but the education imparted is defective and insufficient, as the instructors are conservative, and to some extent jealous. I do not find fault with them. That is the character of the male sex. We must put up with this inconvenience until we have a class of educated ladies to relieve these men. I am neither a Christian nor a Brahmin. To continue to live as a Hindoo, and go to school in any part of India, is very difficult. A convert who wears an English dress is not so much stared at. Native Christian ladies are free from the opposition or public scandal which Hindoo ladies like myself have to meet within and without the Zenana. If I go alone by train or in the street some people come near to stare and ask impertinent questions to annoy me. Example is better than precept. Some few years ago, when

I was in Bombay, I used to go to school. When people saw me going with my books in my hand they had the goodness to put their heads out of the window just to have a look at me. Some stopped their carriages for the purpose. Others walking in the streets stood laughing, and crying out so that I could hear: 'What is this? Who is this lady who is going to school - 267 - with boots and stockings on?' Does not this show that the Kali Ugla has stamped its character on the minds of the people? Ladies and gentlemen, you can easily imagine what effect questions like this would have on your minds if you had been in my place!

"Once it happened that I was obliged to stay in school for some time, and go twice a day for my meals to the house of a relative. Passers-by, whenever they saw me going, gathered round me. Some of them made fun and were convulsed with laughter. Others, sitting respectably on their verandas, made ridiculous remarks, and did not feel ashamed to throw pebbles at me. The shop-keepers and venders spit at the sight of me, and made gestures too indecent to describe. I leave it to you to imagine what was my condition at such time, and how I could gladly have burst through the crowd to make my home nearer.

"Yet the boldness of my Bengali brethren cannot be exceeded, and is still more serious to contemplate than the instances I have given from Bombay. Surely it deserves pity. If I go to take a walk on the strand, Englishmen are not so bold as to look at me. Even the soldiers are never troublesome, but the Baboo boys [6] have their levity by making fun of everything. 'Who are you?' 'What caste do you belong to?' 'Whence do you come?' 'Where do you go?'—are in my opinion, questions that should not be asked by strangers. There are some educated native Christians here in Serampoor who are suspicious; they are still wondering whether I am married or a widow; a woman of bad character or excommunicated. Dear audience, does it become my native and Christian brethren to be so uncharitable? Certainly not. I place these unpleasant things before you that those whom they concern most may rectify them, and that those who - 268 - have never thought of the difficulties may see that I am not going to America through any whim or caprice.

"Shall I not be excommunicated when I return to India? Do you think I should be filled with consternation at this threat? I do not fear it in the least. Why should I be cast out, when I have determined to live there exactly as I do here? I propose to myself to make no change in my customs and manners, food or dress. I will go as a Hindoo and come back here to live as a Hindoo. I will not increase my wants, but be as plain and simple as my forefathers, and as I am now. If my countrymen wish to excommunicate me, why do they not do it now? They are at liberty to do so."

After my return to America I visited her twice at the medical college in Philadelphia, where she became everybody's favorite, being one of the best students that ever crossed the threshhold of the institution. She did not renounce her religion or her habits of life, but observed all of these strictly. After three years of hard study she passed her examination with high standing, and practiced a few months in American hospitals, but she gradually succumbed to the dread disease, pulmonary consumption, and returned to India after an absence of four years, only to die in Poonah, the city where her ancestors had lived as highly respectable people for two thousand years past. She left India with the curse of the Brahmins on her head, but returned as the idol of her people. Thousands upon thousands crowded around her home, almost worshiping the frail, noble being whose youthful life was slowly ebbing away.

Strange are the ways of Providence. When Rev. Dr. Fjellstedt kindled a desire to see India in the bosom of the young country boy, who could then have guessed that this boy was to become a medium to assist that Brahmin woman who was destined to be the first one of the millions of India to - 269 - clear the way to education and liberty for her unfortunate sisters!

Besides my report on wheat culture I sent numerous official reports to our government on different industries, and other matters in India, such as tea culture, the decline of American shipping in Asia, the railroads, the population of India, our commercial relations with India, etc. These reports attracted such attention in Washington that during the month of February, 1883, I received orders from the state department to make a tour of inspection to those provinces and cities which belonged to my district and report to the government anything of national interest. Shortly after receiving this order, which was accompanied by a leave of absence for six months, I also received a cablegram from Holland offering me the position of managing American director of the Maxwell Land Grant Company in New Mexico, whereof more hereafter.

On the 12th of April I turned over all my official affairs to the vice-consul, Mr. C. C. Bancroft, and took the steamer Raipatoonah for Burmah, where I visited the most important seaports, Rangoon, Mulmain, and Akjab. Buddhism is there the prevailing religion, and the caste system, such as is found among the Hindoos, is unknown. The people are more prosperous. The city of Rangoon has, among other notable objects, a celebrated Buddhist pagoda, the great dome of which is covered with solid gold plate. The pagoda is situated on a high elevation above the city, and the dome is one of the most notable and costly works of architecture in the world. It is visible at a great distance out on the ocean, and when the tropical sun throws its rays on it, it looks like a flame of fire, whose splendor is too dazzling for the eyes to endure.

At a dinner party arranged for me by the American consul at Rangoon, I met many of the prominent men in this - 270 - city. Among these a judge of the supreme court, one Mr. Allen, who, late in the evening, at a game of whist, informed me that he had on that day been engaged in the trial of a Birmese prince accused of murder, and that he should pronounce sentence the following day. I could see that he had already made up his mind; still he politely asked me a few questions on international law with reference to the trial. The next day the prince was sentenced to death because he had violated the law of the land, which seems to prove that the English administration of justice in Asia is no respecter of persons.

In Birmah elephants are used for loading and unloading goods in the harbors. In the city of Mulmain I saw some of these wise animals piling up heavy timber in a lumber yard. The elephant put his tusks under the beam and his trunk over it and handled it with great ease. Having lifted the beam on the pile, he looked at it carefully to see if it lay in right shape, and if not, he would move it with his trunk. It was wonderful to see how well these animals seemed to understand what their drivers said. If a very big log could not be moved in the usual manner he would roll it with his feet or shove it with his head, or even put a chain around it and pull it along, and all this at the command of the driver who remained sitting on the head of the animal.

ELEPHANTS PILING TIMBER.

On April 25 I again embarked, this time on the steamer Asia, sailing across the Bay of Bengal, and arrived on the first day of May at the seaport, Bimlipatam, on the Madras coast. It was a pleasant city of white houses and situated at the foot of a high volcano. Here I saw for the first time the notorious car of Juggernaut, in which the image of the god is dragged through the streets. The car is of stupendous size, and rests on sixteen wheels. Thousands of pilgrims followed the car, and formerly many of the worshipers used to throw themselves under the wheels in order to be crushed to death; but this barbaric custom has been prohibited by the English government. The idol of Juggernaut is regarded as very sacred, for according to tradition it contains a bone of Krishna, the Hindoo Apollo, one of the ten incarnations or manifestations of the god Vishnu. This relic worship, which is otherwise unknown to the orthodox Hindoo faith, is a remnant of Buddhism, which formerly prevailed throughout the whole province of Orisa.

THE CAR OF JUGGERNAUT.

On the second day we arrived at Kokonada, where a flotilla of nearly one hundred short-masted sailing vessels of native construction after having received their cargoes lay waiting for us. Again we steamed away along the coast, stopping at the seaports Kalingapatam, Vizagapatam, Masulipatam, and finally arrived at Madras, on the fifth of May. This is one of the handsomest cities in Asia. It is situated near the equator, so that it is very hot there; but the fresh ocean breezes cool the air in the afternoon, and make the temperature particularly delightful.

On the 10th of May I left with the steamer Assam for Ceylon, and arrived at Colombo, the principal city and harbor on this island, on the 13th. Ceylon is called the pearl of Asia, and justly so. I remained there two days, in the company of the American consul, and visited the cinnamon groves, the Buddhistic temples, and other objects of interest. Along the coast south of Colombo is a drive-way for several miles, passing through groves of cinnamon and other spice trees which fill the air with fragrance. There are also artificial lakes, canals, parks and flower gardens in endless profusion; in a word, this place is one of the most delightful spots I have ever seen.

BUDDHA TEMPLE AT CEYLON.

The Egyptian patriot Arabi Pasha was recently banished to this island on account of his taking such a prominent part in the late rebellion in Egypt. I drove out to his fine residence located near the sea, and found him to be a very pleasant and highly educated man, who spoke English fluently, and with whom I soon became on friendly terms on account of my sympathy for the Egyptian people.

Ceylon is the centre of modern Buddhism in India. The temples of the Buddhists are very interesting to see. Many of their priests are men of learning and culture. I spent a few hours with them, and received much attention on their part on account of my being a representative of America. There is an old tradition among the Hindoos that the garden of Eden was situated on the island of Ceylon. The Hindoo narrative of the fall of man has many features in common with the biblical narrative, but with this difference: that Adam, being reproached for his sins, did not, according to the Hindoo legend, put the blame on Eve, but took it all on himself, and said that he alone was to blame, and that the woman should not be cursed. It is further told that when they were expelled from paradise they turned their course northward, and when they came to the shallow water which separates Ceylon from the main land of Asia, Adam took Eve in his arms and carried her across.

Having remained two days at this delightful place we embarked again, and on the 20th of May we were steaming along the coast of Arabia, being within

sight of land the whole morning. In my notbook I find the following lines - 274 - for this day: "Under thick canvass there is a strangely mixed crowd of people on the half-deck, gathered for divine worship, and when they closed the same by singing:
'O, hear us as we cry to Thee
For those in peril on the sea,'
the voices of Mohammedans, Jews, Buddhists and Brahmins from a dozen different countries were blended with those of the Christians."

We spent the 22d of May in the city of Aden, in South Arabia. This place is hot and dreary. Accompanied by one of my fellow-passengers I took a ride on camel-back through the desert to the celebrated water reservoirs. It seldom rains more than once in every three years at this place. To preserve the water that falls on these occasions the Arabians have built a series of cisterns, or large reservoirs, for the water along the foot of a mountain. These cisterns are made with great architectural skill; they are built of stone and cement, and are much more compact and durable than similar works of modern times. Water is a great luxury in Southern Arabia, and it is customary to offer the driver a drink of water for his camel or horse as an encouragement to drive a little faster or to show him a favor. At the same time the driver does not object to a tip, which in oriental countries is called, as in Egypt, "backshish," an expression with which every traveler soon becomes familiar.

From Aden we had a pleasant voyage up the Red sea to Suez. The cholera was, so to speak, in the air, and our steamer was the last one which escaped quarantine. From Suez I traveled in company with some other passengers by rail to Cairo. We stopped an hour at the little city Ismailia, which is situated on the canal, and is a fine place, noted especially for the great fête given by Count F. de Lesseps at the opening of the Suez canal, for which occasion a fine palace was built for the accommodation of Empress Eugenie of
- 275 -
France. On the way to Cairo we passed through the valley which in the Bible is called Goshen, and which Pharaoh gave to the brothers of Joseph to live in, and where the brick yards are located in which the Israelites were compelled to make brick without straw and oppressed in different ways by their task-masters.

During the day I had occasion to see a portion of the canal "Bahr Jussuf," or Joseph's canal, a masterwork some four thousand years old, which the legend ascribes to Joseph, and which still proves what a blessing this man conferred upon the people of Egypt, not only by warding off the dread famine, but also by executing many great and useful works. The canal began at Siut, on the Nile, and meandered through the valley on the west side of the river for a distance of nearly two hundred and fifty miles, until its level was so far above that of the river that its waters could be carried westward into the province of Fajuin, and change its formerly sterile soil into the richest and most fertile fields.

- 276 -

CHAPTER XXVII.

Cairo—Cheop's Pyramid—Venice—The St. Gotthard Tunnel—On the Rhine—Visit in Holland and England—Father Nugent—Arrival at New York.

The train has stopped, and we are in Cairo, the capital of Egypt. The beautiful, the joyous, the memorable Cairo, with its gorgeous mosques, its half mystic, half historical monuments, its narrow streets, and a life, a commotion and an oriental splendor strongly reminding one of the legends "One Thousand and One Nights." In company with a friend from America I visited the principal mosques, bazars, parks and other places of interest, and the next day we drove out to the great Cheop's pyramid, which is located about eight miles from the city. Here I again met with a monument of antiquity which filled me with wonder and admiration. The pyramid of Cheops was built before the birth of Moses,—yes, before Jacob came down with his sons to Egypt,—and it is possible that Joseph pointed out the same to his aged father as a proof of the greatness of the country and its resources.

MOHAMMEDAN MOSQUE.

According to Herodotus one hundred and twenty thousand men were occupied twenty years in building it. Its base covers about eleven acres, and its height is about four hundred and eighty feet. One can get an approximate idea of the enormous mass of material in it, when it is calculated that it contains stone enough to build a wall one and a-half feet thick and ten feet high around all England,—a distance of nearly nine hundred miles.
- 278 -
The renowned Sphinx is hewn out of the solid rock. It is in a reclining position, and, although partly buried by sand, I could easily trace its back for a distance of thirty paces.

At the foot of the pyramid I met an Arabian chief, a gesture from whom showed me that he belonged to the mystic brotherhood of Free Masons, which gave rise to warm handshaking, and an interesting conversation through the aid of my interpreter. In pressing the hand of this son of the desert sighing under despotism, and reading the feelings of his heart through the wrinkles of his face, while he talked of the great country in the West, whence I came, and whose free institutions, granting equal rights to all, were to him a heavenly light pointing forward and upward, I felt more deeply than ever before what a blessing it is to be a citizen of a commonwealth where a man is measured not by his birth or his wealth, but by his own personal merits.

THE PYRAMIDS AND THE SPHINX.

Returning to Cairo the remainder of the day was spent in the Boulak museum, among the most wonderful antiquities - 279 - of the world. Shortly before there had been discovered in the Nubian hills, beneath the temple Dayr-el-Baheree, a burial place containing the bodies of the old Egyptian kings. These had been brought to Cairo, where a separate wing of the museum had been opened for their keeping, and there they lay in their coffins in a fine state of preservation, owing to the Egyptian method of embalming. There were the very men who built the pyramids; there was Amases I., the founder of the new empire, Thotmes III., the great Sethi I., and his famous son Ramses II., and that Pharaoh who is supposed to have brought up Moses; there was also his - 280 - daughter Mirrhis, who afterward became his queen, the same who found Moses as an infant floating in the Nile.

RAMSES II., WHEN YOUNG.

Their bodies—yes, even their features—were well preserved. They lie in coffins of wood, which show skilled workmanship, the corners being carefully dovetailed together. Even their shrouds and ornaments of flowers and herbs show plainly that the style of dressing the dead among the Egyptians four thousand years ago was very much the same as it is now with us.

RAMSES II.

When I stood among the ruins of Pompeii or of the tower - 281 - Sarnath, the home of Buddha, I thought nothing could be more wonderful and awe-inspiring than those hoary monuments; but here lay before my eyes the very man who for many years was a friend and protector of Moses, with his wonderful, commanding features and eagle nose, his long dark hair, which lay in thick folds under his neck. The arms, rings, jewels and other ornaments worn by those kings and their queens, formed part of this wonderful collection, and, by their skillful workmanship, showed the high degree of civilization of the ancient Egyptians.

The following day I took the train for Alexandria. The railroad follows the river Nile in its general course. The valley is densely populated, and wretched mud houses and villages appear in every direction. The cholera had now broken out in its most deadly form, and we saw many dead and dying at the stations. The steamer Tanjore lay ready to sail for Europe, and I was soon comfortably quartered in one of its spacious cabins.

NILE BOAT.
- 282 -

On Sunday, June 3d, a beautiful Italian day, as we were rapidly steaming north through the Adriatic sea, we could see the coast of Greece to the right and that of Italy to the left. We arrived at Brindisi the same afternoon, and at Venice two days later. Surely the beauties of nature and of art that meet the eye in this lovely city seem to be the climax of everything beautiful on earth, and, quietly gliding forward during many hours through numerous canals in a half-dreamy, half-waking condition, with two silent gondoliers at the oars, I could scarcely realize whether this was a beautiful dream, an illusion, or reality.

RIALTO BRIDGE IN VENICE.

The next morning, accompanied by an interpreter, I walked through St. Mark's square, carefully studying its many wonderful attractions, its splendid shops, the clock, the - 283 - thousands of tame doves, the belfry of St. Mark's, the palace of the Doges, the marble pillars of the winged lions, and finally, the most remarkable of all, the wonderful church with its irregular, yet harmonious, unique and impressive architecture. In the church were seen ordinary visitors roaming about under the domes, humble worshipers counting their beads and rosaries, closely-shaved monks and royal officers with clanging sabres, and artists busy with their studies.

With a shudder I crossed the Bridge of Sighs, with its horrid associations, and spent a quarter of an hour in the dark dungeons to which it leads, and in which so many poor mortals, prisoners often without accusers and guiltless of crime, had sighed and suffered through the cruelties of man to man, well knowing that when they crossed that bridge into the dungeon, they had left all earthly hope behind.

In Venice I parted with my American companion, Mr. Robins, in whose company I had traveled all the way from

Madras.

Having promised to be in Holland at an early day, I was compelled to hurry, and left Venice on the evening of the second day. This time I took the route through the St. Gotthard tunnel, which is nine and a half miles long, and through which it takes nearly half an hour to pass. The beautiful lake Como and the grand Alpine scenery have been so often described, that I consider it superfluous to dwell on them in these pages.

In Mayennes I left the railroad and took the steamer down the beautiful Rhine to Cologne, passing the vine-clad hills and the mediæval castles, in delightful conversation with some American and Swedish tourists just returning from the German watering places.

From Cologne I traveled by rail to Rotterdam, where I arrived June 9th, and met my old friend, G. P. Ittman, one - 284 - of the men with whom I formerly had business connections concerning railroad matters in Minnesota. The following day he accompanied me to the Hague to see Baron de Constant Rebeque, one of those European noblemen who would have been a nobleman even if he had been born in a hut. He was then chamberlain of the king, and one of the directors of the Maxwell Land Grant Company, the management of which had been offered to me as already stated.

The next day we all met at the office of the vice-president of the company, the banker Mr. W. F. Ziegelar. The board of directors held a meeting, at which I was elected business manager for America, and it was decided that Messrs. Ziegelar and Rebeque should meet me in America a month later, and that all of us should then proceed to New Mexico to inspect the property and investigate the economical standing of the company, after which I could decide whether I would accept the position or not.

A few days later Mr. Ziegelar accompanied me to London, where one of the directors and many of the creditors of the Maxwell Company resided. Here I also found some friends from India, and in their company spent a couple of days at the beautiful country residence of an English nobleman, Sir Balfour. Among the prominent and excellent men with whom I formed an acquaintance at that place was Maj. Horace Durrant, formerly of the queen's hussars, who was also largely interested in the Maxwell Company, and one of the men from different countries, nationalities and creeds who will always live in my memory like beaming stars on life's varied journey.

Soon afterward I renewed my acquaintance with John Ennis in Liverpool, an Irishman, and a friend of mine for more than twenty years. He is a man who is never happier than when he can do someone a favor, and he has had occasion to do me many. In the evening he took me out to - 285 - see a sight, as he called it, and truly a wonderful sight it was. In a vacant space among the back streets and alleys of Liverpool, near the shipping, stood erected an enormous tent, containing seats for three thousand people. My friend Ennis led me through the back entrance onto the platform, where a few ladies and gentlemen were already seated. The tent was lighted with gas; the people were crowding into it through half a dozen different entrances. I have never seen such a crowd before or since. There were thieves, pickpockets, beggars, prostitutes, drunkards and ragamuffins of both sexes and of all ages, the very slums and filth of that great seaport, laughing, shouting, cursing, weeping, and noisy in every way.

Soon the great tent was filled, and could contain no more.

Then a little man appeared on the platform, whom Mr. Ennis introduced to me as the Rev. Father Nugent, an Irish Catholic priest, very small in stature, but with a countenance beaming with intelligence and benevolence. He stepped to the front, and the moment he was seen by the vast audience order and perfect silence reigned.

Here was another Keshub-Chunder-Sen, but with no new religion or doctrine to advance, only re-echoing what the man of Nazareth had said to the same class of people eighteen centuries ago. This priest has done much noble work, rescued many from a life of degradation, brought up and secured places in America for thousands of street gamins and orphans, and his name is better known, especially among the English-speaking Catholics, than that of any king or emperor. And who would not rather be a Father Nugent than a king?

In the morning of the fourth of July I arrived in New York city, and soon found President Chester Arthur, Gen. Garfield's successor, occupying rooms near my own in the Fifth Avenue hotel. After breakfast I was given an interview with - 286 - him, and, of course, was pleased to learn that he had followed my little work in India with interest, and expressed much regret when I informed him of my intention to resign at the expiration of my leave of absence.

- 287 -

CHAPTER XXVIII.

Home from India—A Friendly Reception—Journey to New Mexico—The Maxwell Land Grant Company—Renewed Visits to England and Holland—Re-elected Secretary of State—Visit of the Swedish Officers in Minneapolis and St. Paul—Two Hundred and Fiftieth Anniversary of the Landing of the First Swedes in Delaware.

On the 8th of July I was again home with family and friends in Minneapolis, and found everything pretty much as I had left it nearly two years previously, except that my good old father had gone to his final rest. A couple of days later I visited my farm, in the Red River valley, and my old and faithful friend Capt H. Eustrom, who lived close by and was then holding an important office, and who had faithfully attended to my interests at that place during my absence.

My Scandinavian friends had meanwhile arranged a reception for me, and on the 11th some eighty of them joined in a banquet at Lyndale Hotel, then situated in the suburbs of Minneapolis at

Lake Calhoun. The afternoon was devoted to a steamboat tour around the beautiful lake, and in the evening the party all sat down to a sumptuous banquet, where many addresses of welcome and tokens of friendship were spoken, read and sung. I had been absent nearly two years, seen and experienced much of the world and enjoyed many pleasures, but I found the old saying true; "There is no place like home." These two years had been of particular - 288 - importance in the history of the cities of Minneapolis and St. Paul. The population had nearly trebled during that time, and such improvements had been made that I could hardly recognize them.

A week after my return my friends from Holland arrived, and we proceeded to New Mexico, where we found the great Maxwell estate, valued at ten million dollars, and containing one and a half million acres of land, consisting of coal fields, gold mines, timber and grazing lands, in a deplorable condition caused by extravagance and mismanagement. We found that there was nearly a million dollars of current debts, while the income was not sufficient to buy postage stamps to carry on the necessary business correspondence.

An agreement was finally effected whereby the former president and American manager relinquished his interest and resigned his position; the Holland directors determined to raise the necessary funds in Europe, and I agreed to undertake the liquidation of the affairs of the company.

Shortly after I repaired to Washington to report my inspection tour in India, and tender my resignation, which was accepted, an unusual courtesy being shown me by extending my leave of absence to January the next year. The following two years were devoted principally to business journeys to New Mexico, England and Holland. I visited the latter countries four times during that period. With the powerful aid of Baron Rebeque, who had spent several months with me in this country in the summer and fall of 1883, a syndicate, backed by several million dollars, was at last formed in Holland, and the whole estate was turned over to it. Having accomplished this, I voluntarily withdrew from the concern, and returned to my own farm and home in Minnesota.

The Maxwell estate is situated within the Rocky mountain region, on an elevation of from six thousand to twelve - 289 - thousand feet above the sea. The climate is delightful and the scenery beautiful, but the country is not fit for cultivation, except such parts as can be irrigated. Hence most of it is devoted to stock raising, and herds of countless cattle were roaming over the prairies, the Maxwell Company alone owning at the time I left its service nearly twenty thousand head.

In the fall of 1886 I was for the second time elected secretary of state by the citizens of Minnesota, re-elected in 1888, and thus made for the third time the head of the state department.

In the fall of 1887 the citizens of Minneapolis were honored by a visit from a large number of Swedish, Norwegian and Danish military officers, non-commissioned officers and soldiers. They arrived by an express train from Chicago, and were met at the union depot by thousands of people. The Swedish Guard, Normanna Infantry, and the society Dania were paraded outside the depot building. The guests were received by a committee, and conducted in procession through the illuminated and crowded streets to Dania hall, where a splendid banquet was enjoyed, while music was discoursed by the Svea and Normanna bands. The city mayor, Dr. Ames, made an address of welcome, after which several Scandinavians made speeches. I had been elected as the spokesman for the Swedes, and expressed myself as follows:

"*Honored Guests from Sweden, Norway and Denmark:*

"From the place where we now stand the roar of the St. Anthony falls may be heard through the still night. You are, therefore, far back in the depths of the American West; and yet this is only the modern gate of entrance to the great North-west.

"A couple of hours ago a half dozen railway trains left our depot over different roads and are now speeding on toward the setting sun, and some of them do not cease their journey until they have passed distances greater than that between London and Rome, through fertile, but, as yet, mostly unsettled regions. Thirty-four years ago I, with a few other of your countrymen, some of the earliest in Minnesota, gazed for the first time at - 291 - the St. Anthony falls. There was no city, not even a sign of a city, on this side of the river; the red man chased his game in the woods where our churches and school-houses now stand; the country west of us was an unknown wilderness, Minnesota did not exist as a state, and many of our western states, which now contain millions of happy inhabitants, were not even projected.

"Now, on the contrary, our state alone is a mighty empire, with a population of nearly a million and a half, and with an assessed valuation of six hundred million dollars. Minnesota now produces a hundred million bushels of grain annually on her fertile fields, six hundred and fifty million feet of lumber from her forests, and her infant iron mines already show an annual production of half a million tons of rich ore. The Scandinavians constitute more than one-fourth of the population of the state, and produce at least one-third of our agricultural products on their own lands, as most of them are farmers. The amount of grain which in Minnesota alone is annually produced, would be more than sufficient to furnish the whole population of Sweden with bread from the beginning to the end of each year.

CAPITOL OF MINNESOTA.

"Our beautiful city of Minneapolis has already a population of one hundred and sixty thousand, of which at least one-fourth, or forty thousand, are Scandinavians or their descendants.

"I hope you will all have an opportunity to see our city with your own eyes before you leave us,—its mills, churches, schools and happy homes,—and will therefore not consume the time by referring to these.

"As to yourselves, gentlemen, we have heard what has been said to you so expressively in Chicago by our friends there, and we join them heartily in their praise.

"When we heard that the soldiers and representatives of Denmark, Norway and Sweden would honor us with a visit we all rejoiced, and we have come together this evening to express our joy in a cordial welcome.

"We have intentionally conducted you to this hall where we may, under our own roof, pay you our homage in the plain manner of our sturdy Scandinavian forefathers, and give you an opportunity to see us as we are in our daily life. We are men of the people; we have come here as poor immigrants, ignorant of the language and of the customs of the country. Our sole heritage was our strong arms and our good cheer,—no, excuse me, another heritage of more worth than gold or genius have we brought from our old homesteads,—our share of Northern fidelity, strength, and virtue; and the talent confided to us we have used in all branches of industry, science, fine arts, in the service of the community, the state, and the Union, in peace and in war, and we perform our share in the great national work, the result of which is a new and powerful commonwealth, the foundation of which lies in the individual worth and right of man.

"I think I can see a Providential dispensation in this, that when the time - 292 - arrived for the new world to take its place among the nations with a new and powerful cosmopolitan race, the Scandinavian people were also chosen to contribute a part in that grand work, and that it was especially reserved for the 'men of the people' to receive in this country free and equal opportunity for their development. Who can fail to see the stamp of the Scandinavian people on the entire social fabric of the new world?

"We would be forgetful if we did not gratefully remember the great good which the fatherland has bestowed upon us from tender childhood to the very hour when we bid it farewell; we would be unworthy of the name and fame of our fathers if we did not honor and love as a dear mother the ever memorable land of our birth, and you, its worthy representatives, as our relatives and brothers.

"Your presence among us is a proud event, and its remembrance shall be cherished as one of the most pleasant. And when you return to those dear places where we took the first steps on life's eventful journey, we wish you to take back cordial greetings from us all, and say to our kindred that we teach our children to love and honor the people and institutions in the Northern lands, although they have never seen them; and say to them that, far out in the wide West by the laughing water of Hiawatha, and hundreds of miles beyond, are friends and brothers whose fidelity and affection neither time nor distance can obliterate."

The address was responded to with much feeling by Col. Liljehök of Sweden The festivities continued amid addresses, music and song until long past midnight. The following day the guests were shown around the city, after which they visited St. Paul, where they also received a cordial welcome, and were presented to the governor.

The following year, on the 14th of September, an event took place which deserves particular mention. It was the celebration of the two hundred and fiftieth anniversary of the landing of the first Swedish settlers on the Delaware. The Revs. J. Enstam and C. J. Petri, together with myself, in the middle of the summer called a meeting of Swedish-American citizens to prepare for such celebration. Committees were appointed and elaborate preparations made, to which nearly all the Swedes lent a willing and helping hand. The great exposition building was given up to our use: bands of music were engaged, a choir of one hundred and - 293 - fifty Swedish singers, mostly from the different churches, was trained, and eminent orators, statesmen and professors were invited. A souvenir badge was sold at the Swedish business places in the city; the net proceeds,—amounting to about eight hundred dollars,—were donated to the fund for the relief of the sufferers by the great fires in Sundsvall, Umeå and Lilla Edet in Sweden.

The program of the day included a fine parade with bands of music and banners; but a heavy rain came early in the day, and the parade had to be abandoned, and the people instructed to assemble at the exposition building at their own convenience, *which they also did*, in such great numbers that before the hour of opening the exercises every seat and standing place in the great auditorium were occupied. Many came from distant towns, cities and states; a special train brought nearly one thousand from St. Paul, with marshals, music and banners; the general council of the Lutheran Church, then assembled in Minneapolis, came in a body and occupied seats on the platform to the right of Cappa's Seventh New York Regiment Band, while the Swedish chorus of one hundred and fifty voices, under Prof. Norman, occupied the platform to the left.

The platforms were decorated with numerous society banners, and the colors of Sweden were seen everywhere. The lofty pillars reaching to the roof were wrapped in alternate stripes of blue and yellow, the national colors of Sweden, and side by side and uppermost were the stars and stripes. A large picture of the old Swedes Church in Wilmington, Delaware, built in 1698 was hung in front of the speakers' platform, and attracted general attention.

As chairman of the committee of arrangements I had the honor to act as presiding officer of the day. The government of Sweden was represented by Consul Sahlgaard, with other distinguished guests, and the historical society of - 294 - Delaware by Maj. Geo. C. White. As near as can be estimated there were fully fifteen thousand people present, and the interest manifested by that vast audience can best be understood from the fact that thousands stood upon their feet during the whole proceedings, which lasted three hours.

OLD SWEDES CHURCH AT WILMINGTON.

The festivities commenced at two o'clock in the afternoon with a musical selection by Cappa's band, at the close of which the audience was welcomed by myself in the following words:

"The discovery of America was the greatest event which had taken place from the days of Christ till it was made, but the settlement of America by the right kind of people was, in its beneficial effects upon the human race, a matter of still greater importance. It seems like an order of Divine Providence that this new world was left in its natural or savage state during all the dark centuries of schooling and experiments in Asia, Africa and Europe, in order that it might remain a virgin soil for the higher civilization which was to follow.

"To establish this civilization, based upon true principles of government required not only wisdom and strength, but toleration, brotherhood, justice and exalted virtue. The people chosen for that great work came from different countries and different conditions of life,—the English Pilgrims to New England, the Dutch, the Swedes and the Quakers to the middle country, the English Cavaliers, the Scotch Highlanders and the French Huguenots to the South,—and in them all, combined and intermingled, were found the elements of body and of mind, which have given to the world its best government, its greatest nation, and its highest civilization.

"Since the English were the largest in number their language became the language of all, and for that reason, perhaps, history has been partial to those who first spoke it. Memorials and anniversaries have often been celebrated over the landing of the Pilgrims and the valor of the knights; their just praise has been written and sung a thousand times, so that their honored names have become precious household words among the generations of our day, while the others have often been forgotten or ignored.

"Fully recognizing the merits of all, we have assembled here to-day from many parts of the United States to commemorate a great historical event,—in celebrating the two hundred and fiftieth anniversary of the landing of the Swedes on the Delaware, and to do honor to their memory in prayer, song and speech, and to this intellectual feast I bid you all a hearty welcome."

This celebration was unquestionably the largest and most important gathering that ever took place among the Swedes in America; great attention was paid to it all over the country, and it contributed greatly toward placing the Swedes rightly in the estimation of the people, throwing a clearer light on the achievements of the past, and emphasizing the importance of the Swedish-Americans of the present.

CHAPTER XXIX.

The Causes of Immigration—American Influence on Europe, and Especially on Sweden—The Condition of the Swedes in America—American Characteristics—Antipathy against Foreigners—The Swedish Press on America—American Heiresses.

Much has been said on the causes of immigration. These are numerous, but the chief cause I have found to be that the people of the old world are now being aroused to the fact that the social conditions of Europe, with its aristocracy and other inherited privileges, are not founded on just principles, but that the way to success ought to be equally open for all, and determined, not by privileges of birth, but by the inherent worth of man. And here in America is found a civilization which is, to a large extent, built on equality and the recognition of personal merit. This and the great natural resources of the country, the prospects for good wages which a new continent affords, and in many cases greater religious liberty, draws the people of Europe, at any rate from Sweden, to this country.

Sweden is a very good country, but more especially so for those who are fortunate enough to be born to title, honor or riches. To be sure, even there instances are known of men from the ordinary walks of life making their way to wealth and prominence; but those are exceptions, possible only in cases of unusually great personal merit. Here, on the other hand, the reverse is the rule; the self-made man accomplishes most, as instanced by the history of our presidents, governors, financiers and other distinguished men. And this is quite natural, for the prospects and possibilities which a man sees before him in this country stimulate his ambition, and arouse his energies to surmount the greatest difficulties.

The new ideas now permeating society in Europe, and which will gradually transform it, have, to a great extent, originated in America, more particularly the idea of brotherhood, the sympathy with equals, the conviction that it is our duty to better the condition of our fellow-men, and not despise them, even if they are unfortunate. In this respect, as well as in many others, America exerts a great influence over Europe. To me the better situated classes of Sweden seem short-sighted in their hostility to emigration, for a man of broad views must admit that emigration has been beneficial even to Sweden herself. It may not have benefited the higher classes directly, as they cannot hire servants and laborers as cheaply as formerly; but the people have benefited by it as a whole, their condition being now better than formerly, when competition between the laborers was greater.

America also exerts a great influence on the mental and moral development of the people of Sweden, although this may not be so apparent on the surface. The thousands and hundreds of thousands of letters written every year by Swedish-Americans to the people of the working classes of Sweden arouse the latter's ambition, and develop liberal, political and religious ideas among them. No one can calculate the scope of this influence, to say nothing of the eloquent language spoken by the millions of crowns which are annually sent home to poor relatives and friends, and which either lighten the burden of poverty or enable the recipients to prepare a brighter future for themselves in this country, and how many a poor, downtrodden fellow, who could expect - 298 - nothing better than the poor-house in his old age in Sweden has become an able and useful citizen in this country!

When the poor young laboring man or woman, who in Sweden has felt the oppression of poverty and looked forward to a life without hope, arrives in this country, the timid, bashful looks give way to hopefulness and self-reliance. It is true that this is often carried too far, especially in the line of expensive and extravagant dress, which sometimes makes the wearer appear ridiculous; but these are trifles, the main thing being that those people learn to know their own worth, and are able to create a brighter future for themselves.

The tact and manner acquired within a short time by common laborers who looked thoughtless and careless while at home, are simply astonishing. A Swedish diplomat, who visited Minnesota twenty years ago, and, among others, met one of his father's former farm laborers, who was now in good circumstances, in an official report to the government of Sweden expressed his astonishment at the change which the Swedish people had undergone in that respect.

It cannot be denied that many among the higher classes in Sweden feel very unfriendly toward the United States, and it was even not long ago a common saying among them, "America is the paradise of all rogues and rascals."

Many Americans suppose themselves to be better than all others, and believe their country and institutions to be perfect. In this they are mistaken, for in several respects this country is as yet in its infancy, and has many defects which the countries in the north of Europe have long since outgrown. As one instance I would mention that the school system is altogether too dependent on local influences, so that while the common schools in the northern cities and towns are very fine,—in some instances perfect,—those in the country rate very low compared with the same class in Sweden, Norway, - 299 - Denmark, and Northern Germany. Another case in point is the system of taxation which notably gives unprincipled men of wealth opportunities for escape, while the poorer classes are taxed for the full amount of their property, the burden thus falling proportionately heaviest where it ought to be lightest, and *vice versa*. Again, the laws which make possible rings, monopolies, and trusts, to the great prejudice of the people, or permit gambling on the produce of the country as carried on in the great commercial marts of America, robbing the producer of the fair wages of his toil, and many other things which would not be tolerated among the nations of Europe. Thus it lies within the power of one man, in this our great state of Minnesota and other states, to make or unmake cities, towns, and communities, by a single edict locating a railroad, fixing a time-table, and in many other ways exercising arbitrary power that no European ruler would think of assuming. The execution of our laws, also, in many places has proven highly unsatisfactory, often making our much-boasted jury system, especially in criminal cases, a farce and a disgrace.

The trouble is that political demagogues and Fourth of July orators continually keep pointing out only the best sides of our institutions, which undoubtedly are both many and great, while few have the courage to speak of the defects and short-comings.

As for the conduct of the native Americans toward the immigrants who settle among them, I venture to say that although they consider themselves very tolerant, and are so in a general way, they are in many respects very intolerant and prejudiced; but this is owing to a lack of knowledge concerning other nations. It is true that the immigrant, especially from the north of Europe, is bidden welcome, and is generally well received, but he is expected to be content with shoveling dirt, chopping wood, carrying water, plowing the - 300 - fields, and doing other manual labor, no one disputing his right or his fitness for these occupations. But when he begins to compete with the native American for honor and emolument in the higher walks of life, he is often met with coldness, mingled, perhaps, with a little envy, and although the adopted citizen may, in many instances, start on an equal footing with the natives in culture, intelligence, and business ability, it is only exceptionally that he will be recognized as an equal socially; and there is scarcely an adopted citizen of the non-English-speaking nationalities who has not deeply realized the truth of this statement.

It may be safely said that it will on an average take two generations before the children of the non-English-speaking immigrants shall cease to suffer more or less from these prejudices. Certainly the children of immigrant parents, although born and brought up in this country, are often subjected to sneers and taunts by their more fortunate playfellows, even within the walls of the American public schools.

This antipathy is most noticeable in places where the number of foreigners is very great, but less where they are few, and may be explained and partly excused by the fact that, when a great number of foreigners live together they are more apt to maintain their customs, language and amusements, which differ from those of the native-born. But the chief reason is that when the immigrants, most of whom belong to the hard-working classes, arrive directly from a long and exhausting journey, they are often poorly dressed, awkward and ignorant of the language and customs of the country, and look forlorn and crestfallen. The first impression which the native American thus receives remains with him, while he does not stop to consider that the same class of people coming from America to Europe would not appear to better advantage if they should go there as immigrants. Nor does he consider the injustice of judging whole - 301 - nationalities by their less favored representatives under such circumstances. There are, of course, many noble exceptions among the native Americans; but as to genuine tolerance between different nationalities, I have seen far more of it in the great cosmopolitan cities of Europe, Asia and Africa, than in America.

But these shortcomings may be easily overlooked for the many noble traits of character which all admit him to possess. And most striking and beautiful of these is the honor and respect he shows to woman. There is no other country in the world where woman is treated with such consideration, and where she is as safe and honored as among Americans, and if we judge nations by the way their women are treated, as I think we should, the American nation has no peer in the world.

But if the Americans have a one-sided and wrong conception of foreigners, so have also many foreign people a wrong conception of America, and we ought not to blame the former more than the latter. The Swedish press, for instance,—with praise-worthy exceptions, of course,—has always shown great prejudice or ignorance in its treatment of America, and especially of the Swedish-Americans. Thus it has always been ready to dwell on the dark sides and keep silent about that which is praiseworthy in this country. If, for instance, a lawless deed has been perpetrated on the frontier it is pointed to as a sample of American civilization, without considering that such things take place only in the western cow-boy or mining life, the days of which will soon belong to the past. And if an immigrant, who, deservedly or undeservedly, has been unsuccessful writes a letter to his old home and slanders America, how eager the newspapers are to rush into print with it. Even if the man has been here only a few months, and seen only a small spot of the country, they are still ready to accept his story as reliable testimony, - 302 - and judge the whole country accordingly. But this by no means applies to Sweden and the Swedish press alone; it may with equal truth be said of the Europeans and the press of Europe generally.

There is no gainsaying the fact, however, that new-comers as a rule must expect adversity and difficulty on account of being strangers, and because of their unfamiliarity with the English language. And such as are unaccustomed to manual labor and have not learned a trade stand a poor chance, especially in the beginning. Book learning is of little use at first, for there is no lack of educated people in America. Hence it is a great mistake for young men with nothing but an education to depend upon to come here with the expectation of making a fortune, for the only way to success will at first generally be by taking hold of the spade or the axe. Have they the courage to do this? Then let them come, for opportunities will open after a while to those who shall deserve them. Certificates of character and recommendation are here of little value; titles and family connections of still less. One cares not much for what you have been; but only for what you are.

In the last civil war a young German officer came to President Lincoln and offered his services as a volunteer in the army. The man had high recommendations, and talked a great deal about his noble birth, and even intimated that royal blood was flowing through his veins. Having patiently listened to all this, Lincoln, putting his hand on the young man's shoulder, said, encouragingly: "Don't let this trouble you, my friend, for I assure you that if you only do your duty well and faithfully, these things will be no impediment to your success. We are not so unjust in America as to think less of a man on account of his European titles. No, I can assure you that you have precisely the same chance for advancement and success as if you had been a man of the people, - 303 - provided you prove as competent and meritorious as one of them."

I have often heard Europeans wonder how it is that with such a democratic spirit so many American heiresses seem anxious to marry European noblemen. But it should be remembered in the first place that there are not many, but comparatively only a few who manifest this desire, and also that those few by no means represent public opinion here. On the other hand, is it not quite natural that when European gentlemen of the highest classes meet and get acquainted with American girls, their social and intellectual equals, that a mutual attachment may in most cases be the true motive for such alliances? For, as the grand Lincoln remarked, when the European nobleman possesses all other requisite qualifications his titles are no barrier to his success, either in the army, in business affairs, or with the fair sex. Old names and titles are usually a guaranty of good education, culture, and other praiseworthy acquisitions.

In my contact with the world and with men of different peoples and races, I have found that it is unjust to judge them by nations or classes, as if one nation or one class were necessarily better or worse than others, for there are both good and bad characters among all, and a good man is just as good, and a bad one just as bad, whether he be Hindoo, Mohammedan, or Christian, American or Swede, nobleman or peasant. Much good may be hidden under a coarse and common exterior, and we must not search for virtue only among the accomplished, the rich, and the fine-looking. Just as much, indeed, is found among the lowly and unobserved; and in the quiet, humble daily walks of life are constantly enacted deeds of heroism and virtue which are never known or applauded by the world, though fully as deserving as many of those which are given an honored place in the annals of history; yes, often much more so.

- 304 -

CHAPTER XXX.
REVIEW.

A few weeks ago I made a short visit to Vasa, our first home in Minnesota. The occasion was the eighty-seventh birthday of my mother, who still lives near the old homestead. [7] With spirited horses I drove in company with a son and a grandson over the same road which was first marked out by our simple ox wagon thirty-eight years before.

What a change! The former wilderness changed into smiling fields dressed in the purest green of early summer, and along the whole road are fine homes, nearly all of which belong to Swedish-Americans, who commenced their career as poor immigrants like myself, or to their children, most of whom are to the manor-born.

We stop twelve miles from Red Wing close to our old farm, at a little cottage surrounded by tall trees. There, by the window, sits greatgrandma, watching eagerly for someone whom she knows always spends that day with her.

Close to the quiet home stands the large Lutheran church, one of the finest country churches in America, and to the peaceful cemetery surrounding it we all soon make a pilgrimage to scatter flowers on the graves where my good father and sister, my wife's parents, sister, and many other near relatives have found a resting place. The little cemetery is clothed in a flowery carpet of nature's own garb, and studded - 305 - with several hundred marble monuments with inscriptions that testify to the Swedish ancestry of those who rest under them.
SWEDISH CHURCH IN VASA.
- 306 - From this place, which is the most elevated point in Vasa, the surrounding country affords a picture of such rural peace and beauty, that even a stranger must involuntarily pause to wonder and admire; how much more, then, I, who was the first white man that trod this ground! Below, toward the south, we see the wooded valley, watered by a little creek from Willard's spring, where we came near perishing that cold January night in 1854; at the head of the valley, the hill where we built the first log cabin; immediately beyond this hill the hospitable home of my

wife's parents, from which I brought my young bride to our own happy little home, which stood on another hill near the same spring, and of which a part still remains; here, just below the church, is the field I first plowed; over there in the grove where we cut logs and fencing material, stands now the orphan home, established by Rev. E. Norelius; and on the other side the road is his handsome residence and garden, but he himself sits inside, frail and suffering on account of the hardships of the first few years.

Close by are the post-office, two stores, a blacksmith shop, a school-house, two smaller churches, one Methodist and one Baptist, and several other public and private buildings, and a few miles farther north, near the Cannon river, are two railroads, running from the Mississippi westward, connecting with other roads which span the continent, and only terminate on the shores of the Pacific ocean.

All around, so far as the eye can see, are green fields, grazing herds of cattle, planted and natural groves, comfortable buildings, and great white-painted school-houses. Not a hill, not a valley or a grove but they call forth touching recollections, some mingled with sorrow and pain, but by far the most bright and cheerful; for here I spent the first hopeful years of my manhood; here we lived, the first Swedes in Minnesota, in a circle of innocent and faithful friends; here I - 307 - won the wife who tenderly and faithfully has shared the vicissitudes of life with me, in sorrow and in joy ever the same; here those of my countrymen who followed me when I was yet but a youth, have acquired independence, happiness, and such esteem that the settlement of Vasa has a reputation among the communities of the state which reflects honor upon the memory of the great king whose name it bears.

But this picture of development, culture and progress is not confined to this settlement, for countless other Scandinavian, settlements in the west and northwest have made as great progress within a comparatively short time.

On my arrival in 1852 the Mississippi river was the north-western boundary line of civilization with the exception of the state of Iowa, which then had only a small population. Since that time twelve new states further west have been peopled and admitted into the Union. There was no railroad west of Chicago; now the immense distance between the Mississippi and the Pacific ocean is spanned by four giant railroads, while more than a hundred trunk and branch lines intersect the country in all directions, and lakes and rivers are navigated by hundreds of steamers, which compete with the railroads in carrying the products of the West to the Atlantic, whence they are distributed over the whole civilized world.

Hundreds of cities that did not exist, even by name, have since sprung up as if by magic, and some of them have already become renowned throughout the world for their industry, commerce and culture. Among them are Minneapolis and St. Paul, already intertwining their arms around each other in an embrace that will soon unite them into one. The former did not exist when I first gazed on St. Anthony falls, which now furnishes motive power for its magnificent mills and factories, and the latter was a town of about two thousand inhabitants. - 309 - Their combined population is now one-third of a million. St. Paul contains a large number of Scandinavians, but Minneapolis seems to be their favorite city, the Swedes alone numbering over forty thousand. They have many churches, private schools, academies and other institutions of learning.

FLOUR MILLS IN MINNEAPOLIS.

The three Scandinavian nationalities agree pretty well in our good state, and have united their efforts in several enterprises of some magnitude. In Minneapolis there are several banks and other monetary institutions owned and controlled by them, not to mention hundreds of other important commercial and manufacturing establishments due to the enterprise of our countrymen. Having gradually learned the language and the ways of this country, a surprisingly large number of the Scandinavians who began their career as common laborers have engaged successfully in business on their own account, and many have devoted themselves to professions demanding a higher education, which is greatly facilitated by a number of excellent academies and colleges established and supported by them in several of the western states. A great number of county offices are filled by the Scandinavian-Americans; in our legislature there are generally from thirty to forty members of that nationality; many of them have occupied positions of the highest trust and honor as officers of the state and of the United States, and no one can deny the fact that they have universally proved themselves fully equal in ability and trust-worthiness to the native born.

But it is not only in Minneapolis or in Minnesota, but throughout the whole country that the Scandinavians have gained such a good name, that in all the recent agitation against foreign emigrants, not one voice has been heard against them. They learn the English language well and quickly, and assimilate readily with the native American element, which is natural enough considering that they are to - 310 - a very large extent of the same blood and ancestry as the English people, and that the English language is borrowed to no small extent from the Scandinavian.

Americans often express astonishment at the ease and correctness with which the Scandinavian immigrants acquire the English language. A little study of philology will readily account for it. If we take, for instance, the names of household goods, domestic animals, and other things appertaining to the common incidents of plain every-day life, we find the English words almost identical with the Scandinavian terms, only varying in the form of spelling or perhaps pronunciation, as those are apt to change with time and locality. For example: English—ox, cow, swine, cat, hound, rat, mouse, hen, goose, chicken; Swedish—oxe, ko, svin, katt, hund, rotta, mus, höna, gås, kyckling. Of implements: English—wagon, plow, harrow, spade, axe, knife, kettle, pot, pan, cup; Swedish—wagn, plog, harf, spada, yxa, knif, kittel, potta, panna, kopp. Or the part of our own bodies, such as: English—hair, skin, eyes, nose, ears, mouth, lips, teeth, shoulders, arm, hand, finger, nail, foot, toe, etc.; Swedish—hår, skinn, ögon, näsa, öron, mun, läpp, tand, skuldra, arm, hand, finger, nagel, fot, and tå. Or of the occupations of the common people, such as: English—spin, weave, cook, sow, sew; Swedish—spinna, väfva, koka, så, sy, etc. In this connection it may not be out of place to quote one of England's most eminent authors and scholars, Edward Bulwer Lytton, who says:

"A magnificent race of men were those war sons of the old North, whom our popular histories, so superficial in their accounts of this age, include in the common name of the 'Danes.'

"They replunged into barbarism the nations over which they swept; but from the barbarism they reproduced the noblest element of civilization. Swede, Norwegian and Dane, differing in some minor points, when closely examined, had yet one common character viewed at a distance. They had the same prodigious energy, the same passion for freedom, individual and civil, the same splendid errors in the thirst for fame and the point of - 311 - honor, and above all, as a main cause of civilization, they were wonderfully pliant and malleable in their adventures with the people they overran.

"At that time, A.D. 1055, these Northmen, under the common name of Danes, were peaceably settled in no less than fifteen counties in England; their nobles abounded in towns and cities beyond the boundaries of those counties, which bore the distinct appellation of Danelagh. They were numerous in London, in the precincts of which they had their own burial-place, to the chief municipal court of which they gave their own appellation—the Husting."

It is, of course, impossible to ascertain the exact number of Scandinavians and their descendants in this country, but we can come very near it by studying the statistics of the United States treasury department, a recent report from which gives the number of emigrants during the last seventy years from Sweden and Norway as 943,330, and from Denmark as 146,237, or a total since the year 1820 of 1,089,567; while the same report gives the number during the same period from Germany as 4,551,719; Ireland, 3,501,683; England, 1,460,054; English Colonies, 1,029,083; Austria-Hungaria, 464,435; Italy, 414,513; France, 370,162; Russia, 356,353; Scotland, 329,192; Switzerland, 174,333.

When we take into consideration the numerous Swedish colonies that settled in Delaware, Pennsylvania and New Jersey in the seventeenth century, and their descendants, together with the descendants of Scandinavian emigrants of the last seventy years, I think it is safe to estimate the total population of Scandinavian descent at over four millions, or fully one-sixteenth of the entire population of the United States. The very fact that the nationality assimilates so readily with the native American element causes it to be lost sight of; and it should be so, for the only desirable immigrants to this country are those who cease to be foreigners, and merge right into the American nation. Such are certainly the Scandinavians. They do not bring over any grievances from the mother country to correct or avenge, and there are no Clan-na-Gael, no Mafia societies among - 312 - them, nor are there any anarchists or revolutionists. They come here to build homes for themselves and their children; they are contented and grateful for the privileges of American citizenship, and make themselves worthy of it by pushing into the front rank in the onward march of education, philanthropy and religion, as well as in material progress.

One illustration, among many that might be given, is found in the report of a late conference of the Swedish Lutheran Church, from which it appears that they have now in Minnesota alone two hundred and forty-five parishes, with one hundred and seventy-nine churches, valued at over six hundred thousand dollars, and all paid for. The Norwegian Lutheran Church would undoubtedly show equal if not better results, though I cannot give the exact figures.

It is a great mistake which some make, to think that it is only for their brawn and muscle that the Northmen have become a valuable acquisition to the American population; on the contrary, they have done and are doing as much as any other nationality within the domain of mind and heart. Not to speak of the early discovery of America by the Scandinavians five hundred years before the time of Columbus, they can look back with proud satisfaction on the part they have taken in all respects to make this great republic what it is today.

The early Swedish colonists in Delaware, Pennsylvania and New Jersey worked as hard for liberty and independence as the English did in New England and in the South. There were no tories among them, and when the continental congress stood wavering equal in the balance for and against the adoption of the Declaration of Independence, it was a Swede, John Morton (Mortenson), of the old Delaware stock, who gave the casting vote of Pennsylvania in favor of the sacred document.

When nearly a century later the great rebellion burst upon - 313 - the land, a gallant descendant of the Swedes, Gen. Robert Anderson, met its first shock at Fort Sumter, and, during the bitter struggle of four years which followed, the Scandinavian-Americans were as true and loyal to their adopted country as their native-born neighbors, giving their unanimous support to the cause of the Union and fighting valiantly for it; nor should it be forgotten that it was the Swede John Ericson, who, by his inventive genius, saved the navy and the great seaports of the United States, and that it was another Swede by descent, Admiral Dahlgren, who furnished the model for the finest guns of our artillery. Surely love of freedom, valor, genius, patriotism and religious fervor was not planted in America by the seeds brought over in the Mayflower alone.

Yes, it is verily true that the Scandinavian immigrants, from the early colonists of 1638 to the present time, have furnished strong hands, clear heads and loyal hearts to the republic. They have caused the wilderness to blossom like the rose; they have planted schools and churches on the hills and in the valleys; they have honestly and ably administered the public affairs of town, county and state; they have helped to make wise laws for their respective commonwealths and in the halls of congress; they have, with honor and ability, represented their adopted country abroad; they have sanctified the American soil by their blood, shed in freedom's cause on the battle-fields of the revolution and the civil war; and though proud of their Scandinavian ancestry, they love America and American institutions as deeply and as truly as do the descendants of the Pilgrims, the starry emblem of liberty meaning as much to them as to any other citizen.

Therefore, the Scandinavian-American feels a certain sense of ownership in the glorious heritage of American soil, with its rivers, lakes, mountains, valleys, woods and prairies, and - 314 - in all its noble institutions; and he feels that the blessings which he enjoys are not his by favor or sufferance, but by right; by moral as well as civil right. For he took possession of the wilderness, endured the hardships of the pioneer, contributed his full share toward the grand results accomplished, and is in mind and heart a true and loyal American citizen.